WITHDRAWN

Old-Time Variety:
an Illustrated History

Dedicated to my family,
Gerry, Claire, Ryan, Roz, Mark, Vinod and Scott

Old-Time Variety:
an Illustrated History

Richard Anthony Baker

REMEMBER WHEN

First published in Great Britain in 2011 by
Remember When
An imprint of
Pen & Sword Books Ltd
47 Church Street
Barnsley
South Yorkshire
S70 2AS

Copyright © Richard Anthony Baker 2011

ISBN 978 1 84468 124 2

The right of Richard Anthony Baker to be identified as Author of this work
has been asserted by him in accordance with the Copyright, Designs
and Patents Act 1988.

A CIP catalogue record for this book is
available from the British Library.

Typeset in 10pt Palatino by Mac Style, Beverley, East Yorkshire
Printed and bound by the MPG Books Group

Pen & Sword Books Ltd incorporates the Imprints of Pen & Sword Aviation,
Pen & Sword Family History, Pen & Sword Maritime, Pen & Sword Military,
Pen & Sword Discovery, Wharncliffe Local History, Wharncliffe True Crime,
Wharncliffe Transport, Pen & Sword Select, Pen & Sword Military Classics,
Leo Cooper, The Praetorian Press, Remember When, Seaforth Publishing
and Frontline Publishing

For a complete list of Pen & Sword titles please contact
PEN & SWORD BOOKS LIMITED
47 Church Street, Barnsley, South Yorkshire, S70 2AS, England
E-mail: enquiries@pen-and-sword.co.uk
Website: www.pen-and-sword.co.uk

Contents

Foreword

Richard Anthony Baker has done it again. He is rapidly becoming **the** chronicler of the show-going public's most popular "hims and hers" – ancient and modern. Not only "hims and hers," but the punters' most popular places to be entertained in, their most popular suppliers of jokes and songs to sing and whistle and the producers who provided just what they wanted to see.

Richard is the author of the two "must have" books on the most fascinating period of our entertainment history – the period that began with music hall and finished with its follow-up, variety. This companion volume to his *British Music Hall: an Illustrated History* is the one all of us fans of the golden years have been waiting for. In that first book, he brilliantly recreated the free and easy, drinks all round, macho music hall for us. Music hall – that hardly anyone alive today can tell us about first-hand, yet still stays in our minds through its unique songs and characters.

Variety came about just after the First World War. It happened, I believe, through blokes wanting to take their wives and sweethearts to less obvious Rabelaisian entertainments. The drinking was banished to the back of the hall and its customers sat in orderly rows. [If they sat in orderly rows, the promoters could get more bums on seats!]

Today, there are lots of people who remember variety very well and for them this book is a treasure trove. Richard's pen portraits of the men and women who filled every town's and city's theatres twice a night will promote many a "I first saw her …," "He used to sing …," "He caught a cartwheel on his head" and "there were about 85 different Bettys." If you weren't around at the time, you missed a treat. Variety, as a big business, was practically all over by the 1960s. I worked with the great Max Miller in 1959 and he used to say at the end of his act "Enjoy it, lady, 'cos, when I'm dead and gone, the game's finished." He got it about right.

Variety ran from around 1918 to the 1960s – a short life, but a gay one [the original meaning of the word]. A typical two-hour show brought into our workaday lives, laughs, romance, mystery, admired dexterity and sexual attraction: comedians, comediennes, vocalists [handsome men and beautiful ladies], magicians, jugglers, acrobats and chorus lines. This book tells you everything you need to know about the highly successful business it was. It will, I think, explain just why mums and dads and grannies and granddads remember so many of its participants with such affection.

Here are the names and stories of the stars [and those who were popular with the public, yet never seemed to get talked about today], descriptions of some of the strangest acts you can imagine and great gossipy, anecdotes, both funny, cruel and heart-breaking. As a dedicated old gossip myself, I loved discovering those nuggets hidden throughout. For example,

> The man who wrote two of George Formby's hit songs was the undertaker who buried him
> Performers who did their acts in front of a cloth that was painted with advertisements for local businesses had special instructions. They were told to keep moving about, so every advertisement had equal time to be seen by the audience.
> And was Lord Reith gay?

Bud Flanagan left in his will just half a share in a betting shop while his partner, Chesney Allen, left the equivalent of £2 million. One of 'em could pick winners and one couldn't.

Richard Anthony Baker has done it again. As always [see his articles in the magazine of the British Music Hall Society, *The Call Boy*], his research is thorough, immaculate and painstaking, but never, ever boring. He, like the folk from the exciting, highly coloured world he writes about, makes facts fun. His love for his subject comes through on every page.

Roy Hudd O.B.E.
Suffolk
2011

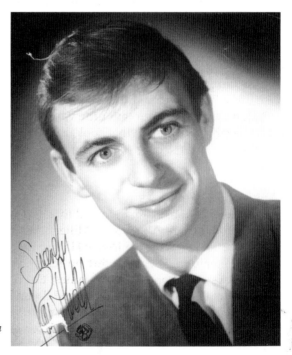

Roy Hudd just as he was about to begin his career in variety.

Introduction

What was the difference between music hall and variety? It is not an easy question. Music hall was a red-blooded, boisterous entertainment aimed at the working man. It was popular from about 1840 to sometime after the First World War. Variety, which took its place, was gentler and more refined. The big theatre owners were responsible for the change. They wanted to appeal to a wider social spectrum. A man was more likely to take his wife or girlfriend to the theatre if there were no risk of anyone being offended by a bawdy comic or a singer revelling in double entendres. That makes variety sound less fun. It was not. There existed as much talent in variety as there was on the halls.

Another problem is dates. When did music hall end and variety start? There was, needless to say, an overlap. Even in the heyday of music hall, the word 'variety' was frequently used. The excellent music hall history written by Joe Mander and Ray Mitchenson lists Danny La Rue, Ken Dodd and Des O'Connor as stars of music hall. Undoubtedly, each of those entertainers would have had a scintillating career on the halls, but it was all over before they even started. Somewhat arbitrarily, I choose 1922, the year Marie Lloyd died, as marking music hall's end.

A further problem is: who was a variety performer and who was not? I have ruled out Arthur Askey, Peter Brough and Frankie Howerd largely because they were better known as radio [and, later, in the case of Askey and Howerd, television] performers. And yet, the BBC was a big supporter and an innovator of variety. There are bound to be anomalies.

You may not find your favourite variety performer in these pages. If everyone worth a mention were in this book, it would be too heavy to carry.

Brackets after sums of money indicate the approximate current-day equivalents.

Acknowledgements
In writing this book, I am indebted to John Adrian, of the Grand Order of Water Rats; the late Clive Allen, Max Miller's last pianist; Geoff Bowden, the editor of *The Call Boy*, the British Music Hall Society's magazine; Martin Breese; Dora Bryan; Peter Burgess, an expert on female impersonation; Wyn Calvin MBE; James Casey, the son of Jimmy James; Frank Cullen, the leading authority on vaudeville; the late Florence Desmond; Ryan Edwards and Mark Macnaughtan for technical help; John Fisher, Peter Lane and John Wade of the Magic Circle; the George Formby Society; Caroline Gibb for invaluable genealogical assistance;

Gerald Glover, the co-founder of the British Music Hall Society; Joan Hollman, the daughter of Gladys Morgan; David Howe, of the Savage Club; Roy Hudd OBE for his magnificent foreword; Christine Kimberley, the daughter of Bobbie Kimber; Belinda Langford, the daughter of Saveen; Angela Levin, niece of Issy Bonn; Pamela Loveday, the daughter of Tony Fayne; Richard Mangan, of the Mander and Mitchenson Theatre Collection; the Max Miller Appreciation Society; Norman Morrison; the late Chubby Oates; the late Robert Nesbitt; the late Patrick Newley, *The Stage* columnist, who gave freely of his time and expertise; Ray Pallett, of *Memory Lane*; Alf Pearson; Michael Pointon, a close friend of Max Wall; the late Beryl Reid OBE; the late Joan Rhodes; Simon Rooks and Jill Collins of the BBC; the late Don Ross of *Thanks for the Memory*; the impresario, Keith Salberg; the Scottish Music Hall Society; my perceptive agent, Robert Smith; Jackie Snow, the daughter of Michael Carr; Mary Todd, of the Old Mother Riley Society; the late Wendy Toye CBE; Max Tyler, the historian of the British Music Hall Society and co-editor of *Music Hall Studies*; the Max Wall Society; the late Elsie Waters; Alan Watts for information about Gaston and Andree; Barry Wiley; Michael Worsley, the son of Arthur Worsley; the late Fred Yule of *ITMA*; the staff of the Bodleian Music Library, the BBC's Written Archives Centre, the British Film Institute, the British Library, the British Newspaper Library, the Family Records Centre, the London Library, the London Metropolitan Archive and Tower Hamlets Central Library.

Richard Anthony Baker, Leigh-on-Sea, 2011

CHAPTER ONE

New Readers Start Here

The Stage is Set

It was a day popular performers thought they would never see. Reviled over many years, music hall, that rumbustious and vulgar entertainment of the late Nineteenth Century, had finally been accepted by the Establishment: the first Royal Command Performance was to be staged before George V and Queen Mary at the Palace Theatre, Cambridge Circus, on 1 July 1912. Such comics as George Robey, sometimes a little saucy, but never salacious, and Harry Tate, with his up-to-the-minute parody on motoring, were allowed their moment of glory. Interestingly, those two men attracted more laughter that evening than anyone else on the bill and were the only entertainers who successfully carried their careers on from music hall to the variety theatre.

In spite of losing some of its bite, music hall was still popular in the years immediately preceding the First World War. In the year of the Royal Command, there were 48 music hall theatres in London alone. Each night [and often twice nightly] they played to 70,000 people. In the world at large, everything appeared normal. Smart hotels held Tango Teas at which women wearing skirts slashed to near the top of the leg danced with young men known as Nuts and, if the tango appeared too complicated, there was another innovation, the foxtrot:

> But everywhere a restless spirit was perceptible, as of people waiting on some impending climax. Nobody knew that we had reached the end of an age, yet everybody in his bones and blood was sensible of something disconcerting, some hovering and pervading disquiet.[1]

On the first night of the Great War, there were lengthy queues outside the most popular halls in the West End. At the Palladium, Little Tich, the four foot six comic who danced in boots nearly half that length, appeared as Miss Turpentine.

Harry Tate: again in mechanical difficulties.

At the London Pavilion, the much loved Marie Lloyd sang *I'd Like to Live in Paris All the Time*. The only concession to international tension was that, at the end of the evening, the national anthems of Russia and France were played, as well as that of Britain.

Once the call-up began, the young men of Britain marched to war belting out the latest music hall songs they had heard: *Pack Up Your Troubles*; *Good-Bye-Ee*; *Take Me Back to Dear Old Blighty*; and this:

> Send out the Army and the Navy.
> Send out the rank and file.
> Send out the brave old Territorials.
> They'll face the danger with a smile.
> Send out the boys of the Old Brigade,
> Who made old England free.
> Send out my brother, my sister and my mother,
> But for Gawd's sake don't send me.

Come 1918, it did not seem so funny. Nearly three-quarters of a million British soldiers had died, about two-thirds of them in their twenties.

During the course of the war, so many young men were overseas that their girlfriends and wives had to make their own lives, eating out with each other, some of them drinking and smoking for the first time. Between 1914 and 1918, the consumption of alcohol actually fell by about a half, although smoking increased. Pubs, which had closed at 12.30am, now had to shut at 10pm. A similar curfew was imposed on all places of entertainment, but music halls still drew big audiences, as did cinemas and theatres staging a new type of entertainment, revue. People needed escapism.

By the end of the war, movies were becoming big business. Several music halls had already been converted into cinemas: the Balham Empire; the Bradford Empire; in Brighton, the Empire and the Alhambra; the New Star, Bristol; the Alhambra, Edinburgh; the Hippodrome, Gateshead; the Savoy, Glasgow; the Tivoli, Liverpool; the Grand, Sheffield; the Variety, Shoreditch; and the Empire, Stockton-on-Tees. More importantly, 3,500 purpose-built cinemas were constructed between 1910 and 1914.

Revues, speedy concoctions of unlinked sketches and songs, had been staged at the Empire, one of three major halls in Leicester Square, since it re-opened after refurbishment in 1906. The first, *Rogues and Vagabonds*, was written by George Grossmith, a leading player in the earliest musical comedies produced by George Edwardes at the Gaiety Theatre. Grossmith also wrote part of the Empire revues, *Hello ... London!* [1910] and *Everybody's Doing It* [1912], built around one of Irving Berlin's earliest hits. By 1912, the craze for revue had London in its grip. At the end of that year, Albert de Courville, who ran the London Hippodrome, staged *Hullo, Ragtime!* his first big spectacular revue, which capitalised on the fashion for ragtime. It ran for 451 performances and de Courville followed it with *Hullo Tango!* in which Harry Tate gave an impersonation of how George Robey would play his sketch about golf. *Hullo Tango!* did even better: 485 performances.

In the years following the war, the revues, the movies, the dances and music hall all reflected the spirit of the age, but times were changing rapidly:

> The old order had gone … Restrictions imposed in wartime were never quite lifted.[2] That centuries-old feeling of security had vanished … Life was no longer simple. It was sharper and more brittle. The old code of morality had slackened … and the days of national pride had been veneered over with self-restraint … The conditions which created music hall no longer existed. There was a new thing called sophistication. The old insularity had gone. Men who had never been further than Margate now knew all about Mesopotamia. It was a different world.[3]

The stars were dying off, too. After years of alcoholism and nervous breakdowns, music hall's pre-eminent comedian, Dan Leno, had died of syphilis in 1904 at the age of 43 and, after the First World War, Marie Lloyd, now weary and bloated, was showing signs of the maltreatment inflicted on her by two brutal husbands. She died in the arms of one of her sisters in 1922, aged 52.

The night she died, a young Lancashire woman, who was in the fifth year of a touring revue that was to make her name, was appearing in Swindon. Once she was famous, people began to refer to her as Marie's successor. She was Gracie Fields.

CHAPTER TWO

Amazing Gracie

Top of the Bill: Dame Gracie Fields

That was an enormous compliment to Gracie, if unwelcome. Comparisons are odious. The eminent critic, James Agate, who rated Gracie so highly that he believed she should play George Bernard Shaw's St Joan,[4] dismissed the allusion succinctly: 'London impudence and Lancashire cheek are poles apart'[5] And Gracie was pure Lancashire, as the northern playwright, J.B. Priestley, who co-wrote the scripts of her films, *Sing As We Go* and *Look Up and Laugh*, pointed out:

> Listen to her for a quarter of an hour and you will learn more about Lancashire women … than you would from a dozen books … All the qualities are there: shrewdness, homely simplicity, irony, fierce independence, an impish delight in mocking whatever is thought to be affected and pretentious.[6]

Gracie was born in the mill town of Rochdale three years before Queen Victoria died. Life was tough, but the no-nonsense kindness of its people made it bearable. If a woman fell ill, her front step was scrubbed, her washing up was done and a stew was left to simmer on the hob. Often, the bedridden woman did not even know who was being so kind. In spite of this close-knit cosiness, one woman, Jenny Stansfield, craved a better existence: 'We're going oop in t'world, not down,' she constantly told her family.

Jenny, a fiercely ambitious and stage-struck woman, introduced Grace, one of her daughters, to the world of show business by way of the Rochdale Hippodrome. Jenny scrubbed the theatre's stage every Sunday. Grace joined her with a duster and a brush. Then, Jenny began doing the laundry for entertainers at the Hippodrome. All the time, she was teaching Gracie the songs she knew and encouraging her to sing them as loudly as she could. The laundry was returned to the Hippodrome every Friday and Saturday and Jenny and Grace were allowed to stand in the wings and watch the shows. Watch everything you can, Jenny told Grace. It's the only way you'll ever learn. After each show, Grace was interrogated: What were the entertainers wearing? How did they look? And, most importantly, what did they sing? If there was a new song, Grace learned it instantly and sang it on the way home. She also learned to impersonate those she saw.

Jennie also exhorted Grace to sing [loudly] outside theatrical digs. One day, the ploy paid off. A music hall singer from the Midlands, Lily Turner, was

Gracie Fields [Grace Stansfield]

- Born Rochdale, Lancashire, 9 January 1898
- Married [1] Archibald Selinger [professionally known as Archie Pitt], Clapham, South London, 21 April 1923 [His previous wife was May Deitchmann] Divorced 1939, died 12 November 1940
- Married [2] Mario Bianchi [professionally known as Monty Banks], Santa Monica, California, 19 March 1940. Born Nice, France, 18 July 1897. [He had previously been married to Gladys Frazin, who killed herself in New York in March 1939] Died Arona, Italy, 7 January 1950
- Married [3] Boris Abraham Luigi Alperovici, 18 February 1952. Died Capri, Italy, 3 July 1983
- Dame Gracie Fields died Capri, Italy, 27 September 1979
- Left over £4 million [£15 million]

impressed by what she heard and suggested that Grace entered a singing competition at the Hippodrome. Grace tied for first place and won 10s 6d [£30]. This even impressed Grace's hard-drinking father, who up to then had foreseen her working life in bleak terms: Shove 'er in t'factory. For a time, Grace worked with Lily Turner. Then, at the age of 10, she joined in succession two juvenile troupes. At about this time, the Stansfields' neighbour, old Fred, moved in with them as he was no longer able to look after himself. Grace sang to him and did impersonations and was encouraged by his toothless chuckle. One night, he said that he had heard that Jessie Merrilees,[7] who was due to appear at the Hippodrome, had been taken ill and that the manager was frantically looking for a replacement. 'Young Grace Stansfield, Rochdale's own girl vocalist' filled the bill and was paid 35 shillings [£60] for the week's work. Grace's father, who had a job at an engineering works, was then earning 30 shillings a week.

Soon, Grace Stansfield became Gracie Fields. Jenny was told that a shorter name would stand out better on billboards. At the age of 14, Gracie began a two-year tour with Charburn's Young Stars and impersonated many of the stars she worked with: George Formby senior [see Chapter 10]; Victoria Monks, who sang *Bill Bailey, Won't You Please Come Home?*; Maidie Scott, whose speciality was *The Bird on Nellie's Hat*; and Gertie Gitana, best known for *Nellie Dean.* [Years later, Gertie Gitana imitated Gracie.]

There followed a season with a Pierrot concert party near Blackpool and a pantomime in which Gracie had a small part. Then, the work dried up. In 1915, old Fred died and left Jenny £100 with a note that read: Tha knows how best to spend it. She did indeed. After paying for Fred's funeral, she settled the family's debts, stocked up the larder and took Gracie every day to Manchester to learn tap dancing. Within six weeks, Gracie had mastered all the steps she was to use later in her movies.

After that, a wad of letters was written to agents, one of whom, Percy Hall, asked to see her. He offered her six weeks' work at £5 a week and then proffered a 10-year contract. Under its terms, Gracie would earn not less than £5 a week. Anything over that sum was to be shared equally by Hall and Gracie. Ill-advisedly, Jenny and Gracie signed.

At the end of the six-week engagement, Hall found her a part in a new revue, *Yes, I Think So,* starring Archie Pitt, a comedian, who had worked as a shop assistant and a travelling salesman before turning to the halls. Pitt was the first professional to recognise Gracie's potential, but she neither found him funny nor even liked him much:

> He sang a song, *Does This Shop Stock Shot Socks with Spots?* that made me smile a bit, but the rest of his act seemed like rubbish. When I sang my couple of songs, I noticed he watched me keenly … He disturbed and unsettled me. His eyes were constantly upon me, too penetrating.[8]

Pitt was not interested in Gracie's looks. She herself admitted that she was not pretty. She was slender, quite tall, with a slight stoop, thin lips and strongly marked, somewhat pointed features. What Pitt saw was a performer with two great gifts: a sense of homely fun and an exceptionally beautiful and flexible voice with an astonishing range, a voice that prompted the coloratura soprano, Luisa Tetrazzini, to suggest that she should abandon music hall for grand opera.

Gracie celebrated her 16th birthday during the tour of *Yes, I Think So.* Archie threw a party for her and wrote a message in her autograph book: To Gracie Fields. One day, you are going to be a big star. *Yes, I Think So* toured all over northern England for 18 months and at one point in 1915 went into the Middlesex Music Hall in London's Drury Lane. At the end of the run, Percy Hall found another revue for Gracie, but Archie wanted her to join a show he had written. Gracie thought she would have to do Hall's bidding, but Archie bought her out of the contract and Gracie opened in *It's A Bargain,* which toured for two-and-a-half years. This was followed by another revue written by Archie, *Mr Tower of London,* which proved even more successful than its predecessors. During its fifth year of touring, Gracie married Archie:

> Archie insisted. I am easily dominated and Archie dominated me. For nine years, since I was 16, Archie had drilled me, encouraged me, driven me, helped me and filled my life with work, work and still more work. There had been nine years of touring with him. Nine years of travelling from one cold damp little theatre to another; no heating, no hot water, sometimes no theatre even, just a hall for which we had to hire a piano. Bad food, bad digs and two, sometimes three shows a day and then Archie would keep me up to till one and two in the morning helping him think up new ideas for sketches.[9]

During six years of touring, *Mr Tower of London* took more than £250,000 [£7.5 million]. When Oswald Stoll booked it for a week at the Alhambra, *The Era* seemed uncertain about Gracie: 'her inimitable manner of ornamenting a song one could never overlook. Nor could anyone fail to note her ability to play 101 tricks with her voice. Perhaps, for these very reasons, her potentialities as an actress may be overlooked.'[10]

Stoll was more certain. During each performance of *Mr Tower of London*, Gracie had a 25-minute break. Stoll asked her to fill part of the time by doing a 10-minute act at the Coliseum. She was paid £100 [£3,000] for the week.

Gracie was going 'oop' in the world. For appearing in the first half of a play, *S.O.S*, at the St James's Theatre, the actor-manager, Sir Gerald du Maurier, paid her £100 [£3,000]. Each night, she went straight on to the second house at the Alhambra, where she earned £200 [£6,000]. The evening ended with a £300 [£9,000] cabaret appearance at the Cafe Royal. Gracie had made Jenny's dream come true.

George Black, who ran the London Palladium from 1928, was delighted to book Gracie on his opening bill, her first appearance at the world's most famous variety theatre. George had seen her work in the Cumbrian town of Barrow-in-Furness when she was still unknown and had long tried to work out the secrets of her charm and power. Those secrets, he said, allowed her to break all the rules:

Any manager could have told her that to turn her back on the audience and walk upstage before the applause and laughter were over was one certain way of ruining an act. She did it and it was one of the most remarkable things I have ever seen her do. With her back still to the audience, she paused a moment and began to sing. The crowd, prepared to laugh again, were brought to silence by the clear liquid notes – that 'third voice' of hers – of a plaintive melody, *Three Green Bonnets*. At exactly the right moment, known to her by instinct, she turned her head, then her body and began to walk down the stage singing. The house was hushed, breathless. As the last notes died away, I heard a gasp. And I, who had been a hard-boiled showman since boyhood and thought I knew all the tricks of the trade, felt what the audience felt. For here was no trick. This was blazing sincerity, a heart speaking to the hearts of the world.[11]

Archie was doing well too. After *Mr Tower of London*, he put several more touring companies on the road and relished the trappings of success. In Bishop's Avenue in Hampstead, he built a 28-room mansion with a marble bathroom for every bedroom, crystal chandeliers in the reception rooms, a huge ballroom and a magnificent staircase: all this for a girl who had been born above a chip shop. In addition, there were a housekeeper, a butler, two cooks, maids and a chauffeur, who drove Gracie round in a Rolls Royce. She told Archie it was like riding in the back of a hearse. If she was being driven to a theatre, she felt uncomfortable about making the chauffeur wait all evening for her. So, she sent him off and travelled home on the bus. That sort of behaviour drove Archie mad.

Part of Gracie's appeal was that she never forgot her roots or the down-to-earth people she grew up with. She felt intimidated by Archie's mansion. In any case, the couple were growing apart. Archie became increasingly close to Annie Lipman, a chorus girl who had been part of the *Mr Tower of London* company, and Gracie fell in love with an artist, John Flanagan, whom she met at the Café Royal. Two weeks before the opening of Archie's latest revue, *The Show's The Thing*, he and Gracie had a fierce row. She packed a bag, walked out and caught a boat train for France, where Flanagan was on holiday. By the time she reached Paris, she knew she was doing wrong. She could not disappoint the cast of *The Show's The Thing*. From Paris, she phoned Archie to say she was returning and, as she made her way back to London, she wept and wept. The Hampstead mansion was put on the market, Archie set up home with Annie Lipman and Gracie moved into a studio apartment in St John's Wood.

The Show's The Thing was another success. It opened at the Lyceum in August 1929 and then transferred to the Winter Garden, where it ran until February 1930. Later that year, Gracie accepted a two-week booking at the Palace Theatre, New York, where, at first, she was not a success. She introduced Americanisms into her act and sounded insincere. She quickly reverted to doing what she did best, being herself, and ended the fortnight amid great acclaim.

By the end of 1930, Gracie was a theatre star; she was also a radio star, having made her wireless debut in February 1927; she was selling gramophone records too [four million between 1928 and 1932]; and she had proved that she knew how to handle an American audience. There was one more medium to overcome, the movies.

Gracie made her first feature film in 1931, *Sally in Our Alley*, co-starring the impressionist, Florence Desmond, and produced by Basil Dean, who had founded Associated Talking Pictures, later to become the Ealing Studios. Dean had many skills, but dealing with people was not one of them: in the words of one film historian, 'he was an autocratic manager of people, he had a talent for wounding sarcasm and a reputation for reducing his employees to tears.'[12]

Gracie hated both the routine of making films and the lack of contact with a live audience. In one small scene, she had to greet a taxi driver with the words 'Good morning, George.' Two days were spent trying to complete the scene. Gracie told Dean that from then on he would have to accept either the first or second take. She earned herself the sobriquet 'One Take Joe'.

She was propelled into a second film, *Looking on the Bright Side*, another feel-good movie aimed at dispelling worries about recession and unemployment – and another huge success. As a result, her agent, Bert Aza, told her that Archie had negotiated a contract for six films to be made over the coming six years. The purse: £72,000 [£2.5 million]. Gracie turned it down. 'Tell Archie I won't sign with him, Bert. No hard feelings, but I can't live that sort of life for the next six years.'[13] A week later, Bert phoned her in some excitement to say that RKO had offered her £20,000 [£700,000] to make *This Week of Grace*. But the ordeal proved just as unbearable and, when it was over, Gracie told Bert: 'We'll never sign for another film … I'm really only happy on the stage. So, turn all film offers down.'[14]

Gracie Fields' filmography

[The movies, the studios, the well-known songs, any other variety performers]

1931   *Sally In Our Alley* [ATP (Associated Talking Pictures)]. Director, Maurice Elvey. *Sally*, written by Will Haines, Harry Leon and Leo Towers. Florence Desmond [see Chapter 21], wrote 'What a dear Gracie was to work with and what energy she had! She never seemed to get tired. A rehearsal was a performance to her.'[15]

1932   *Looking On The Bright Side* [ATP]. Co-directors, Basil Dean and Graham Cutts. Julian Rose.

1933   *This Week of Grace* [RKO]. Director, Maurice Elvey. Vivian Foster and Henry Kendall: 'Gracie was always cheerful and smiling, although her language occasionally made even the electricians blush. She would smooth everything over by inviting the whole production unit over to the local for drinks all round. No wonder she was worshipped by everyone who worked with her.'[16]

1934   *Love, Life and Laughter* [ATP]. Director, Maurice Elvey. Horace Kenney and Robb Wilton [see Chapter 7].

1934   *Sing as We Go* [ATP]. Director, Basil Dean. *Sing As We Go*, written by Harry Parr Davies. Stanley Holloway: '[Gracie] is generous in the way she gives of herself and her affection to her friends and her public ... I think this sort of big-heartedness is partly what's made her loved all over the world.'[17]

1934   *Look Up and Laugh* [ATP]. Director, Basil Dean. Robb Wilton and Harry Tate. 'Harry Tate, poor fellow, could not remember a single line for more than a few minutes together ... This great comedian [has] now lapsed into senility.'[18]

1936   *Queen of Hearts* [ATP]. Director, Monty Banks.

1937   *The Show Goes On* [ATP]. Director, Basil Dean. *I Never Cried So Much in All My Life*, written by Will Haines, Jimmy Harper and Harry Castling. Billy Merson.

1938   *Keep Smiling* [Twentieth Century Fox]. Director, Monty Banks. Eddie Gray [see Chapter 5].

1938   *We're Going to be Rich* [Twentieth Century Fox]. Director, Monty Banks. *Walter, Walter (Lead Me to the Altar)*, written by Will Haines, Jimmy Harper and Noel Forrester.

1939   *Shipyard Sally* [Twentieth Century Fox]. Director, Monty Banks. *Wish Me Luck as you Wave Me Goodbye*, written by Phil Park and Harry Parr Davies. Oliver Wakefield [see Chapter 17].

1943   *Stage Door Canteen* [Sol Lesser Productions]. Director, Frank Borzage.

1943   *Holy Matrimony*. Director, John M. Stahl.

1945   *Molly and Me*. Director, Lewis Seiler.

1945   *Paris Underground*. Director, Gregory Ratoff.

Gracie's other well-known comic songs included *The Biggest Aspidistra in the World*, written by Jimmy Harper, Will Haines and Tommie Connor; *I Took My Harp to a Party*, written by Noel Gay and Desmond Carter; and *Turn 'Erbert's Face to the Wall, Mother*, written by Max Kester, William Ellis and Ronald Hill.

She was then offered £25,000 [£875,000] and, after that, £30,000 [£1 million]. Gracie capitulated and made two more films. 'Now, that's the lot.' Bert nodded. 'I know how you feel, Grace. If anybody asks, I'll tell them you won't make another film for less than £40,000.'[19] A few days later, Bert told her he had an offer for four films, each worth £40,000 [£1.35 million]. 'Now, I know they're all barmy,' Gracie said.[20] Barmy or not, by the end of the 1930s, Gracie became Britain's highest paid film actress. Her appeal was neatly summed up by a cinema magazine:

You need look no further than to Gracie herself. She is big because she doesn't care a jot [about] whether she is earning a fortune or not. Gracie is always just herself.[21]

It was through her seventh film, *Look Up and Laugh*, that Gracie met Monty Banks. He had just directed his first film for Associated Talking Pictures and Basil Dean wanted him to direct Gracie. They gelled instantly and, in Dean's words, this jolly little 'cosmopolite', an Italian citizen with an American accent and a British passport, made Gracie laugh at a time when she had great need of laughter. Monty was known as both a gambler and a womaniser, but in 1940 he and Gracie married.

Shortly after the outbreak of the Second World War, Gracie sang at as many troop concerts as she could. Arthur Askey[22] witnessed her indefatigability:

Often, when I'd had enough and they said, "There's a bit of an isolated camp down the road," she'd go … She could be tired out, but she'd climb into the lorry … and, when she got on the stage, no matter how rough and improvised it might be, she seemed to shed that tiredness and become a different person.[23]

But once Italy joined the war in support of Germany, everything changed. As an Italian, Monty instantly became an

Gracie's second husband, Monty Banks.

enemy alien and could have been interned. Gracie was faced with a dilemma. Should she stay in Britain or go abroad and be with her husband? She chose the latter and became the focus of questions in Parliament and ill-informed criticism by journalists who accused her of deserting Britain.

In fact, across Canada and America, she staged concerts in aid of Britain's war effort. Once America declared war on Japan at the end of 1941, the situation eased for Gracie. By then, Monty had become an American citizen and the couple were able to travel the world entertaining the troops.

Even so, Gracie was granted only a temporary British passport, which she had to renew every six months. In 1945, she applied for British nationality, but was refused because of Monty's American citizenship. Shamefully, the Foreign Office recommended that she should be treated as an alien. She withdrew her application and remained an Italian citizen until she died. Gracie herself said 'I may have an Italian passport, but no matter what is written in it, I am British at heart.'[24]

Her reputation had been damaged, however, and, when she returned to the Palladium for a fortnight's engagement in 1948, no one was sure how she would be received. She discussed every moment of her act with Bert Aza, but refused to say which song she would open with. She chose *La Vie En Rose* with its opening line, 'Take Me In Your Arms Again'. By the time she finished, both Gracie and her audience were in tears.

Two years later, Gracie and Monty were travelling to Italy on the Orient Express when Monty suffered a heart attack. Before medical assistance could be summoned, he died in her arms. Gracie was a widow at the age of 51.

Her work continued, but at a more leisurely pace. Gracie had not expected to marry again, but she fell in love with Boris Alperovici, who first visited her home in Capri to mend her record player. After they married in 1952, Britain saw increasingly less of Gracie, although she appeared from to time on the religious television programme, *Stars on Sundays,* in the 1970s.

Gracie died in 1979. Three days later, the *Sunday People* began an extraordinary series of articles based on interviews she gave to a writer who had made a television documentary about her 10 years previously. Gracie agreed to the interviews with one proviso: that their contents were kept secret until after her death. She disclosed that, during large parts of her life, she had been desperately unhappy. What she called her marriage of convenience to Archie Pitt had been loveless; Monty Banks had gambled much of her money away; and Boris Alperovici was a snob, who did not like the working class English – my sort of people: he wants to keep them as far from his snooty Italian society friends as he can.

But, during Gracie's lifetime, that was all kept from the public. What they saw was what J.B. Priestley saw too:

[Gracie] was independent, saucy, sharply humorous, bossy, maternal, blunt in manner, but deeply feminine in her rapid alternations of sentiment and derisive laughter … In the years just before the war, when she was often … desperately tired, she was compelled to maintain this character off as well as on stage, to be both candid and high-spirited, generous with her time and attention.[25]

CHAPTER THREE

Funny Girl

Female Fun: Hylda Baker, the Houston Sisters,
Gladys Morgan, Beryl Reid, Tessie O'Shea,
Suzette Tarri, Joan Turner, Revnell and West,
Elsie and Doris Waters

For most variety performers, Britain was divided in two. From each direction, Birmingham seemed to be the cut-off point. In general, entertainers made famous in the north found that they were not understood south of the city and those who had conquered the south soon knew that anywhere north of the city was a wilderness. But the rule did not apply to Gracie Fields; nor did it to Gert and Daisy, two Cockney women, who, by chatting about back-street life and everyday events, became a mainstay of variety bills for more than 40 years.

Gert and Daisy were the creation of two Cockney sisters, Elsie and Doris Waters, whose humour has barely dated. They joked with each other in a quiet and confidential manner about Gert's permanent fiancé, Wally, Daisy's lazy husband, Bert, and their nosey neighbour, old Mother Butler, and, in the words of the arch-nostalgist, Denis Gifford,[26] brought an air of neo-realism to the stultified Oxford English of Reithian radio.

Elsie and Doris came from a musical family. Their mother, Maud, was a fine singer and their father, Ted, whose job was to supply brass plates to undertakers, filled his spare time singing with a minstrel troupe. He made all six of his children learn to play the piano plus one other instrument. Elsie chose the violin and Doris the tubular bells. [Their brother, Horace, learned both the violin and

Elsie Waters [Florence Elsie Waters]

- Born Bromley-by-Bow, East London, 19 August 1893
- Elsie Waters died Worthing, Sussex 14 June 1990
- Left £216,787 [£320,000]

> **Doris Waters** [Doris Ethel Waters]
>
> - Born Bromley-by-Bow, East London, 20 December 1899
> - Doris Waters died Worthing, Sussex 18 August 1978
> - Left £35,138 [£130,000]

viola. In time, he changed his name to Jack Warner and became a radio star in *Garrison Theatre* during the Second World War and a television star as *Dixon of Dock Green* from the mid-1950s to the mid-1970s]. The family called themselves E.W. Waters' Bijou Orchestra and, on one occasion, played for 1,400 inmates of the Poplar Workhouse.

Elsie and Doris studied at the Guildhall School of Music, but, instead of becoming serious musicians, they joined a seaside concert party at Southwold in Suffolk, where they wrote their own material and were each paid £4 a week. For a number of years, besides the concert parties, they performed at concerts, dinners and Masonic functions. Then, in 1927, they appeared on BBC Radio for the first time and released their first gramophone record two years later. In 1930, they were working on an act involving two Cockney women when they were asked to write and record something quickly for the Parlophone studios. They came up with *Wedding Bells*. They sang briefly at the start and end of it. In between, they indulged in East End banter about weddings. It was an immediate success and, within a short time, their concert audiences were calling out for them to 'do the Cockney women'.

> There seems to have been a rift between the sisters and Jack Warner later in life. According to the actor, Michael Kilgarriff, there were two attempts in the 1980s to present stage versions of the careers of Elsie and Doris. Both apparently foundered as a result of Elsie's refusal to permit any mention of Jack or of the sisters' apparent long-standing relationship with the same man.

Their names were made. In 1934, they appeared on the first of the *Guest Night* programmes with the bandleader, Henry Hall; in the Second World War, they broadcast daily cookery hints; they made some excellent movies, including *Gert and Daisy's Weekend* [1941]; and in the 1950s they starred in their own radio sitcom. A taste of their act can be savoured in a radio recording from Blackpool in 1952, introduced, as always, by a few bars of *Daisy Bell* (Daisy, Daisy, Give Me Your Answer, Do):

Isn't it grand to be on holiday? We've had some good food.
   What do you think we had for dinner yesterday? Some tripe. I've never had tripe before.

Never had tripe?

I didn't know what it was. I thought it was hanging up in the shop for the butcher to wipe his hands on …

Do you remember before you went away you lost your swimming costume?

What, my bikini?

Yes. Did you find it?

Yes. When I got here, there it was in my purse all the time.[27]

Elsie and Doris appeared in their first Royal Variety Show in 1934. Three years later, it was the turn of another female Cockney double act, Ethel Revnell and Gracie West. With Ethel standing just under six feet tall and Gracie nearly five feet, they dressed as a couple of small girls, billed as The Long and The Short of It.[28]

Ethel Revnell

- Born London 12 July 1896
- Died London 24 August 1978
- Left £27,382 [£105,000]

Their act always opened with their signature tune:

> Oh, we do see life! Yes, we do see life.
> Though we haven't got a man to call us wife,
> We don't pine or make a shine.
> Life's worth living and we think it's fine.
> We don't play golf upon on the links
> And we only drink the softest drinks,
> But we stay up late playing tiddleywinks.
> Oh! We do see life.[29]

Ethel met Gracie at the very first audition she attended. They then appeared in the same summer show, *The Margate Pedlars*, and were persuaded to team up. They got their big break in 1928 when they were cast in a touring production of the C.B. Cochran revue, *One Dam Thing After Another*. There followed some

---

Gracie West [Grace West]

- Born Portsea Island,Hampshire, 21 January 1890
- Died Portsmouth 10 April 1983

successful pantomime appearances under the direction of one of the kings of panto, Julian Wylie. Then, in 1934, they arrived at the top pantomime venue, the Theatre Royal, Drury Lane, where they appeared as the Ugly Sisters in *Cinderella*, the first women ever to have played those parts at the Lane.

Time and again, BBC Radio tried to book them, but they thought their act was too visual. They eventually relented:

> To our surprise, the act, after being modified and re-written here and there, turned out to be admirable radio material. The only thing that didn't please me, though, was the thought of broadcasting. Grace seemed all right. She didn't worry very much. For myself, I almost fainted in front of the mike on the night of the broadcast.[30]

In 1946, Gracie retired through ill health, leaving Ethel to pursue a successful solo career, at one point appearing alongside the suave Jack Buchanan in his last revue, *Fine Feathers*, at the Prince of Wales Theatre.

Another 'Cockney' comedienne, Suzette Tarri, had to wait until she was 57 before becoming a star. For years, she worked in concert parties, singing sentimental duets with her accompanist, David Jenkins, whom she later married. Little by little, Suzette introduced comedy into the act. When David went into music publishing, Suzette continued as a solo artiste appearing at concerts, dinners and dances.

Towards the end of 1937, she and David were given an audition by a talented and innovative BBC radio producer, Ernest Longstaffe. They sang a Negro spiritual. Longstaffe asked for something else. They tried a more modern song. Longstaffe still wanted something different. David mentioned that Suzette did some comedy. Longstaffe wanted to hear it and Suzette, seized with nerves, launched herself into some patter. Longstaffe laughed, took a gamble and immediately put her in a show called *Lightning Variety*. She was an instant success. Other radio shows followed; she appeared at variety theatres under Jack Hylton's management; joined a road show with the Two Leslies [see Chapter 24]; and began releasing 78s.

Suzette Tarri [Ada Barbara Henrietta Tarry]

- Born Hoxton, North London, 2 January 1881
- Married [1] Thomas Copeland in Islington, north London, 30 December 1905
- One son, Kenneth, who emigrated to Canada
- One daughter, who died in Hollywood
- Grandson, Wellington White; grand-daughter Alissande White
- Married [2] David Edmund Jenkins
- Suzette Tarri died Southgate, Middlesex, 10 October 1955
- Left £17,911 [£300,000]

Suzette developed a turn as a Cockney charwoman, Our Ada. Much of her comedy was drawn from real life. She once overheard a woman giving advice to a neighbour:

> Keep your own teeth as long as you can, dear. You've no idea what a trouble plates are. I've got sets and sets of teeth all standing grinning at me on my kitchen dresser. [Suzette] reproduced it almost word for word.[31]

In the guise of Our Ada, she began telling stories about her husband, Alf:

> The only bit of luck I ever had was when I won £5 at a bazaar. It was for a funny make-up competition. Course, it was odd my winning because I wasn't competing. I was only looking on at the others. But they made me take the prize. So, Alf said, 'You'd better let me handle the money. I'll invest it in land.' So, he went out and bought a plot of ground for a grave for hisself. Just like Alf to think of his own comforts first.[32]

Oddly enough, Suzette sang her closing song not in the guise of Our Ada, but in her own somewhat cultivated tones.

The climax of her career was an appearance at the London Palladium, sharing a bill with Danny Kaye. During her last three years, she suffered from cancer. She made her final stage appearance at the Theatre Royal, Portsmouth, in December 1954 and her last radio appearance in a Henry Hall *Guest Night* at the end of that month.

There were two Welsh comediennes in variety. One, Tessie O'Shea, made no play of her Cambrian roots. The other, Gladys Morgan, did – eventually.

Gladys, who was the same height as Gracie West, had a trademark, an uncontrollable shriek of laughter. It was made all the more unusual in that it emanated from such a tiny frame. The laugh was infectious. As soon as she let it rip, she had the audience on her side. Her bill matter told the whole story: Gladys Morgan: Variety's Longest Mirthquake.

At first, Gladys hid her Welsh lilt in a northern accent as she found most of her work in northern clubs. Her heroes were, in any case, such northern comics as Frank Randle and Albert Modley [see Chapter 11]. She made her name in 1946 when Mai Jones, the co-writer of the unofficial Welsh national anthem, *We'll Keep a Welcome (In the Hillside)*, auditioned her for the BBC radio programme, *Welsh Rarebit*. At first, Mai did not like her act. It seemed to be part Yorkshire/part Wales, she felt. Gladys reverted to her natural accent and adopted a signature tune, *Let a Smile Be Your Umbrella*. She was an instant success and stayed with *Welsh Rarebit* for three years.

Gladys had had a long showbiz apprenticeship. She had been touring in revues and concert parties for years. When she married a fellow comic, Frank Laurie, they formed a double act: Frank, the funny man; Gladys, the feed, but, when an agent saw them play Liverpool during a week of cine-variety,[33] he suggested that they changed roles. They took his advice and the act worked much better. During the Second World War, their talented daughter, Joan, joined the act. All three worked for ENSA and met Bert Hollman, ENSA's entertainments

Gladys Morgan [Gladys Mabel Morgan]

- Born Swansea 9 November 1898
- Married Francis Lorriman [professionally known as Frank Laurie] in Bristol 7 November 1923 [He died in Worthing, Sussex, 26 May 1967]
- Daughter, Joan, born Bristol 26 January 1924. Married Bertram Frederick Hollman [professionally known as Bert Hollman] in Leeds 21 April 1952 [He died in Worthing 16 April 1988]
- Son, Graham, who had a short-lived double act with Bud Flanagan's son, Buddy.
- Gladys Morgan died Worthing, Sussex, 16 April 1983
- Left £4,259 [£9,250]

organiser for north-west England, who, in time, married Joan. He also joined the act, which was then billed as Gladys Morgan and Family. In South Africa, they had their own series on Springbok Radio, *The Morgans*, scripted by Joan. Audiences were then segregated through apartheid. Back home, Gladys had to put up with abusive anonymous phone calls.

Gladys also appeared with Frankie Howerd, a committed fan; on BBC Radio's phenomenally successful *Educating Archie*; and at the London Palladium with the singer, Frankie Vaughan, the high point of her career.

The axiom of Tessie O'Shea, more Blackpool than Cardiff, was 'Laugh and Grow Fat'. She reckoned she weighed 17 stone [238 lbs], but she looked less than that. No matter. Years before obesity became an unpleasant buzzword, she championed the cause of the larger woman:

Being plump has nothing at all to do with glamour or charm. You don't have to be a skinny rake to be beautiful. Charm and beauty … express themselves in the little details and in your personal tastes and habits.[34]

Tessie O'Shea [Teresa Mary O'Shea]

- Born Cardiff 13 March 1913
- Married David Halsel Rollo in Blackpool 31 July 1940 [dissolved 1950]
- Tessie O'Shea died Leesburg, Florida, 21 April 1995

With her signature tune, *Two Ton Tessie from Tennessee,* Tessie radiated verve and fun. She was only five when she sang and danced at local charity concerts in south Wales. By the time she was 12, she had appeared at the Bristol Hippodrome and the Chiswick Empire. At first, she modelled herself on the similarly rotund Lily Morris, who sang *Why Am I Always the Bridesmaid?* and *Don't Have Any More, Mrs Moore.* But she soon found her own stage persona. Accompanying herself on the banjulele, she bounced along with such songs as *It All Belongs To Me, I'm Worth My Weight in Gold,* and *A Little Bit of Something that the Others Haven't Got.* She was soon a star.

In a revue, *High Time,* at the London Palladium in 1946, she made her entrance on top of an elephant. At the time, nobody knew that the animal was pregnant and, when Tessie became too much for her, she was thrown off. Tessie was supposed to recuperate for three months, but, when she heard she had been selected for that year's Royal Variety Performance, she threw away her crutches and made a triumphant comeback.

As variety dwindled, Tessie found herself reduced to the occasional movie or television appearance. Come 1963, however, Noel Coward took her to America to appear in his musical, *The Girl Who Came to Supper.* Her role was Ada Cockle, who sold fish and chips to the crowds lining the route for George V's coronation procession. At the show's out-of-town try-out in Philadelphia, it was clear that Tessie, singing *London is a Little Bit of All Right,* was going to steal the show. Coward wrote:

> The star of the evening was Tessie O'Shea, whose ovation during and after 'London', held up proceedings for almost five minutes. I have never heard such cheering. She fully earned it because she was warm, friendly and gave such a perfect performance. Not unnaturally, she got all the notices. It was truly thrilling to see that rumbustious, bouncing old-timer, after some years of limbo, come back and tear the place up.[35]

Praise from the Master is praise indeed. Tessie earned good money and Florida could be a nice place in which to end one's days. But she spent the last few years of her life in straitened circumstances, living in a converted shop with a man who once abandoned her for a younger woman he had made pregnant. The only sign of her previous wealth was an old Bentley.

Two Scottish girls took London by storm. The Houston Sisters, Renee and Billie, had been on stage since their infancy. By the time they reached the London Coliseum, they had mastered their trade and, with a refreshingly new act, they became stars overnight.

Their parents, Jim and Liz, ran a theatre company, presenting songs, comedy and drama. During the summer, they accepted only seaside bookings so their daughters could be with them. At home, the girls staged their own shows. Renee thought up sketches, chose the songs and made the costumes. The yard behind their home became a stage and the whole neighbourhood turned out to see them.

On one occasion, when Jim and Liz were due to play Airdrie in north Lanarkshire, they caught flu and persuaded the theatre manager to let the girls

Renee Houston [Catherine Rita Murphy Gribben]

- Born Johnstone, Renfrewshire, 24 July 1902 [The maiden name of Renee's mother was Houston]
- Married [1] George Alexander Joseph Balharrie in Glasgow 19 February 1925 [Dissolved] (Miss Houston said the marriage was unconsummated)
- Married [2] Patrick de Lacy Aherne [professionally known as Pat Aherne] in London 28 November 1932 [Pat Aherne, a movie actor, died in Los Angeles 30 September 1970]
- Married [3] Donald Wintermute [professionally known as Donald Stewart] in central London 7 August 1948 [died 3 March 1966]
- Renee Houston died in north-west Surrey 9 February 1980

go on in their place. From that moment, the Houston Sisters were born, Renee, playing a small girl in a gingham frock, Billie, an immaculately clad boy. After years of touring, they were spotted by agents for Stoll, who booked them for the Coliseum in October 1925:

They had built outsize tables and chairs for us to make us look smaller and I remember I had to come on and try to climb into a couch … I slipped onto my backside, tried again and landed on my face … It was simple stuff … But it was funny – at least they must have thought it was for they were paying us the enormous sum of 50 guineas a week.[36]

Billie Houston [Sarah McMahon Gribben]

- Born Shettleston, Glasgow, 28 April 1906 [The maiden name of Billie's mother was Houston]
- Married [1] Robert Wilton Smith [the son of the comedian, Robb Wilton] at Brompton Oratory 25 December 1928 [Dissolved 1933] [Robert Smith died 7 August 1943, aged 36. See Chapter 7] [At her first wedding, Billie Houston gave her name as Sarah Cecilia Maria McMahon Gribben]
- Married [2] [Richard James Shapland Cowper [professionally known as Shapland Cowper, an actor]. Separated [After an argument with Miss Houston, Cowper committed suicide by taking poison, Paddington, West London, 21 July 1938, aged 34]
- Married [3] Paul Wills-Eve, an Australian journalist [Died Chertsey, Surrey, 6 July 1973, aged 59]
- Billie Houston died Walton-on-Thames, Surrey, 30 September 1972 [On her death, her forenames were registered as Sarah Cecilia Maria]

The Houston Sisters' act relied very much on spontaneity: 'They never wrote a word of [it] in advance. They … simply chose the songs, worked out very roughly the situations – and left the rest to their native wit.'[37]

Backstage, Renee and Billie argued ceaselessly. The act apparently went well until ill health forced Billie to leave the act [or so the official version has it]. From then on, Renee appeared on stage with her third husband, Donald Stewart; scored a personal hit in a Noel Gay show at the London Hippodrome, *Love Laughs!* [1935]: [her four minute song, *Love Laughs at Locksmiths*, in which she sang both beautifully and raucously, threw in a few impersonations and exchanged banter with both the musical director and members of his orchestra was a tour de force]; made movies as disparate as *A Town Like Alice* [1960] and *Carry On at Your Convenience* [1971]; and introduced herself to a new generation of fans in a BBC Radio panel game, *Petticoat Line*, a light-hearted female version of *Any Questions?* The Chairman was the former dance band singer, Anona Winn, but Renee, a member of the panel, was the undoubted star, offering blunt advice to listeners who had written in. So many listeners found her forthright language unacceptable that she was eventually limited to two swear words per show. Anona and Renee could not bear the sight of each other.

Long before winning recognition as a serious actress, Beryl Reid appeared in variety as a ghastly schoolgirl, Monica, and a love-struck Birmingham teenager, Marlene. In *Educating Archie*, Monica was the girlfriend of Peter Brough's dummy; she dressed in the gymslip and boater she had worn at school, even though it was radio. Brough, not the most adept ventriloquist, once asked Beryl whether she ever saw his lips move. 'Only when Archie's talking,' she told him. Beryl based Marlene partly on a landlady at theatrical digs in Birmingham and partly on her dresser at the city's Theatre Royal:

> One way or another, I'm determined to land Perce this year. Ooh, he's lovely is Perce. He rides a motorbike now. He looks sensational in the gear – dressed in leather from head to foot. Leather helmet, leather jacket, leather trousers. If he comes off his bike, we just have him soled and heeled.[38]

Beryl was particularly successful in revue: *After the Show* [1951] at the St Martin's; *Rocking the Town* [1956] at the London Palladium; and *One to Another* [1959] at the Lyric, Hammersmith.

Alan Melville, who wrote sketches for revue and became one of Britain's first television stars, reckoned Beryl was hugely underrated:

> One of the inexplicable ingredients [of intimate revue] is that the leading comedienne, having had them rolling in the aisles all evening, should suddenly still the congregation by doing a serious number … [Once, when] Miss Reid had to appear in a Wren officer's uniform … the audience sat back for another belly laugh. She stilled them in a matter of seconds and all through the item – a sad little monologue about a woman whose life had gone very agley – there

Beryl Reid [Beryl Elizabeth Reid]

- Born Hereford 17 June 1919
- Married [1] William Lister Worsley [professionally known as Bill Worsley, the producer of *Workers' Playtime*] 1 October 1949. [Dissolved]
- Married [2] Derek Harold Franklin of the Hedley Ward Trio in Blackpool, 23 August 1954. [Dissolved]
- Beryl Reid died 13 October 1996
- Left £420,219 [£500,000]

was not a sound in the house until the applause cracked out after the long silence she held at the end of it.[39]

Beryl's abilities as an actress were finally recognised in *The Killing of Sister George* [1965], in which she played the lesbian star of a soap opera and Joe Orton's outrageous *Entertaining Mr Sloane* [1975].

Joan Turner seemed to have everything going for her. She was pretty, she sang operatic arias with a wonderful clarity and then switched to comedy, mocking everything, chiefly herself. But she felt her life needed greater stability. She married and had two children, but found the lure of showbiz too great and went back to performing. When she escaped from her career a second time, she fled to America. That venture ended in even greater personal tragedy.

As a child, Joan found she had a talent for mimicry and perfected imitations of local shop-owners. By the age of 13, when she was trying to find work as a performer, her audition piece included impersonations of Gracie Fields, Shirley Temple and Jessie Matthews. There followed years of touring in road shows and pantomimes, but the hard work paid off. Before she was 21, she was a well-known name, a comedienne with a vocal range of four octaves and a billing that undersold her abilities: The Wacky Warbler. When a young solicitor proposed marriage, though, she decided to leave the stage and settle down at Bracebridge Heath, near Lincoln. But the offers of work kept coming. In 1954, she starred alongside Tony Hancock and Jimmy Edwards[40] in a revue, *The Talk of the Town*,

Joan Turner [Joan Teresa Turner]

- Born Belfast 24 November 1922
- Married [1] William Hugh Christopher Page in Bournemouth 7 September 1946. [Dissolved]
- Married [2] Leslie Cocks
- Three daughters, Susanna, Joanna and Amanda
- Joan Turner died 1 March 2009

in Blackpool. When the show transferred to the Adelphi Theatre in London, Joan could not resist the temptation.

She rented an apartment in London and hired a nanny to look after her baby daughter. Her husband felt aggrieved and sued for divorce on the grounds of desertion.

For the next 20 years, Joan could do no wrong. She was on television and radio; she appeared in variety and pantomimes; she also staged her very funny one-woman show. The money poured in. Joan was seen in fashionable night clubs and restaurants; she owned a Rolls Royce and a Bentley; she bought mink coats; and her hairdresser attended to her every day. But no money was saved and she was eventually declared bankrupt.

Once she was discharged, she headed for the United States, but work was hard to find. Feeling homesick, she sank rapidly and finally hit rock bottom, scavenging for an existence as a bag lady in Los Angeles. By the time she returned to Britain, she had a serious drink problem. She moved into sheltered accommodation and attended meetings of Alcoholics Anonymous.

Then, in 2002, she announced that she was co-writing her autobiography. Her collaborator, the actor, Harry Dickman, said they hoped to have it published the following year. In 2005, she again staged her one-woman show at the tiny Jermyn Street Theatre in the West End. It was not a success. At a matinee, she abandoned her first number halfway through, saying that she had had enough of 'that fucking song'. It went from bad to worse. Her accompanist walked out and her mike was switched off. The theatre's manager said afterwards: 'It was awful ... She was like Joan Rivers on speed, [but] without the professionalism.'

In 2006, Joan announced that she was [still] writing her autobiography. It promised to be a kiss-and-tell effort. She had been to bed, she said, with Hancock, Terry Thomas and others, but they had all been too drunk to do anything.

Hylda Baker was one of the funniest women in variety and one of the least popular. When she was chosen as a victim of *This Is Your Life*, 35 people approached by researchers declined to appear. She became famous as a result of one television appearance in the BBC's ersatz music hall show, *The Good Old Days*, in 1955. But Hylda Baker was no overnight sensation. She had been on the stage since the First World War.

Hylda was the daughter of Harold Baker, a comedian-cum-dancer, known as Chukky. By the time she was three, he had taught her to dance. Aged 10, she made her stage debut at the Opera House, Tunbridge Wells, where she danced, sang three songs and performed some comic impersonations, including one of Charlie Chaplin. By the age of 14, she was a leading lady and went on to write, produce, direct and star in her own touring shows.

On the way up, she felt she had to fight for everything she wanted. This made her aggressive and suspicious of everyone she worked with. She was also marred by two family tragedies. In 1924, her father was hit by a sandbag that fell from a theatre's flies. He never worked again. His character changed and doctors diagnosed acute melancholia. He was admitted to a lunatic asylum, as they were then called, and spent the rest of his life there. Less than 10 years later, one of Hylda's brothers unexpectedly committed suicide.

Hylda Baker [Hilda Baker]

- Born Bolton 4 February 1905
- Married Ben Pearson at Doncaster 12 January 1929. [Dissolved 1933]
- Hylda Baker died London 1 May 1986

As short as Gladys Morgan and Gracie West, Hylda was naturally drawn towards comedy. Offstage, she was eccentric, taking her pet monkeys with her everywhere and, as a result, denied accommodation at hotels. It was her routine with Cynthia, a tall blonde, always played by a man, which brought her lasting success. Cynthia never spoke in spite of every effort made by Hylda to coax her. Hylda always arrived first on stage, dressed rather down-at-heel. Her efforts to speak posh usually collapsed in a welter of garbled gobbledegook:

Have you seen my friend? She's tall and blonde with aquamarine features. We're only in London for the day and I've spent an hour and a half at the lost property office. We were just coming out of Euston station when all of a sudden she said, 'I've lost them.' I said, 'What, again?' I mean I wouldn't care, but she couldn't remember whether she'd put them on or not. I said 'Why don't you buy yourself some woollen ones? Then you can feel whether you've lost them or not.' Well, you can't go about losing kid gloves like that.[41]

Cynthia would then walk slowly on, looking simple. Hylda believed she had to speak loudly to get through to Cynthia and exaggeratedly mouthed her lines, a technique she had learnt while working in an impossibly noisy factory: I said, 'Be soon, didn't I? Beeee sooooon!'

Hylda had all the conversation to herself until the end of the sketch when she confided in her audience: 'She just looks straight through you. I wouldn't care, but she knows, y'now.' Those last few words became her famous catchphrase.

Hylda invented Cynthia in 1950. The part was played by a fast-moving succession of men, as Hylda made it clear that part of their job was to have sex with her. In the end, she regarded Cynthia as her Frankenstein's monster. Her escape from the sketch came in 1968 with a Granada TV series, *Nearest and Dearest*, which teamed her with Jimmy Jewel, the variety comic whose act with his cousin, Ben Warriss, had abruptly ended [See Chapter 24]. Hylda was cast as Nellie Pledge, who ran a pickle factory with her brother, Eli. Differences between them materialised at the second rehearsal. Hylda counted the lines that got laughs to make sure she had as many as Jimmy. When *Nearest and Dearest* became a stage show, Hylda was spotted standing on a chair outside the theatre measuring the lettering on the posters to check whether the 'J' of Jimmy was no larger than the 'H' of Hylda. By the time *Nearest and Dearest* was made into a feature film, Hylda and Jimmy were not speaking to each other. Finally, Jimmy could take no more and his place in a show on the North Pier, Blackpool, was taken by the emollient Ken Platt. At the end of the 22-week run, Platt called the experience a living nightmare.

CHAPTER FOUR

Black and Blue

Two Monoliths: the London Palladium and the BBC

The greatest and most famous variety theatre in the world is [or, more precisely, was] the London Palladium. Every big star, British and American, aspired to play there and, for many years, it staged the most lavish and spectacular pantomimes in the land, but it was not always so successful. The low point came in 1928, 18 years after it opened.

The Palladium was the brainchild of Walter Gibbons. With the encouragement of his father-in-law, George Adney Payne, one of the leading variety managers of his day, Gibbons formed a public company, the London Theatres of Variety, to take over 15 music halls, all but one of them, the Holborn Empire, in the London suburbs and run them as a circuit. [The main circuits, Moss Empires founded by Edward Moss, and the Stoll Group, under Oswald Stoll, had merged in 1898. The main Moss Empires theatres were the London Hippodrome and the Victoria Palace. Others were spread right across Britain. Stoll's chief theatres were the London Coliseum and the Hackney Empire.] Gibbons also wanted to build a new theatre in the heart of London. This was the Palladium, designed by the leading theatre architect, Frank Matcham, at a cost of £250,000 [£14 million].

Once it opened, Gibbons spent his money unwisely. For one week, for example, he paid an eminent American soprano, Edith Walker, £600 [£33,500]. By 1912, it was clear that he was incapable of putting the Palladium on a sound financial footing. Approaches

Managing Director,
CHARLES GULLIVER

PRICE 3ᴰ·

were made to Stoll, who agreed to run LTV temporarily, but only if Gibbons left. He got his way. A statement was issued announcing that Gibbons was resigning through ill health. He returned to his chief interest, cinema, and tried again and again to bring sound to silent movies by synchronising them with gramophone records. Here, too, he failed.

Under Stoll and his young company secretary, Charles Gulliver, the Palladium was soon prospering. There were strong variety bills, a series of spectacular revues and, in 1927, the Palladium's first musical, *The Apache*, starring the heart-throb, Carl Brisson, a former Danish boxer, who sang with a rich tenor voice. In anticipation of a big success, Gulliver doubled seat prices. But *The Apache* ran for only 166 performances.

Worried about the enormous success of the first talking picture, *The Jazz Singer*, Gulliver then turned to a man who knew all about movies, the disgraced Walter Gibbons. Together with a financier, Gibbons bought LTV back for £1,570,000 [£45 million] with the aim of staging cine-variety. Gibbons was happy to choose the films. He entrusted the selection of variety acts to a young man in Gulliver's office, Val Parnell. He also began searching for provincial variety theatres to add to his chain.

He became particularly interested in a northern circuit, which was experimenting with cine-variety with great success. It was run by three brothers, George, Alfred and Ted Black, who agreed to sell provided George was given a job in London. Gibbons agreed and a new company was formed, The General Theatre Corporation. Gibbons was the managing director and Black was given a place on the board. Cine-variety was to go ahead at the Palladium, but, in the meantime, Gibbons became fascinated by *Dawn*, a film starring Sybil Thorndike as the First World War heroine, Edith Cavell, who was executed by the Germans for helping hundreds of Allied troops to escape from occupied Belgium.

Dawn caused enormous controversy. Germany wanted Britain to ban it and, even though he had not seen it and refused to do so, the Foreign Secretary, Sir Austen Chamberlain, agreed. Sybil Thorndike sought the opinion of Shaw and managed to arrange a screening at a small theatre in Soho. Simultaneously, the British Board of Film Censors, was to view the film at its headquarters opposite the theatre. There was only one print available. So, after Shaw had seen each reel, it was rushed across the road. At the end of the screening, Shaw proclaimed the film a masterpiece, but the censors supported the ban, leaving the director, Herbert Wilcox, with only one option:

to try to persuade the London County Council to approve it. By a majority of one, they granted the film a licence. Highly excited by this outcome, Gibbons offered a record fee for the rights and, a few hours after the vote, *Dawn* was being shown at the Palladium.

Gibbons gleefully predicted a six-month run, but the Palladium, everyone agreed, was the wrong venue. Within 10 days, the film was transferred to a cinema a couple of miles away. Its failure at the Palladium marked Gibbons' final decline and fall. His associates demanded his resignation and he left, complaining that he was being ordered around by amateurs. Five years later he died, a disillusioned disappointed man.

It was now George Black's job to run the Palladium. He not only saved the theatre, but safeguarded the future of variety itself. When George was 10, his father invested in a waxworks show that he presented at fairgrounds. George was put in charge of collecting admission fees, but the show was not a success. Neither was the next venture, a touring show featuring an animatograph, an early motion picture device. At one point, George, his father, plus Alfred and Ted spent two days walking to the Devon resort of Ilfracombe, giving 13 performances along the way and earning a total of 10 shillings. Black senior decided to return to Sunderland, where he was born, and open a cinema. He found an old church and gave George the job of demolishing the altar, putting up a screen in its place, writing advertising posters, singing to audiences between films and operating the projector.

This time, the Blacks succeeded. Two new cinemas were bought and, after Black senior died, the three brothers acquired a circuit of 13 cinemas, which they sold in 1919 for £280,000 [£6.75 millions]. George, who was now 28, need never have worked again. Instead, he built up another circuit of 11 cinemas, the ones he sold to Gibbons. George had learned how to be a businessman and how to be a showman too. At Christmastime, many of his cinemas staged pantomimes in which variety acts appeared.

George's acumen was doubted only once when he paid the startling sum of £4,250 [£127,500] for the English rights of an American film. It was *Tillie's Punctured Romance*, the first feature-length comedy movie from Keystone, directed by Mack Sennett and starring Charlie Chaplin, Mabel Normand and Marie Dressler. George recouped his investment many times over.

When George took over the running of the Palladium, he was instantly welcomed by variety entertainers, who recognised him as a man bursting with ideas. In language better suited to a politician, he explained his intentions:

It is not enough for the old Variety to return with its cobwebs and dust, its go-as-you-please methods and monotonous similarity of turns. A new structure is being built on the old foundations, replete with new ideas, new methods, renewed vitality and, above all, fresh powers of amusement. The old gloomy temples of Momus[42] with their sombre furnishings are no fitting habitation for the new Variety. We must have bright, joyous decorations, the acme of artistry in lighting, in scenery and stage dressing and orchestras that provide real music.[43]

George was determined to make the Palladium the world's greatest variety theatre. He set 3 September 1928 as the date when the new era would begin. In the weeks before, London was plastered with posters that announced: Variety is coming back. Later, the words, To the Palladium, were added. His opening bill included Ivor Novello in a one-act play [his attraction then was as a cinema idol] and Gracie Fields. Wearing a magnificent new gown, she made her entrance past rows and rows of swathes, swags and chiffon and then confided in her audience: 'Ee, ba gum. It's all too grand for me.'[44]

George's big idea was to quicken the pace of shows. It sounded simple enough, but it was a necessity noted by Sophie Tucker, the Last of the Red Hot Mammas, on her first visit to Britain in 1922. She was taken to the Coliseum, which she likened to the Palace in New York.[45] The seats were big and comfortable; the lighting system was better than in America; and the drop curtains, which had scenery painted on them, were richly coloured. But for Sophie, who was always magnificently accoutred, none of the acts dressed smartly or looked up to date. None of the men wore tuxedos and the gowns the women wore looked as if they had been bought in second-hand clothes shops:

> The show … was very much like our bills, with the acrobats to open, the neat dancing girl, the street comedians, the jugglers, the monologuist, the women singers, the comedienne, the ballroom dancers … the comedy sketch, the dramatic sketch, then the headliner and the standard act. But there the likeness ended … The songs were drawn out from eight to ten minutes. While performers made changes, there were many stage waits. It all seemed slow and draggy to me.[46]

George agreed and the changes he introduced were welcomed by audiences, performers and reviewers alike, among them, the BBC's first drama critic, Archibald Haddon: 'The first necessity of the dying music hall, if its life were to be saved, was to quicken the show. Black did that. Variety sat up and gasped and its pulse began to beat more regularly.'[47]

A leading columnist of the day, Hannen Swaffer, agreed: '[George Black] saved variety by making artists work together, one introducing the next … He stopped the long dreary waits, during which the last chorus would be played by the orchestra over and over again. He made artists smarten themselves up, buy better costumes.'[48]

George Black knew he had to battle against the increasing competition of cinema, but there was another problem for him, the growing popularity of radio. In 1922, 35,000 people had wireless licences. Within the space of five years, that figure rose to more than two million. Uncharacteristically, George could not make up his mind about radio. Before he took control of the Palladium, LTV had imposed a ban on all broadcasts from the theatre because it was felt that routines by comics, for instance, could become stale in one night. George lifted the ban, arguing that, if comics were forced to find new material, everyone would benefit. He changed his mind when he came to realise that people were staying at home, listening to their favourite entertainers for free, rather than paying to see them at the theatre.

From the outset, the entertainers' trade union, the Variety Artistes' Federation, was stubbornly opposed to radio:

> The artiste who is in demand and who is identified with material of an original and distinctive character would be most unwise to broadcast such material, since, by doing so, he would not only shorten the life of his material, but also lessen the value of his act as a going concern.[49]

Stoll felt the same, believing that, when broadcasting reached a high state of perfection, 'the best singers, actors, lecturers and orators will be listened to by ten million people at a time, but all the lesser fry in artistry will be wiped out. No one will have any use for them.'[50]

As it turned out, people hearing new entertainers on the radio then went to the theatre to see them as they wanted to know what they looked like. In the 1930s, Palladium playbills advertised Elsie and Doris Waters as Radio's Gert and Daisy and the comedian, Tommy Handley[51] as the Famous Radio Star.

The fledgling BBC soon found that listeners rated variety shows as their favourite programmes. It began finding its own entertainers, men like Norman Long ['A smile, a song and a piano'], who first broadcast from Marconi House in 1922. His radio appearances led to a recording career. Between 1925 and 1940, he made 52 mildly amusing records, including one that lampooned the BBC, *We Can't Let You Broadcast That*; Mabel Constanduros, who had written sketches about the fictional Buggins family to amuse her mother and sisters, first broadcast them in 1925; and John Henry played a hen-pecked Yorkshireman who told tales of his exploits with his friend, Joe Murgatroyd, and of disagreements with his wife, Blossom. In the late 1920s and the early 1930s, the BBC auditioned between 1,500 and 2,000 would-be entertainers every year, but less than one per cent of them were accepted.

In the early years, leading lights in the variety world despaired at the lack of experienced producers at the BBC. One showbiz newspaper complained that the BBC's variety was as much like variety as Poplar was like Paradise. The criticism was unsurprising. The Corporation's first Director General, John Reith, loathed variety as much as he did jazz.[52] He described George Formby's song, *When I'm Cleaning Windows*, as disgusting. It was not until 1933 when Eric Maschwitz[53] was

Norman Long; a smile, a song and a piano.

appointed its first Head of Variety that the BBC started to behave more professionally.

Even then, Maschwitz complained that it was difficult to find good entertainers 'except the Director General's great friend, Sir Harry Lauder, with whom he had done a private deal. We had old Sir Harry twice a year, shouting at us, running us around the place and arguing with everybody. A terrifying event that was.'[54] Lauder himself, who w:s first heard on the air in December 1925, made a good case for broadcasting:

Eric Maschwitz: song and variety supremo.

I have the opportunity of playing to tens of thousands of folk who would never otherwise have had the chance of hearing Harry Lauder. I thought of the people in the lonely glens far removed from town and village, of the sailors on the sea, of the men on the lighthouses and lightships, of the villagers and rural workers, of all the vast scattered peoples who never have a chance from one year's end to another of attending a music hall or other place of entertainment. And I also thought of the thousands of sick and ailing ones … to whom the coming of wireless has been indeed a boon and a blessing.[55]

In time, the BBC became a major employer of variety entertainers. *Music Hall*[56] [1932–1952], one of the first programmes to be recorded before an invited audience, was followed by *Workers' Playtime*[57] [1941–1964] and *Variety Bandbox*[58] [1942–52], all immensely popular shows. The BBC was as strict with its performers as George Black, a stern disciplinarian who cut any dubious line from a comic's script. In its earliest days, the BBC told its entertainers there were to be no references to politics, no vulgar or distasteful material and no Biblical quotations.

In 1932, George Black became even more powerful when the General Theatre Corporation merged with Moss Empires. Six years later, he was made managing director of Moss Empires. A splendid example of his sense of showmanship came with the abdication of Edward VIII in 1936. After a patriotic scene had been staged at the Palladium, he stopped the show. The cast, assembled on stage, stood to attention while the abdication speech was broadcast throughout the theatre. Immediately it ended, a singer dressed as Sir Francis Drake led the cast and audience in *Land of Hope and Glory,* followed by the National Anthem. By the time this shameless stunt had been staged, George's days were sadly numbered. He was only 54 when he died after an operation in 1945.

Val Parnell was a worthy successor. Like George, he had been steeped in the theatre since he was a child. His father was the world-famous ventriloquist,

Fred Russell, a stalwart of the Variety Artistes' Federation. When he was a boy, Val's Christmas presents were often toy theatres. At the age of 13, he started work in the office of Sir Walter de Frece, who ran a circuit of northern music halls. Later on, as the booking manager of the General Theatre Corporation, he looked an unlikely figure. Quiet and unobtrusive in appearance, he might have worked in banking. Although he was a first-rate talent scout, he was tough, he bore grudges and he made enemies. One unnamed performer turned up at the Palladium with a revolver and threatened to shoot him. Parnell sent him a note that read 'For that privilege, you will have to wait your turn in a pretty lengthy queue.'[59]

Val Parnell: of the Parnell showbiz dynasty.

In the late 1940s, when he felt there were not enough British variety stars, he turned to the United States and brought over a string of American names to top the Palladium's bills: Frank Sinatra, Ella Fitzgerald, Judy Garland, Jack Benny, Jimmy Durante, Nat King Cole, Benny Goodman, George Burns and Gracie Allen and many more.

Val concentrated on the Palladium. He entrusted Moss Empires' other theatres to his chief booking manager, Cissie Williams, a martinet in the variety world. She could make or break careers. Craven advertisements placed by entertainers in Christmas theatre papers always acknowledged the debt they owed to Miss Williams: not Cissie, always Miss Williams or Myth Williams, as Beryl Reid styled her. [In fact, she was not Cissie Williams at all. She was born Lydia Hobden, a greengrocer's daughter]. A smart woman with her hair swept back, she could, according to one colleague, be a screaming harridan. Neurotic, both shrewd and naïve, she was most importantly incorruptible. Florence Leddington, her counterpart in the Syndicate Halls circuit, expected a gift to be left on her desk when she absented herself for a few moments while interviewing a new act.[60] No one ever dreamed of trying to bribe Williams.

On her death in 1966, Jimmy Jewel paid tribute to her:

> Cissie could be terribly hard and, if you committed the unforgivable by over-running your time, she was on the phone the next day with a big stick. But she could also be kind and understanding and you could always go up to the office and get her to listen sympathetically to your problems.[61]

Cissie had a thing about shoes. In 1954, three years before the start of *Hancock's Half Hour* on BBC Radio, Tony Hancock was about to join a Moss tour that began at the Shepherd's Bush Empire. In a run-through at a theatre near Sloane

Square, Hancock ambled on stage in an ill-fitting suit and a pair of down-at-heel shoes. Williams watched his act in silence. At the end, she turned to his agent, Phyllis Rounce, and said: If he dresses in those shoes, he will not be allowed on the stage. Rounce bought him new shoes, but he found them uncomfortable and, when he next appeared before Williams, he wore his old ones. Her only reaction was a roar: Get him off!

An agent persuaded her to see two girl dancers. They're pretty and they're good, she conceded, but I can't use them. They have dirty shoes. We don't book acts with dirty shoes. She could have told him to make the girls clean their shoes, but her view was that they should not have worn dirty shoes in the first place.

An elderly comic appeared with a neat patch sewn into his trousers after he had fallen over drunk. Williams' solution: Buy him a new pair. Deduct the cost from his salary and tell him that, if he does it again, he is out. A comic whose patois was pure Geordie received a similarly brusque verdict: Tell him he can play Newcastle and Sunderland, but the rest of his dates are cancelled.

The comedian, Barry Cryer, likes to tell the story of the outrageous Northern comic, Frank Randle [see Chapter 11], who was badly received by an audience at the Finsbury Park Empire. They stamped their feet and threw coins at him until the management tried to drop the fire curtain in front of him. Randle quickly ducked under it, scowled at the audience and shouted Bastards! The next day he was summoned to Williams' office. She told him she would never countenance swearing, even bringing herself to repeat the offending word. No, no, my dear, replied Randle. Have you the Italian? I was shouting 'Basta, basta. Enough, enough.'

On the other hand, when the great Tommy Cooper told a notoriously Anglophobic audience at the Glasgow Empire to fuck off, Williams backed him up: 'Great. It's about time someone told those bastards to fuck off.'[62] [There is more about the work of Cissie Williams in Chapter 19].

Norman Hoskins worked for Williams producing Moss Empires' box office cards. His biggest problem was to make it look as though more than one entertainer was topping the bill. In addition, Williams insisted that only one comic could appear as a comedian. Others had to be content with being described as a humorist, a laughter raiser or something similar. The amount of space allotted to any artistes who appeared on the cards was in strict proportion to their fees and popularity. Norman Hoskins transgressed only once. In the Autumn 2009 edition of the British Music Hall Society's magazine, *The Call Boy*, he wrote:

Although Hylda Baker was only a medium priced act at the time, I thought that, as she was wowing audiences, she should receive enhanced billing. Cissie, however, did not agree and consistently reduced her space. Foolishly, I persisted, not appreciating that Hylda was in the doghouse. Doubtless, she had committed the unforgiveable sin of over-running her act. The result? I had the dressing down of a lifetime. 'You must be in love with this bloody woman,' shrieked Cissie. 'The next time she comes in, I'll bring you two face to face.' It was a terrifying spectacle. I backed away murmuring apologies.

Tommy Cooper notwithstanding, Moss Empires was as strict about bad language as the BBC. If anyone appearing on the radio had sworn, they would never have broadcast again. But then, people expected higher standards from an entertainment beamed straight into their homes and the BBC tried to meet those standards. Among the complaints:

- **1935** A clergyman from Devon protested about a joke told by Clapham and Dwyer:

What is the difference between a Champagne cork and a baby? A Champagne cork has the maker's name on the bottom.

Two nights later, during a news bulletin, the BBC broadcast an apology for 'highly objectionable remarks, violating standards that have been firmly established.'

- **1940** The Assistant Director of Variety, Pat Hillyard, instructed all variety producers to scrutinise the scripts of the comedian, Billy Danvers, and, in the words of one who clearly did not understand double entendre, 'make certain that he does not slip anything in on the night.'
- **1943** Tessie O'Shea was banned for her 'partiality for innuendo' and Tommy Trinder pulled out of a new series, *Tommy, Get Your Fun* because one of his jokes had been cut:

I was walking down Whitehall the other day when an American soldier came up to me and said 'What side is the War Office on?' I said 'Our side, I hope.'

- **1946** The Chairman of the BBC, Lord Inman, wrote from his hospital bed to complain that his 18-year-old son, 'a perfectly normal boy [who] enjoys good fun,' was disgusted by a joke told by [again] Clapham and Dwyer:

When I got into my hotel bedroom last night, I found a lady's nightdress on the bed and I rang the bell.
 What for? To ask them to take it away?
 No. To ask them to fill it.

So, in 1949, the BBC decided it needed to lay down stricter and more specific rules for variety producers about the subjects it considered unsuitable for humour. It was known as the Green Book, devised by the Director of Variety, Michael Standing. In one section, it decreed that there was a ban on jokes about immorality of any kind, effeminacy in men; lavatories; on suggestive references to prostitution, ladies' underwear, honeymoon couples, chambermaids, fig leaves, animal habits, lodgers and commercial travellers. In addition [it added], extreme care should be taken in dealing with references to or jokes about marital

Cross-talking comics Clapham and Dwyer.

infidelity and pre-natal influences. The 'vulgar' use of such words as 'basket' was also banned.

In light entertainment, such words and phrases as 'God', 'Good God', 'blast', 'Hell', 'damn', 'bloody', 'Gorblimey' and 'ruddy' were to be deleted from scripts and innocuous expressions substituted. There were to be no references to Negroes, although, in a weird concession, 'nigger minstrels' was to be allowed.[63]

A list of banned songs was maintained and constantly updated. It included *One for the Road, She Had to Go and Lose it at the Astor, Only a Glass of Champagne*, and *Please Do It Again*. Some restrictions were difficult to understand. *Mandy is Two* was allowed, but only on the Home Service, the forerunner of Radio Four.

On a quiet night, John Reith can be heard turning in his grave at great speed.

CHAPTER FIVE

Gang of Six

Court Jesters Flanagan and Allen, Nervo and Knox, Naughton and Gold [not forgetting Monsewer Eddie Gray]

George Black's most triumphant achievement was to nurture and develop the Crazy Gang, three double acts, who believed that comedy should have no rules. When he told friends he was putting six comedians in the same show, they told him it would be disastrous. The comics would try to ruin each other's acts and audiences would stay away in their thousands.

> Jealousy has always been the curse of the theatre and comics are the biggest problem of all. It has long been proverbial among managers that two comedians on one bill are too many for comfort. They fight about dressing rooms, billing and 100 other things. Put them on the stage together and each would do his best to turn the other's performance into a lugubrious exhibition.[64]

The three acts were Nervo and Knox, Naughton and Gold, and Flanagan and Allen. Everyone now assumes that Flanagan and Allen were the senior partners because they became well known through recordings of their songs, most notably *Underneath the Arches, Run, Rabbit, Run, We're Going to Hang out our Washing on the Siegfried Line* [for these last two, see Chapter 9]; and many others.[65] In fact, Nervo and Knox, although first among equals, always had the number one dressing room.

Jimmy Nervo was the son of Captain George Holloway, who ran a circus. By the age of nine, Jimmy had mastered juggling, acrobatic dancing and tightrope walking. He was nicknamed Nervo after an accident-prone cartoon character.

Teddy Knox also came from a theatrical family. His father was an actor and, as a

Jimmy Nervo [James Henry Holloway]

- Born Hackney, north London, 2 January1897
- Married Minnie Schimmler in Worthing 2 October 1939
- Jimmy Nervo died London 5 December 1975
- Left £99,978 [£550,000]

youngster, Teddy was part of a juggling and balancing act. The two men teamed up in 1919, appearing as gymnasts and knockabout comedians in variety and revue and playing a season at the Ziegfeld Follies. Black was a big fan of both men. He believed they were capable of anything on stage. In the Crazy Gang shows, they even became female impersonators, Jimmy appearing as Jean Harlow and Teddy as Marlene Dietrich. Black especially admired Teddy's ability to speak fake gibberish incessantly. 'He can go on for hours in that meaningless, but highly expressive language, explaining, gesticulating, denying, affirming and saying nothing.'[66]

Nervo and Knox invented slow motion wrestling, which is more difficult than it sounds. To wrestle at a fraction of the speed takes far more energy than the real thing. At the end of their act, they were dripping with sweat. Both men had been brought up tough. When they learned that another act, the Jerez Brothers, were copying them, they intercepted them near a theatre they were playing and beat them up.

Charlie Naughton and Jimmy Gold worked as painters and decorators before becoming slapstick comedians. Prior to the Gang, they were best known for a burlesque about labourers, *Turn it Round the Other Way*, in which they made out that a plank, for instance, would be shorter [or longer] if it were turned round.

Teddy Knox [Albert Edward Cromwell-Knox]

- Born Newcastle-upon-Tyne 12 July 1897
- Married [1] Clarice Mabel Tate [née Dulley] [professionally known as Clarice Mayne {1886 – 1966}, the widow of the songwriter, James W. Tate] in Sussex, 6 September 1934
- Married [2] Betty Reeves in central London 7 March 1969
- Teddy Knox died Salcombe, Devon, 1 December 1974

Charlie Naughton [Charles John Naughton]

- Born Glasgow 15 December 1886
- Married Alice Martin in Glasgow 16 September 1909
- Son killed in Second World War
- Charlie Naughton died in London 11 February 1976
- Left £4,076 [£20,000]

Naughton had a habit of going to a nightclub after the theatre and not arriving home until four in the morning. Thinking of the neighbours, he stopped his taxi at the end of the road and walked the last few yards. If he was unsteady on his feet, a couple of policeman on their beat often helped him to reach the front door. After falling ill, his doctor told him to give up drinking and nightclubs, go home early, get up at dawn and walk smartly round his local park.

> Much against his will, Charlie decided to give it a try. That night, he went straight home after the show. Next morning, about seven, he walked down to the bottom of his road, where the two policemen were waiting for him and promptly took him by the arm, as usual, and helped him straight back to his house.[67]

Bud Flanagan's partnership with Chesney Allen was based on a successful blend of opposites. Bud, the son of Jewish refugees from Poland, grew up in terrible poverty. At the age of 14, he ran away from home and reached New York, where he found work as a taxi driver and a boxer, all the time trying to establish himself as a comedian. Ches, a former actor on the 'legitimate' stage, was the ideal foil. Their personalities were summed up in the way they dressed: Bud in a moth-eaten fur coat and an old straw hat; Ches in a neat suit and a trilby. Their singing voices were also well matched. Bud had a light voice

Jimmy Gold [James Joseph McGonigal]

- Born Glasgow 21 April 1886
- Married [1] Anna Bachman in Glasgow 19 February 1016
- [2] June/Betty Nowland
- Son, James
- Jimmy Gold died in Harrow 7 October 1967
- Left £9,903 [£120,000]

Bud Flanagan [Reuben Weintrop]

- Born Whitechapel, east London, 14 October 1896
- Married Annie Quinn, known as Curly, in Chester-le-Street, Durham, 8 November 1924
- Son, Robert [died Los Angeles 29 February 1956, aged 30]
- Bud Flanagan died in Kingston-upon-Thames 20 October 1968

Chesney Allen [William Ernest Allen]

- Born London, 5 April 1894
- Married Aleta Cosetta Turner in Leeds 6 March 1922
- Chesney Allen died in Chichester 13 November 1982
- Left £92,813 [£2 million]

---

modelled on the music-hall singer, Alec Hurley. Ches's was deeper. He did not sing so much as slide up to a note.

The two men met twice before teaming up, first in France during the First World War and then near the Criterion Theatre in Piccadilly Circus where Ches was appearing [possibly understudying] in a Feydeau farce. By the early 1920s, Ches was part of a company run by the music hall singer, Florrie Forde. Bud was invited to join the company at the Glasgow Empire and Flanagan and Allen made their first appearance together at the Keighley Empire in 1926.

An honorary member of the Gang was 'Monsewer' Eddie Gray, whose French was not so much fractured as smashed to smithereens. Gray was a one-off, a genuine eccentric who was as funny offstage as on. He also began his career as a juggler. His cleverest trick was to juggle three apples, one of which gradually disappeared as he took bites out of it. Sporting a grotesque moustache and a battered top hat, he widened his scope as his career progressed. He gave

---

Eddie Gray [Edward Earl Gray]

- Born Pimlico, London, 10 June 1898
- Married Marie Cecilia Loftus Pasquali, formerly Jones, in Lambeth, south London, 3 October 1931 [died 1994]
- Eddie Gray died in Shoreham-by-Sea, Sussex, 15 September 1969
- Left £6,733 [£67,500]

mock-Shakespearean recitations and worked with performing [or more truthfully, non-performing] dogs.

A priceless piece of film shows him vainly trying to persuade a bored and tired-looking dog to jump through an impossibly small hoop. When the dog lies down, Gray gets his audience to stand in order to encourage the poor creature to do the same.[68]

Eddie first used his version of Franglais to try to make French stagehands understand him. It soon became an integral part of his act:

Now, ce soir – that's foreign for this afternoon – moi's gonna travailler la packet of cards – une packet of cards, not deux, une. Now, I have 'ere an ordinaire packet of playing cards – cinquante-deux in numero – fifty-two in number – ein, swine, twime and every card parla la meme chose.[69]

Offstage, the Gang spent Sunday afternoons at boxing matches at the Ring in Blackfriars. One week, a dreary match followed the same pattern, round after round. During the eighth round, Eddie threw a set of door keys into the ring. The match stopped and the boxers looked at Eddie in surprise. 'I'm going now,' he said. 'Lock up when you've finished.'[70]

A stage-struck girl, who wanted to be a dancer, arranged an interview with Eddie. When she went to his dressing room, she found him completely naked. She did her best to pretend that everything was normal and Eddie promised to do all he could to help her. As she was leaving, he said, 'I wonder whether you would close your eyes for a minute. I want to put my trousers on.'[71]

Uncharacteristically, George Black was unimpressed by Eddie's stage act. Throughout his career, Eddie refused to sign a contract with any management. Black disliked such unusual independence. After the Gang's last show, Eddie carried on working. He refused to take holidays. In 1969, he played a week at Brighton and then went to see Elsie and Doris Waters at the Hippodrome in Eastbourne. When he was invited on stage, he received a standing ovation. Those cheers may have been ringing in his ears three days later when he died. Eddie was the comedian's comedian. Tommy Trinder once said: 'The critics call me a God of comedy. Well, Eddie Gray is Einstein.'[72]

George Black believed that, for any audience, the show should start as soon as they arrived at the theatre. On that, at least, the Gang agreed with him. They often stood in the queue for their own show before taking their place in the stalls and loudly heckling the other acts. At other times, they welcomed theatregoers in the foyer, sold them inaccurate programmes at inflated prices and directed them with great politeness to the wrong seats.

Nervo and Knox more or less originated the Crazy Gang's formula. In 1925, they were touring with their own revue, *Young Bloods of Variety*, a fast-moving show in which they took part in other acts. Val Parnell saw it and, in November 1931, George Black decided to try it out for a week at the Palladium, adding Naughton and Gold, another double act, Billy Caryll and Hilda Mundy,[73] and Eddie Gray to the cast.

The show was popular enough for another Crazy Week to be staged the following month. The team's sense of anarchy began to materialise as Gang members interrupted Robb Wilton's sketch, *The Charge Officer*, and tried to lay bets on races that had already been run. Tommy Handley came in for the same sort of treatment. Nervo, Knox and Caryll appeared as girl guides in Handley's sketch, *The Disorderly Room*. Eddie Gray's juggling clubs were greased and cabbages were released from the flies just as someone was about to sing.

In 1932, Flanagan and Allen joined the team, but without the approval of the others, who felt they might slow the show up. They were wrong. Flanagan and Allen fitted in perfectly and Crazy Weeks became Crazy Months, regularly attracting 30,000 people a week to the Palladium. Bills advertising the shows perpetuated the crazy sense of humour. Nervo and Knox were billed as 'fresh from their South African deportation' and Flanagan as 'staying until his coat been deloused.'

The Story of a Song

The Ritz I never sigh for.
The Carlton they can keep.
There's only one place that I know
And that is where I sleep.

Underneath the Arches
I dream my dreams away.
Underneath the Arches
On cobblestones I lay.
Ev'ry night you'll find me,
Tired out and worn,
Happy when the daylight comes creeping
Heralding the dawn.
Sleeping when it's raining
And sleeping when it's fine
[I hear the] trains rattling by above.
Pavement is my pillow,
No matter where I stray.
Underneath the Arches
I dream my dreams away.

Bud's song about a down-and-out sleeping rough became an anthem of the Depression years. He maintained he had written it in a dressing room at the Hippodrome, Derby, in 1926 or 1927 and had sung it at the Pier Pavilion, Southport, the following week. Strangely, it was not published until 1932. Some song-sheets list Reg Connelly [see Chapter 9] as the co-author. The

Arches, incidentally, are the railway arches near Charing Cross station in London. In America, the song flopped at first because 'arches' there mean 'feet'. As a result, the US songwriter, Joseph McCarthy, was brought in to Americanise it. Cleverly, he left the chorus as it was, but rewrote the introduction to explain arches and remove references to the Ritz and the Carlton, which were also beyond the comprehension of Americans:

> The bridge down by the river
> With arches overhead:
> It's home-like there to me
> That's where each night I make my bed.

By 1934, the shows began to have proper titles. *March Hares* was the first, followed by *Life Begins at Oxford Circus*, *Round About Regent Street*, *All Alight at Oxford Circus* [all 1935]; *Okay for Sound* [1936]; *London Rhapsody* [1937–38]; *These Foolish Things* [1938–39]; and *The Little Dog Laughed* [1939–40]. Black had a rule about how long a show should run. When it had taken £25,000 for stalls seats alone, he announced its closure. Bear in mind that the top price of a seat at the Palladium was then six shillings [30p] {£10.50}.

During the run of *The Little Dog Laughed*, George Black announced that the Gang was about to play to its one-millionth theatregoer. A middle-aged couple had just bought their seats when the Gang descended on them. The woman was given a huge bouquet of flowers, the man, a big box of cigars and both were escorted to George Black's box. At the interval, they were invited to Bud's dressing room for a drink. About 15 newspaper photographers were there too. As Bud recalled, it was then that the man piped up:

> 'I can't have any pictures taken. You see, I don't know this woman. In fact, I only met her ten minutes before the show at Oxford Circus tube station. What will my wife say?' I told GB, who smiled wryly and said, 'Sorry, boys, no pictures.' With those few sad words, about £10,000 worth of publicity went down the drain.[74]

On the outbreak of the Second World War, the Crazy Gang went their separate ways. There was talk of them reuniting once peace was declared, but Val Parnell, said: 'I don't want a lot of old men running around my theatre.'[75] The impresario, Jack Hylton, then stepped in and offered the Gang the Victoria Palace. The first show there was called *Together Again* [1947–49]. It ran for 1,566 performances, making it second only to *Beyond the Fringe* [1961–64] as the most popular revue ever seen in Britain, although the two were hardly comparable. There followed: *Knights of Madness* [1950]; *Ring out the Bells* [1952–54]; *Jokers Wild* [1954–56]; *These Foolish Kings* [1956]; *Clown Jewels* [1959]; and *Young in Heart* [1960–62].

The Gang made five movies, *Okay for Sound* [1937], *Alf's Button Afloat* [1938], *The Frozen Limits* [1939], *Gasbags* [1940] and *Life is a Circus* [1958]. They loved practical jokes, some of them funny, most of them cruel. Val Guest had a hand in writing all five films and, when he arrived on the set one morning, most of the Gang complimented him on a sports shirt he had just bought from Simpson's. Teddy Knox was not so sure. He ran his fingers over it, declared it was made from poor material and could easily tear. Val disagreed. The shirt was made from textured linen. Teddy then grabbed hold of one collar and tugged it, practically ripping the shirt in half. Jimmy Nervo pulled at the other collar and, in minutes, the shirt was in ribbons.

The wardrobe mistress, who was looking on, suggested Val collected another shirt from wardrobe. Ten minutes later, he reappeared wearing a silk beach top, assuring Teddy that this item could definitely not be torn. Again, Teddy reduced it to thin strips of material and, when the laughter had subsided, suggested Val should collect another shirt from wardrobe. Val had the last laugh: 'It doesn't belong to wardrobe,' I told him. 'It's yours. From the cupboard in your dressing room.'[76] Touche!

Chesney Allen, who had suffered from rheumatism for years, retired from the stage on doctor's orders in 1945 and became the Gang's agent and manager. When the television writer, Jimmy Perry, was working on the first series of the Home Guard comedy, *Dad's Army*, in 1968, he wanted Flanagan and Allen to sing the signature tune he had composed [*Who do you think you are kidding, Mr Hitler?*] He phoned Ches and put the idea to him, but was turned down. Ches said he had been ill and was too weak. Bud recorded the song on his own. The recording was the last work he did. He died a short time afterwards.

In 1975, a stage show of *Dad's Army* was put on at the Shaftesbury Theatre with the whole cast dressed as Flanagan and Allen singing *Home Town*. Jimmy phoned Ches again and asked him to appear on the first night. That was impossible too. Ches was quite ill, but he eventually agreed to do just one night. A seat in the front row of the stalls would be set aside so that he could easily reach the stage. Ches said 'No' to that. He would be too recognisable and would detract attention from the stage. When the time came, he joined Arthur Lowe on stage. There was a short silence and then everybody in the audience burst into applause and gave him a standing ovation. In 1982, when Roy Hudd played Flanagan in *Underneath the Arches* at the Prince of Wales, Ches again made the odd appearance. He phoned to say when he would be in London and then suggested that he took part. Whenever he did, he brought the house down. He died that year, the first of the Gang to retire and the last to die.

CHAPTER SIX

There'll Never Be Another

Cheeky Chappie Max Miller

Max Miller knew the meaning of innuendo and it wasn't the Italian for 'suppository'. Max was the greatest stand-up [or front cloth] comic of all time. He had a reputation for being dirty, but he never told a blue joke. A gag might look as though it was heading for a doubtful conclusion, but Max always stopped short and, if the audience laughed, he accused them of having dirty minds. 'You wicked lot. It's your sort who get me into trouble.'[77]

No other comic before or since established such a quick and magical rapport with his audience. From the moment he was on stage, he had the audience, to coin a cliché, in the palm of his hand. His entrance was nicely stage-managed. Before he came on, the stage was blacked out for about ten seconds and the music stopped, leading the audience to think something may have gone wrong. The band then played Max's signature tune, *Mary from the Dairy*, a spotlight hit the prompt corner and, at just the right moment, Max would walk on grinning from ear to ear. He was a good-looking man, six feet tall, with broad shoulders and a narrow waist. He had clear blue eyes and he made himself up to resemble an old-fashioned chorus boy.

He wore a range of extraordinary costumes, a white trilby, jauntily tilted, co-respondent shoes, an extravagant kipper tie, silk suits with enormous plus fours, even an outfit depicting white daisies against a blue background, and then began the act. The playwright, John Osborne, was a fan:

> He talked about girls. Unwilling girls, give-her-a-shilling-and-she'll-be-willing girls, Annie and Fanny, girls who hadn't found out, girls on their honeymoon, fan dancers minus their fans, pregnant girls and barmaids the stork puts the wind up every six weeks.[78]

This was typical:

> I like the girls who do.
> I like the girls who don't.
> I hate the girl who says she will
> And then she says she won't.
> But the girl I like the best of all
> And I think you'll say I'm right
> Is the girl who says she never does
> But she looks as though she m…. 'ere, listen![79]

Everyone knew what he was talking about. Sex. But nothing was explicit. In between the gags, the verses and the songs were some throwaway lines that became Max's catch phrases: You can't help liking him, can you? There'll never be another. They don't make 'em any more, duck. All clever stuff – no rubbish. In spite of this aggressive display of heterosexuality, Max displayed a curious sexual ambivalence. Take the costume for a start – and remember, we are talking about a time when a man who wore a shirt other than white was a definite queer. Max might adopt a certain stance and say: What if I am? I don't care.

In writing a joke, Max enjoyed challenging his censors:

> If I buy a present for a girl, I buy it according to what dress she's wearing. Yesterday, she was dressed for tennis. So, I bought her a racquet. Next time I met her, she was dressed for golf. So, I bought her some clubs. I called on her one night and I didn't have to buy her anything. She wasn't in. You'll get me into trouble. I'll have you censored. So, I waited for her. When she came in, she said her hands were cold. So, I rubbed her hands. Then, she said her back was cold. So, I rubbed her back. She then said she was cold all over. So, I bunged her in the oven.[80]

On paper, who could object to that? The audience guessed how the gag might have ended and they laughed uproariously. But a censor has no jurisdiction over an audience.

Max was born into a very poor family. His father, who was of Romany origin, was a hard-drinking man who beat his wife. The family lived in rented accommodation on the Sussex coast. They always kept a handcart in the back yard. So that, if they were short of cash and the rent was due, they waited until late at

Max Miller [Thomas Henry Sargent]

- Born Brighton 21 November 1894
- Married Frances Kathleen Marsh [born 26 October 1896] in Torquay 17 February 1921 [She died in Hove 24 January 1979]
- Max Miller died in Brighton 7 May 1963
- Left £28,091[81] {£400,000}

night, loaded the cart with their few belongings and moved from Shoreham, say, to Portslade and then to Hove and Brighton before moving back again.

Max left school at the age of 12. He was barely literate. He worked first as a milkman's boy, earning three shillings [£8] a week. Then, he helped out in a fish and chip shop and, after that, he became a motor mechanic and a chauffeur. What Max relished, though, was going to local pubs in the evening and singing the popular comic songs of the day, one of them, Fred Barnes'[82] *The Black Sheep of the Family*. Come the Great War, he was posted to Mesopotamia and then to India. He also appeared with amateur concert parties and, when he returned home, he said he wanted to make show business his career.

His great idol was the black-faced song-and-dance man, G.H. Elliott, another Brighton resident. He said many times that he would not have even considered becoming an entertainer without Elliott's influence: 'I used to watch him every evening in Brighton, then go off and practise his dances under the pier.'

Since 1903, holidaymakers in Brighton had enjoyed seeing concert parties run by Jack Sheppard. After the war, Jack advertised for performers. Max applied and Jack took him on as a song-and-dance man, paying him £2.10s [£140] a week. Another of Jack's artistes was a contralto, Kathleen Marsh. In 1920, they toured together in a revue and, when they reached Devon, they married. They formed a double act called Kitty and Max, but they were not successful. Kathy, as she was known offstage, had the foresight to realise that Max had a big future as a comic. From then on, she took over. She devised his stage name and, when she saw him referred to in a review as a cheeky chappie, she thought that was ideal bill matter. Kathy looked after Max's finances, handled his correspondence and fan mail, made his outrageous costumes and even signed his autographs.

During the late twenties, Max toured with a number of revues. It was not until he changed agents and became represented by Julius Darewski that his fortunes started to change. In 1929, he appeared at the London Palladium for the first time. He was there again the following year:

Max, who brings with him a … novel style of humour, soon had the house with him, not only for his crisp burlesque of the American-style vocalist, but also for his cheeky style of divulging his own personal secrets concerning his "affairs" and those amazing plus-fours.[83]

Within two years, he became a very big name indeed, commanding a salary of £100 [£3,500] a week. [In time, that grew to £1,000 a week].

Max was at his best with an audience. Between 1932 and 1958, he regularly cut 78 rpm records, but, even when the band was instructed to laugh, these were stilted efforts. The same was true of his movies. Between 1933 and 1942, there were 14, six of which are, unbelievably, missing believed lost. One of the problems was that Max talked too quickly. His early stage career is to blame for that. He tried to fit in as many gags as he could in the time allowed him.

As with Harry Lauder and the American comedian, Jack Benny, there were allegations that Max was mean. One story tells of Max chatting with fellow comics in a bar and bragging about the number of houses he owned in Brighton. Ted Ray interrupted him: 'Why don't you sell one and buy us a drink?' Max refused to buy drinks for his fans, as he told the actor, Alfred Marks:

If I go into a bar, am I expected to buy 15 people a drink? No. They pay me for the privilege of having a drink with Max Miller. It gives them pleasure.[84]

He also refused to tip backstage staff. 'They don't do anything for me. They drop my cloth in from the flies. Then they sod off to the pub for a quarter of an hour while I'm working … If it wasn't for me, they wouldn't bloody well be working.'[85]

It is difficult to put behaviour of this kind into context. As a child, Max had known real poverty. Once he was successful, financial stability was understandably important to him. His acts of charity went unpublicised. Shortly after his death, Kathleen said he regularly gave money to the blind. He had been badly shocked when he was temporarily blinded in the First World War. He made regular donations to a group of 'pensioners',[86] 'people he had heard were in desperate need. He helped scores of people in his time … old troupers who were hard up and others.'[87]

Max was distinctly generous with advice for younger comedians, as a young Cyril Fletcher discovered when he shared a bill with Max:

[Max said] 'There are lots of little bits in your act which I enjoy tremendously and which I think could be improved. For instance, if you put this story in front of

Cyril Fletcher.

that story, you'll find it'll go better. And this tag. We'll rephrase it. Now, if you try that at your next performance, you'll find that it goes better." He reshaped my act and I thought that was extraordinarily generous.[88]

Bob Monkhouse, too, had a comic master-class when, as a youngster, he shared a bill with Max at a charity concert at the London Coliseum. Bob had already written some gags that Max had used. When they met, Max told him there were rules about comedy that could be bent, but never broken. First, keep your material simple, clear and sharp. People will not laugh if they cannot understand you. Secondly, use energy. Be crisp and animated. Thirdly, give your audience a chance to laugh. If they do not, stare them out. Take them into your confidence. Be likeable and, if they do not take to you straightaway, act happy as if you do not care. Fourthly, let your audience see you are taking a chance. There were other rules, too, about avoiding repetition, except where it lends build-up and emphasis, and about using movement to create a mental picture.

Max dissected one of Bob's jokes:

Her father said, 'Have you the means to make a woman happy?' I said, 'Yes. They always laugh at it.' [Max said:] No, it's wrong coming from a clean-cut lad like you. The word 'it'. Too brutal. No subtlety. You want to hint at what you mean. And 'means'. That's the wrong word for the set-up. Try it like this: Her father looked at me. He said, 'Have you got what it takes to make my daughter happy?' I thought to myself 'Oh, yes. I've got that all right!' Now, pause there. Give 'em the eye. Let 'em catch on to what you mean. 'I've got what it takes to make her happy all right! Not just happy. The first time she laughed her head off!'[89]

Gracie Fields and George Formby have each been the subject of three biographies, but there has been only one of Max. There are two reasons for that. One was that offstage Max was essentially a dull man. He played the Cheeky Chappie for about 30 years or so and he was enormously successful. That basically was the whole story. The second reason is that no one can rely on anything published in Max's sole biography.

That was written by the mysterious John East,[90] who claimed that Max virtually adopted him when he was a boy of nine. He gives some perceptive accounts of Max as a performer, but there are pages and pages of stories about Max from people who, it appears, answered a letter from East in a newspaper. If East knew Max so well, why did he seek the reminiscences of others?

The biography is highly suspect. Let us examine one incident in particular: whether Max did or did not tell a joke on BBC Radio that led to him being banned from broadcasting in Britain for several years. The joke is, by now, notorious: that Max was walking along a narrow mountain precipice when he met a beautiful naked girl coming towards him. He did not know whether to block her passage or toss himself off. Max Wall said the joke was sometimes attributed to him and, after repeatedly denying it, he found it easier to admit it. Clive Allen, Max's last pianist, said Max had told him it was untrue: somebody had made it up and, after a time, it had become an urban myth. Plenty of Max's followers agree it was not his style. He did not tell dirty jokes, not even at 'stag' [all-male] functions.[91]

So, who provides evidence to the contrary? Almost solely, John East, who devotes three rather confused sentences to the incident.[92] Writing in 1977, he put a date on it: 1944. A BBC producer, on hearing the first few lines of the gag, faded Max off the air. Max was then banned for five years. It was a different story in 1978 when East told BBC Radio Manchester that the joke had been transmitted, not in 1944, but in 1940. Max, he said, was escorted from the premises by the announcer, Stuart Hibberd, who said John Reith had already been on the phone to say he would ensure that Max would never work again. Come 1994, the centenary of Max's birth, East elaborated further. Speaking on BBC Radio Two, he said that he was actually present when the joke was told; that there was pandemonium; that the programme was taken off the air; and that years later, Reith told East he had sent Max a telegram that read: Will send wreath [Reith] to your funeral.

All good stories. So good, in fact, why did not East include them in his biography? In trying to find the truth of the matter, the BBC's file on Max is useful. Between December 1942 and July 1949, there is no mention of Max. That is the period during which he was banned. The BBC acted against him after one of his broadcasts was faded out halfway through because he had not adhered to the agreed script. So, to make it clear: the notorious joke was not heard, but, because he did not stick to his script, Max was kept off the air for six-and-a-half years.[93]

Max made his reappearance in *Fanfare*, a show from Manchester transmitted in August 1949. In December 1949, he was featured in a Henry Hall *Guest Night*. His return was celebrated by one of the most popular journalists of the day, Collie Knox:

> The BBC has always been the tiniest bit nervous of letting loose … Max Miller. His brand of humour is, if I may so phrase it, apt to put the cat among the chickens … It was clever of Henry Hall in his comeback *Guest Night* to include Max. He said nothing of which "Father of Seven" or "Indignant Taxpayer" could possibly disapprove and was extremely funny … I waited in an ecstasy of anticipation for him to say something awful. He didn't. But he never does.[94]

Given the length of his absence from the BBC, one might have thought that Max would be on his best behaviour from then on. Not so. At the end of 1949, he was invited to take part in a Christmas edition of *Variety Bandbox*, which was to be recorded at the Camberwell Palace a few days earlier. According to the producer, Max arrived demanding 15 minutes for his act, instead of the eight originally negotiated. Max also said he would sing two songs that had not been submitted in advance. After further disagreements, the producer decided to drop him from the show, phoning his agent, Julius Darewski, to tell him that the recording would be infinitely better without him.

There were more negotiations and Max was eventually reinstated, but his act did not last eight minutes. It lasted 15 and, while the announcer was introducing the next performer, the musical comedy actress, Binnie Hale, Max reappeared on stage, gave a V-sign and shouted, 'If you've time for her ....' The BBC's Head of Programme Contracts summoned Darewski, who said that Max was upset that the compere of the show, Frankie Howerd, was given more to do than him. Max denied giving a V-sign and said he had come on stage again merely to collect his coat.

Darewski said: 'Please try to humour him. You can lead him anywhere, but he will not be driven.' The following month, the Head of Variety, Michael Standing, wrote to Darewski: 'I am prepared to accept things were said that fermented an already troubled situation.' [Of all the broadcasts Max made, only three have been retained in the BBC Archives: on radio, his appearance in *Festival of Variety* in 1951;[95] and on television, *Celebration Music Hall*,[96] in 1954 and *This is Your Life*, when Max Bygraves was honoured in 1961. Max's problems with the BBC continued until the very end. An LP, recorded at a hotel near Brighton in 1961 and entitled *That's Nice, Maxie*, was banned by the Beeb 'on the grounds of general good taste.']

The amount of time Max needed for his act became something of an obsession with him, especially if there was another comedian on the bill. When he took part in the 1950 Royal Variety Show at the London Palladium, he deliberately ran over the time he had been allotted.

He was angry that Jack Benny had been allocated 20 minutes, while he was given only six. He abandoned the routine he had rehearsed. The audience loved it, but, by the time he had overrun by five minutes, the frantic stage director was in the wings, shouting at him to come off. Max told him that the Americans had had their chance. Now, he wanted his. When he eventually left the stage, Val Parnell roared at him, 'You'll never work in one of my theatres again.'[97] Max was unrepentant: 'You're £25,000 [£500,000] too late.'[98] But, within two-and-a-half years, Max was back at the Palladium topping the bill. As Max Bygraves commented, if you make money for people, they have a wonderful way of forgetting.

When John Osborne wrote *The Entertainer*, there was confusion over whether the central character, a broken down music hall comedian, Archie Rice, was based on Max. In an interview, Max said that Kathy had been to see Sir Laurence Olivier, who was playing Archie. Olivier, who was fascinated by music hall comics, particularly Sid Field, [see Chapter 25], admitted that he had imitated some of Max's mannerisms. 'I know it isn't all that flattering,' Max said. 'But, between you, me and the lamppost, to be insulted by Sir Laurence Olivier – that's a compliment.'[99] Osborne himself refuted the theory. Archie was a man, he said. Max was a god, a saloon-bar Priapus.

John Osborne was not the only man of letters who was enthralled by Max. When Max was in *Apple Sauce*, George Orwell was a reviewer: 'So long as comedians like Max Miller are on the stage, one knows that the popular culture of England is surviving.'[100]

Max's career was, in effect, halted by a heart attack. It may sound cruel to say so, but the decline in his health may have been fortuitous. As a good-looking young man, Max could play the sex-mad Cheeky Chappie, but now he was 65. The youthful Lothario would be seen as a dirty old man. Max attributed his heart attack to hard work:

> It was trying to stay on top that knocked me. For years, I played the Holborn Empire once every three weeks and always with new material – maybe five new songs I'd written myself. That's a lot of hard work.[101]

But even at that late stage, Max was planning a comeback: 'I can't afford to retire. What would the other comics do for gags?'[102]

CHAPTER SEVEN

A Class of their Own

Unrivalled Billy Bennett, Issy Bonn, Claude Dampier, Freddie Frinton, Jimmy James, Gillie Potter, Joan Rhodes, Jimmy Wheeler, Robb Wilton

While Max was consolidating his status as a star of the variety theatre, Leicester Square in the very heart of London was undergoing a transformation. The Empire, where Dan Leno made his first West End appearance, was rebuilt as a cinema in 1927/28; the London Pavilion, the hub of West End life, was converted into a cinema in 1934; and the Alhambra, where Leotard, the original Daring Young Man on the Flying Trapeze, performed, became the Odeon cinema in 1936.

The changes were reflected across the whole of Britain. More and more people were going to the cinema. Between 1932 and 1934 alone, 300 new cinemas were built in Britain and, from then until 1938, the total number of cinemas increased from nearly 4,500 to nearly 5,000. By 1939, the cinema industry reckoned about 23 million people went to the movies every week.

During the 1930s, these were just some of the variety theatres that were converted into cinemas: the Tivoli, Barrow-in-Furness; the Grand, Birmingham; the Edmonton Empire; the Exeter and Manchester Hippodromes; the Mile End Empire; the Rochdale, Rotherham, Sheffield and Southend Hippodromes; the Star, Stockton-on-Tees; and the Grand, Walsall.

While the theatres were closing, the world of variety was still producing some tremendously talented entertainers, one of them, a momentous comic figure, now best remembered for his Home Guard sketches that always began: 'The day war broke out ...' Before the war, Robb Wilton portrayed bumbling, incompetent officials, a magistrate, perhaps, or a fireman or police officer. These sketches stand the test of time since dithering bureaucrats, like the poor, will always be with us.

As a young man, Robb abandoned a promising career as an engineer to join a local repertory company. He usually played the villain in bloodthirsty melodramas. One account recalls that, when he went on stage inadvertently wearing a hat that was too small for him and began getting laughs, he opted for comedy, but that sounds a little too convenient. Another account says that, when he first played Dame in pantomime, he decided to switch to the halls. It is more likely that his future wife, Florence Palmer, an actress he met at the Alexandra Theatre, Hull, persuaded him to branch out into comedy as she recognised that melodrama was going out of fashion.

Robb Wilton [Robert Wilton Smith]

- Born Liverpool 28 August 1881
- Married Florence Ann Barker [professionally known as Florence Palmer] in Stalybridge 21 January 1904 [She died in Liverpool 5 February 1956]
- Son, Robert, born Liverpool 20 June 1907. Died London 6 August 1943
- Robb Wilton died Liverpool 1 May 1957
- Left £28,605 [£420,000]

The music hall proprietor, Walter de Frece, saw Robb when he was appearing in Liverpool and gave him a three-year contract. In 1909, Robb, billed as the Confidential Comedian, made his London debut at the Holborn Empire. After three years working on his own, he started playing in sketches he had written and was usually joined by Florence.

In one unforgettable routine, she arrives at a police station to confess to poisoning her short, bald, knock-kneed, toothless husband with a wart on his nose. Robb, characteristically stroking his chin or passing a hand over a perplexed forehead, knows exactly what to say:

I think you did the best you could with him. [But] I don't know what to do. You see, up to now, as far as we've gone, we've got no proof. How do I know – what proof have I got that you really have poisoned your husband? Anyone might walk in here and say they've poisoned their husband ... If I took everybody's word, we'd have the station full in no time.[103]

In another sketch, Florence rushes in to a fire station to report that her house is on fire. After randomly shuffling piles of paper from one tray to another and trying to make small talk, Robb gets round to shouting down a speaking tube to his assistant, Arnold, who is busy organising a football sweep. 'You mustn't let things like that interfere with duty.' A pause, perfectly timed, follows before Robb asks, 'What have I drawn?'[104]

When Robb took part in the Royal Variety Show of 1926, he played another much-loved character, the Magistrate. Timing problems cut the act short and it took another ten years or so before Robb launched himself as Mr Muddlecombe J.P. This character proved so successful on radio that the Magistrates' Association formally complained to the BBC.

One myth, still current, is that leading variety performers could tour the halls with the same sketch year after year. In truth, many tried hard to refresh their act. Once, Robb was booked to appear at the Alhambra, Bradford. The contract stated: in the fire station sketch. Robb crossed the words out and wrote 'new sketch' in its place. The manager immediately contacted Don Ross, who was Robb's agent at the time, to find out why the change had been made. Don told him Robb had a new sketch he wanted to do. He never liked to return to a theatre with material he had used there previously. The manager made it clear that, as he was paying Robb £300 [£10,000] a week, he thought he had the right to tell him what he wanted. Robb was very troubled, but eventually gave way. After the opening night, a Bradford newspaper criticised Robb for using old material. He was furious.

Robb's humour was international. He and Florence enjoyed great success in America, Canada and Australia, but, in their private lives, they experienced tragedy. Their only son, Robert, fell 25 feet [eight metres] from a second floor window in Maida Vale in 1943 after a night out with friends. He broke his pelvis and died of his injuries. He was only 36. Florence never recovered from the loss and took to drinking heavily. Robb carried on working as a solo turn and kept audiences laughing through the worst years of the Second World War:

> The day war broke out, my Missus looked at me and said, 'What good are you?' I said, 'What do you mean? What good am I?' 'Well,' she said. 'You're too old for the Army. You couldn't get into the Navy. And they wouldn't want you in the Air Force. So what good are you?' I said, 'I'll do something.' She said, 'What?' I said, 'How do I know? I'll have to think.' She said, 'I don't know how that's going to help. You've never done it before. So what good are you?' I said, 'Don't keep saying "What good am I?" There'll be munitions.' She said, 'How can you go on…?' I said, 'I never said anything about going … There'll *be* some.' She said, 'Well, all the young fellows will be called up. You'll have to go back to work.' Oh, she's got a cruel tongue.[105]

Robb's was a caustic, quick-witted sense of humour. Towards the end of his career, he appeared at a footballers' social club, which had a corrugated roof. Soon after he started, it began to rain heavily, the sound of the rain amplified by the roof. Next door, the local Boys' Brigade were having music practice, playing trumpets and beating drums. Then, someone at the bar dropped a full tray of drinks. Robb's reaction: 'I think they're trying to train me to be a police horse.'[106]

Robb[107] was a master anecdotalist, but, at dinner parties, he had an enemy, Lily Morris. She harboured a lifelong grievance against male comics because she believed they always quashed any comedy she wanted to introduce into a show. Don Ross saw her in action:

> Robb would be telling a story and every story has a tag line. [At the crucial moment], Lily would invariably move a glass or drop her handbag. She'd do anything to distract and kill it. And my wife [Gertie Gitana] said: 'You know, Lily. You're a right bitch.'[108]

One of Robb's favourite comedians was Jimmy James and Jimmy felt the same about Robb's work. Their comedy was similar. Neither told jokes. Today, they would be described as comic actors and, if they were still working now, they would be in great demand.

If Robb's wartime monologues will live forever, then so will Jimmy's most famous routine, *[Animals] In the Box*. Wielding a cigarette in an apparent attempt to keep himself vertical, Jimmy stood between two stooges, one, tall, stooped, painfully thin and wearing a deerstalker, was called Bretton Woods, after the venue of the wartime monetary conference. The other, in a long overcoat and carrying a shoe-box, was named Hutton Conyers, after a village in Yorkshire.

For a time, a young Roy Castle played Conyers. Jimmy's nephew, Jack Casey, who was often referred to as 'Eli' or 'Our Eli', played Woods. Conyers claims to have just returned from Africa with two man-eating lions that he keeps in the box. 'I thought I heard some rustling,'[109] Jimmy comments. As the nonsense continues, Conyers discloses that the lions are not only the animals in the box. A giraffe and an elephant are there too. 'Is it male or female?' 'No, an elephant.' 'I don't suppose it makes any difference to you whether it's male or female.' 'It wouldn't make any difference to anyone but another elephant.'[110]

Roy Castle, who took a year off from his career to play Conyers, used to say the routine grew from a two-minute joke told by the 1950s singer, Dickie Valentine. Jimmy apparently acquired a shoe-box and the joke was worked up into a 12-minute act. But Jack Casey and Jimmy's son, James Casey,[111] who played Conyers before Roy Castle, said Roy had heard the joke in America. One Wednesday in 1956, according to this second version, Roy told Jimmy he believed it could form the basis of a sketch. The following Sunday, they performed it on radio's *Billy Cotton Band Show* for the first time.

Jimmy started out in show business as Terry, the Blue-Eyed Irish Boy, in 1904. [His father was an amateur clog dancer]. Later, he teamed up with his great-uncle, Jimmy Howells, in a double act, the Two Jimmies. In 1929, an agent for George Black saw him performing solo at the Sunderland Empire and booked him for the London Palladium at £100 a week. Nearly 20 years later, Jimmy's support of the American star, Mickey Rooney, saved a Palladium show from

Jimmy James [James Casey]

- Born Stockton-on-Tees, County Durham, 20 May 1892
- Married Isabelle Darby 1921
- Son, James, born 1922
- Jimmy James died in Blackpool 4 August 1965

disaster. After the first night, Rooney asked Jimmy, who was second on the bill, what had gone wrong with his act. Jimmy was straight with him: 'You haven't got one.' He worked with Rooney, making suggestions and trying to improve the act, but, after two weeks, Rooney returned home and was replaced by Sid Field.

In 1953, Jimmy appeared at the Royal Variety Performance with another great routine, in which he expatiated on the occupational hazards of preparing chips: the risk of losing fingers, the 'chipster's elbow' and 'the fish fryer's wink'. Many years after his father died, James Casey revived the box sketch. It was part of the Royal Variety Show of 1982 and was as funny as ever.

Jimmy excelled at improvised claptrap. One BBC producer asked him to describe his act. Jimmy said: 'I'm glad you asked me that. It's been worrying me for years.' He went on to describe how his company opened in Chinese costume, harmonising *Sleepy Lagoon*. They finished by spinning 'bowls of goldfish from strings held in our teeth.'[112]

Jimmy, a teetotaller, was also magnificent at playing a drunk. He toured with a sketch, *The Spare Room*, in which a bridegroom gets drunk at the reception and finds himself locked out on his wedding night. It began with Jimmy reeling on stage to the melody of *Three O'Clock in the Morning*.[113]

James Casey once said that his father was self-absorbed, first as a performer, secondly, as a gambler. In the 1930s, Jimmy won £30,000 [£1 million] on a seven-horse accumulator, but he was involved in bankruptcy proceedings in 1936, 1955 and 1963. He owed the Inland Revenue more than he could ever earn. In an ideal world, the taxman would recognise that special exemptions should be made for a man capable of improvising such flights as fancy as this:

> I used to be an actor myself, you know. You may have seen me. I was in a thing called *The Lighthouse Keeper's Daughter*. It ran three nights. It would have gone four only the vicar wanted the hall for the Harvest Festival. You see, I'd be sitting on this settee with the lighthouse keeper's daughter when he'd start to come down the steps from the top of the lighthouse. He'd been up there trimming the wick. Anyway, he had a wooden leg, you see. So there was a clonk and then a soft one. So that gave me plenty of time to get down to the other end of the settee. Well, one night he shouted down for me to row ashore for a pint of paraffin oil for the lamp. Well, I was adamant. I said 'No.' I mean, I'd been twice – once for the papers and once for the milk and it was a four-mile pull each way.[114]

Jimmy's practical jokes were more inventive and less cruel than those of the Crazy Gang. One week, he was at the Gaumont, Southampton, where a young Petula Clark was topping the bill with her accompanist and partner, Joe 'Mr Piano' Henderson. At the Monday morning band call, Pet left her band parts with the musical director. With a sly wink to the conductor, Jimmy started rehearsing them, such songs as *The Little Shoemaker* and *May Each Day*. Joe, followed by a tearful Pet, came rushing on to tell Jimmy these were her songs. Jimmy affected not to understand, explaining that Eli was now a pop singer. He's recovering in his dressing room, Jimmy explained; the fans have just ripped off all his clothes at the stage door. Joe and Pet still did not realise they were the victims of a hoax until Pet saw that the band parts in the pit were hers. Pet and Jimmy kissed and made up. Ill health forced Jimmy to retire in 1964, 60 years after he first went on stage.

Another stage 'drunk', Freddie Frinton, became a cult figure, not in Britain, but in Germany. In a film of a short sketch, *Dinner for One*, he played James, an old butler loyal to his mistress, Miss Sophie. Each year, she holds an imaginary dinner party for four gentleman admirers, all long dead. James becomes increasingly tipsy as he toasts their health.

On New Year's Eve, the sketch is shown repeatedly on German television channels. It is also transmitted in at least 20 other countries, but, oddly, never in Britain.

Freddie began his working life at a fish processing plant in Grimsby. There, he is said to have entertained his workmates with jokes and parodies, but he was fired. During the Second World War, he appeared in George Black's forces' revue, *Stars in Battledress* and, after the war, he toured in the revues, *Strike a New Note*, *Strike It Again* and *Sky High*. *Dinner for One* was written by Laurie Wylie for the Duke of York's Theatre revue, *Four Five Six!* which ran from March to December 1948. In that production, James was played by Bobbie Howes and Miss Sophie by Binnie Hale. When Noel Coward, as President of the Actors' Orphanage, presided over the *Night of a Hundred Stars* at the London Palladium in 1955, the sketch co-starred Boris Karloff and Hermione Gingold. Freddie bought the rights of the sketch some time later. In 1963, the producer and compère of a German variety show saw it and persuaded Freddie and the actress, May Warden, to travel to Hamburg and record it.

A decade earlier, Freddie was finding work hard to come by. He had just decided to leave show business when he saw that Arthur Haynes, with whom he had appeared in *Stars in Battledress*, was working at a local theatre. Haynes

---

Freddie Frinton [Frederick Bittiner Coo]

- Born Grimsby 17 January 1909
- He was the illegitimate son of a dressmaker, Florence Coo. It appears that he was fostered at an early age and that he then assumed the name of his foster parents, Hargate.
- Married [1] Maisie Elizabeth Basil in Grimsby 13 September 1931 [Dissolved]
- Married [2] Nora Mary Gratton at Brentford 3 July 1945
- Two daughters, Susan, born 1946, and Marilyn, born 1949
- Two sons, Stephen, born 1952, and Michael, born 1954
- Freddie Frinton died London 16 October 1968
- Left £32,277 [£363,000]

was delighted to see him again and offered him a part in two series of his ATV show, which ran from 1957 to 1966. This led to Freddie's best-known work, a starring role with Thora Hird in BBC Television's sitcom, *Meet the Wife* [1963 to 1966]. Here again, his character, a northern plumber, is over-fond of drink. In real life, Freddie was, in fact, teetotal. In 1968, he had just recorded the pilot of another TV sitcom, *Thicker than Water*, when he died from a heart attack during a summer season in Bournemouth. The television show went ahead with Jimmy Jewel taking Freddie's role.

Claude Dampier specialised in 'silly arse' characters. His face was his fortune. Chinless and with protruding teeth, it was easy to believe he was daft. After some theatrical experience in Britain, Claude spent most of his 30s and 40s in South Africa and Australia. In 1925, he took the leading role in a silent movie, *The Adventures of Algy*. A young blonde actress, Billie Carlyle, made her screen debut in the film and Claude was so pleased with her work that he suggested they formed a double act. By May 1926, they were starring at a theatre in Sydney in an act called *The Professional Idiot*, a phrase Claude also used as bill matter.

Claude Dampier [Claud Conolly {sic} Cowan]

- Born Clapham, south London, 23 November 1878
- Married [1] Irene Vere [Daughter professionally known as Dorothy Dampier, who married Herbert Edwin Hare, professionally known as Bertie Hare]
- Married [2] Doris Davy [professionally known as Billie Carlyle born Adelaide, Australia, 1901, died Staines, Middlesex, 23 July 1991]
- Claude Dampier died Stanmore, Middlesex, 1 January 1955
- Left £3,461 [£60,000]

Once, while they were performing in New Zealand, Billie was late arriving on stage. Claude had to ad lib and immediately invented a non-existent character in the audience whom he called Mrs Gibson. When Billie eventually made her entrance, Claude introduced her to Mrs Gibson, who remained part of their act until their last appearances in the 1950s. Claude returned to Britain with Billie in 1927. They toured and broadcast regularly, but unfortunately, they made too much of Mrs Gibson and the repeated references to her became tiresome. This was the sort of routine audiences laughed at in 1943:

I was out in the garden the other day when, what do you think, I lost my voice. Couldn't smell a thing. So, I got Mrs Gibson to look after me. She did all my smelling for me and she put me on a diet too. Did me a lot of good.

Vegetables. Nothing but green vegetables. She had an awful job dying the potatoes green.[115]

Through Mrs Gibson, Claude was banned from broadcasting on BBC Radio for three months after he referred to squeezing her oranges. Neither he nor Billie knew of the ban until the BBC phoned to arrange bookings for shows to be aired once the ban was over. Billie took the call:

'What ban?' I asked. 'Well, for Mr Dampier saying he was going to squeeze Mrs Gibson's oranges,' was the reply. 'Oh, what lovely publicity,' I said. 'I must give that to the papers.' Panic! Three times the BBC rang, but I said I would have to wait until Mr Dampier got home for him to make the decision. But, as the chappy with whom I spoke was going to get into trouble for mentioning the ban, we decided to let it go.[116]

Claude Dampier is best appreciated now for his film appearances, particularly his role as a manic piano tuner in *Radio Parade of 1935*.

CDs of the Jewish entertainer, Issy Bonn, singing his own brand of sentimental ballad, still sell well. But the other half of his act, in which he told stories about his friend, Finkelfeffer, is almost forgotten:

His boy, Jaky, said to him one day, 'I want an encyclopedia for school.' He said, 'You walk. It's good for you.' … He was walking along the street with a sad face. I said, 'What's the matter?' He said, 'There'll be trouble at the grocer's. His wife has just had a baby girl and he's had a notice in the window for the whole week [saying] "Boy wanted".'[117]

As a youngster, Issy, a butcher's son, was part of an act called the Three Rascals that combined music with comedy. In time, he turned solo and worked as Benny Leven, [almost] his true name. He made his first broadcast in 1935 and became one of the most popular singers on *Variety Bandbox* with such numbers as the Sophie Tucker song, *My Yiddishe Momme* [1925], written by Jack Yellen and Lew Pollack, and his signature tune, *Let Bygones Be Bygones* [1946] [Joseph Gilbert].

Issy was as popular in South Africa as he was in Britain: 'Issy Bonn sauntered on to the stage with his friendly smile and his billycock hat and effortlessly filled the hall with that amazingly flexible voice of his … Mr Bonn could have been a Tauber, but he prefers to be a male Gracie Fields.'[118]

There is no doubt that Billy Bennett was in a class of his own in both appearance and repertoire. His appearance was neatly summed up by James Agate: 'that rubicund, unaesthetic countenance, that black, plastered quiff, that sergeant-major's moustache, that dreadful dinner-jacket, that well-used dickey and seedy collar, the too-short trousers, the hobnailed boots [and] the red silk handkerchief tucked into the waistcoat.'[119] And the repertoire? Largely melodramatic monologues turned into doggerel-cum-gibberish. For instance, Milton Hayes' *The Green Eye of the Little Yellow God* became *The Green Tie on the*

Issy Bonn [Benjamin Levin]

- Born Brick Lane, Whitechapel, east London 21 April 1903
- Married Marie Florence Fitzgerald in Liverpool 11 March 1927
- Son, David Jacob, born east London 16 July 1929 [Died 24 October 1945]
- Issy Bonn died London 21 April 1977

Little Yellow Dog [see Chapter 17]; George R. Sims' *Christmas Day in the Workhouse* became *Christmas Day in the Cookhouse*; and Tennyson's *Charge of the Light Brigade* became *Charge of the Tight Brigade*.

At least, his act was clean. Well, nearly. There is this line in *The Green Tie*: 'There's a cock-eyed yellow poodle to the north of Gongapooch', which is Hindi slang for 'anus'. Perhaps that is why Billy styled himself Almost a Gentleman.

Billy came from theatrical stock. His father was John 'Jock' Bennett, one half of a knockabout double act, Bennett and Martell. As a boy, Billy wrote parodies for his father's friends on the halls. He was trained as an acrobat, but was unhappy. He ran away from home and joined the Army, but found military life tougher than trampolines and wall-bars. He returned to the career his father had mapped out for him, appearing in sketches and singing comic songs. Just as he was becoming established, the Great War broke out. Billy felt it was his duty to rejoin his old regiment, the Sixteenth Lancers, and, with them, he served in several campaigns on the Western Front, seeing action at Ypres and Somme. During the First World War, he spent some time in a concert party, entertaining

---

Billy Bennett [William Robertson Russell]

- Born Glasgow 21 November 1887
- Died Blackpool 30 June 1942
- Left £38,874 [£1 million]

---

troops in schools, barns, aircraft hangars and open fields, often accompanied by only a tin whistle.

Resuming his career in 1919, he appeared as the Trench Comedian, performing a soldier act wearing the khaki he had worn in France. At the Theatre Royal, Dublin, where British soldiers were none too popular, he was advised to do something else. Billy had to think quickly. Either he changed his act immediately or he left the show:

> 'The best thing you can do,' said the manager, 'is to disguise yourself.' I immediately left the hall, bought a false moustache and pulled down my hair, just as I do now and have done ever since, and hey presto! I had a make-up. When I changed my soldiering act to a burlesque one, I went to Liverpool, my native city, and bought a second-hand evening dress of ancient vintage, which fitted everywhere it touched, and with my Army boots and socks, I completed my present outfit.[120]

Billy claimed to have written all his own material. That is not quite true. He relied to a great extent on T.W. Connor,[121] who wrote for many music hall entertainers.[122]

In 1930, Billy was growing tired of monologues. He had broadcast some time previously and wanted to do it again, but not in his customary guise. He went to see his agent, Archie Parnell, who was in a nursing home, recovering from a serious operation. He told Archie about his plans, saying he wanted to assume another name. Archie said, 'No.' Billy's contracts forbade it. He then suggested he would talk with a dialect. Again, 'No.' Audiences would soon realise it was him. Billy finally suggested he would change his name, talk in dialect and find someone else to form a double act. Archie thought he might just get away with that. But which dialect? Scottish? Irish? Jewish? Yorkshire? In each case, there were already double acts specialising in those dialects. But not black-face. There had not been a black comic cross-talk act since Brown, Newland and le Clerq played the halls.

An appointment was made with the BBC. All Billy needed now was a partner. An American actor, James Carew, the third husband of the eminent actress, Dame Ellen Terry, agreed to do it. They would call themselves Alexander and Mose, 'Alexander' from *Alexander's Ragtime Band* and 'Mose' from *Mumbling Mose*, a minstrel song from the early 1900s.

> Right from the start, the keynote of the Alexander and Mose act has been simplicity. We are just two simple coons,[123] one semi-educated, using long words he doesn't understand, and the other, the poor mutt who falls for everything. Subtlety would be out of place. Frankly, we did not set out to cater for a Ritzy West End audience, but rather for the country farmer by his fireside, the ordinary worker and the average willing-to-be-amused City man.[124]

When Carew left the act, his place was taken by the Australian singer, Albert Whelan. The couple made five 78s in 1931 and 1932, but the novelty was relatively short-lived.

Besides the monologues, Billy had some good songs. Two were written by those masters of the comic song, R.P. [Bob] Weston and Bert Lee, *She Was Poor, But She Was Honest* and *Please Let Me Sleep on your Doorstep Tonight*. The author's favourite is a satire on the so-called wickedness of the theatre. Billy stops at nothing to conceal from his mother how he earns his living:

> The day she met me out with Gladys Cooper,[125]
> She started screaming 'Murder' and 'Police'
> And would have caused a dreadful scene in public.
> So, I told her that the girl was Crippen's[126] niece.
> 'Cos my mother doesn't know I'm on the stage
> And, when I draw £600 each week,
> If she knew where it came from, she'd shoot me like a dog.
> So, I said I stole the money from an Irish synagogue.
> She can think that I'm a murderer before she'll know the truth.
> I have to have respect for her old age.
> She knows that I'm a bigamist, a blackguard and a crook
> But Thank Heavens she don't know I'm on the stage.[127]

No wonder Agate credited Billy with raising 'every night of the week to the level of Saturday night.'[128]

Gillie Potter was a curious figure to be found in the variety theatre. He was witty, rather than comical, and required those watching him to have been sufficiently well educated to appreciate him. Dressed in a Harrovian straw boater, rimless spectacles, a blazer and Oxford bags, he addressed his audience in a superior, rather schoolmasterly way. Consequently, he was not universally popular, especially in northern England.

The son of a Methodist minister, Gillie went to Worcester College, Oxford, but did not complete his degree. He made his London stage debut as a cowboy in *The White Man* at the Lyric in 1908; he was an eccentric dancer in a tour of the Seymour Hicks/Arthur Wimperis musical, *The Gay Gordons*; and he joined a concert party at the Alfresco Pavilion in Shipley, West Yorkshire. After a pantomime in Exeter, he was booked by Stoll to tour in variety and in 1916/17 he understudied George Robey in *The Bing Boys Are Here* at the Alhambra. Gillie supplied his own potted biography to the *Radio Times*:

Gillie Potter [Hugh William Peel]

- Born in Bedford 14 September 1887
- Married Beatrice Fanny Scott in Southport 16 June 1912
- Died in Bournemouth 4 March 1975
- Left £11,274 [£55,000]

At Oxford, Cambridge, Salamanca and Old Heidelberg, his student career ran merrily until in each case [it was] interrupted by an organised suspension of credit. During a period of protracted unemployment, Mr Potter married the beautiful Miss Fuller, daughter of the famous Fuller, who discovered the Earth. Miss 'Porky' Fuller, his daughter, is extremely artistic and travels all over the country painting the same gorgeous sunset, irrespective of the actual state of the weather or the time of day. Mr Potter is now on the second of at least 30 farewell tours, to be followed, should these prove successful, by another 30.[129]

Gillie Potter's career moved sharply ahead after the success of his appearance at the Royal Variety Show in 1930. Queen Mary was reported to have rocked with laughter at him. Within a year, he broadcast for the first time. His talks centred on the mythical village of Hogsnorton and its squire, Lord Marshmallow. He looked on Hogsnorton as 'England in microcosm … a reflection of the true heart of England … There was nothing in it that would offend either a child or a bookmaker.'[130] The opening line of the sketch became Gillie's catch phrase: Good evening, England. This is Gillie Potter speaking to you in basic English.

Gillie was one of the first comedians to appear on television. He took part in experimental transmissions from Crystal Palace. Then, between 1936 and the eve of the Second World War, he made a number of 10- and 15-minute appearances from Alexandra Palace.

Of his recordings, the author's favourite, for geographical reasons as much as anything, is *Mr Potter Goes to Southend*:

In the train, I asked a man what the time was. He said, 'Why do you want to know the time?' I said, 'Well, I've not got my watch with me and I want to know how late the train is.' He said, 'On this line you don't need a watch. You need an almanac.' Well, we saw the New Year in and we got down to Southend … We went on what they call the seafront and watched them ploughing. There was some talk about going to the sea itself, but the man who knew the way was ill.[131]

In his private life, Gillie Potter was a learned man, deeply interested in church history, archaeology and heraldry. He was a frequent contributor to the letters pages of *The Times*.

Jimmy Wheeler could not have been more different. He was the last of the red-nosed comedians, robust and down-to-earth. With a pork-pie hat, a shaggy moustache, a rasping Cockney accent and wielding a violin he threatened to play, his style was unmistakeable.

Jimmy's father was one half of a double act, Wheeler and Wilson, named after the old Wheeler and Wilson sewing machines. Jimmy's parents taught him to dance and paid a shilling [£1] a week for him to have violin lessons.

After Frank Wheeler died, Jimmy took his place in the double act, combining

Jimmy Wheeler [Ernest Alfred Henry Remnant]

- Born Battersea, south London, 16 September 1910
- Married Elizabeth Webb in London 5 July 1931
- Daughter, June, born 1933, married Leo Bassi. [Son, Leo, comedian and actor, born 1952].
- Jimmy Wheeler died in Brighton 8 October 1973

comic cross-talk with slapstick, music [violin and ukulele] and finishing with a song. By the time he was 21 Jimmy had made films and had toured South Africa. Now, there was a new challenge, television. In 1932, Jimmy and his father were paid five guineas [£180] to appear in one of John Logie Baird's experimental transmissions from Broadcasting House to the Radio Exhibition at Olympia.

In 1949, when Jimmy and his father were appearing at the Grand, Brighton, the manager asked them to do two spots. Jimmy's father was against the idea. So, Jimmy made a solo appearance. He was seen by one of Val Parnell's representatives and was 'tried out' at halls in Huddersfield, Halifax and Doncaster; then, the Finsbury Park Empire; and ultimately, the London Palladium. One of his favourite routines saw him as a rent collector on a council estate:

> I found the first house just as the coalman was delivering the coal in the bathroom. I said to the lady of the house, 'I'm the rent collector and I've been told to raise your rent.' She said, 'That's a good job because I can't.' ... The next house I banged and banged on the door until finally a man came out with a mallet in his hand. I said, 'You missed me last week.' He said, 'Well, stand still. I won't miss you this week.'[132]

Jimmy wrote most of his material, but, when he was given his first TV series by the BBC, he was supplied with some first-rate writers, Talbot Rothwell, who was responsible for the scripts of 20 Carry On films, Sid Colin, who worked with Rothwell on Frankie Howerd's TV series, *Up Pompeii*, and John Antrobus, who wrote the script of the satirical play, *The Bed Sitting Room*, with Spike Milligan.

In time, Jimmy became a prodigious drinker. When he first saw hoardings proclaiming Drink Canada Dry, he saw it as a challenge. Will Wyatt,[133] who was a young producer on BBC Television's arts programme, *Late Night Line-Up*, witnessed the problem:

I remember two great comedians, Arthur Askey and Jimmy Wheeler, both arriving very early for a discussion about music hall. Wheeler was already plastered. So, trooper that he was, Askey said, 'Leave him to me,' and took him off to the canteen to pour coffee into him in a [successful] attempt to save the show.[134]

In 1956, Jimmy heard that he was to be part of the bill for the Royal Variety Show. Laurence Olivier and Vivian Leigh, Gracie Fields, the Crazy Gang, Max Bygraves and the honky-tonk pianist, Winifred Atwell, were appearing too. At the top of the bill was the outrageously camp American pianist, Liberace, who took a train from Los Angeles to New York and then a ship to Southampton, a total of nine days' travelling.

The dress rehearsal had just finished when Val Parnell received a message from Buckingham Palace. British and French forces had invaded Egypt in response to President Nasser's nationalisation of the Suez Canal, in which an Anglo-French company held the controlling shares. The Soviet Union was threatening to retaliate. As the international crisis deepened, the Queen felt unable to attend the show. It was cancelled.

Liberace burst into tears and was comforted by Gracie. The rest of the cast were equally depressed. Jimmy decided to dispel the gloom. He marched into the main dressing-room with his violin and announced, 'I've rehearsed this bloody thing for a fortnight. So, somebody's gonna hear it.'[135] The disaster soon gave way to hysteria. Winnie Atwell invited everyone back to her home for champagne and at four o'clock in the morning, she and Liberace were sitting at her piano playing *Chopsticks*. Undoubtedly, Jimmy left the party enunciating his catch phrase 'Aye-aye. That's your lot.'

Joan Rhodes had the sort of childhood that keeps psychologists and psychiatrists in business. She was abandoned by her parents and was brought up by an aunt, who hated her. She overcame this terrible start to her life to become one of variety's brightest stars and travelled the world, working in more than 50 countries. Joan was a strongwoman. She tore telephone directories in half, bent steel bars, broke six-inch nails and invited four beefy men on

Joan Rhodes [Joan Louisa Ada Taylor]

- Born Catford, south London, 13 April 1921
- Died London 30 May 2010

stage to have a tug of war with her. She always won. The real attraction of her act was that she did not look strong. A stunning blonde, she appeared in a glamour girl's costume, fishnet stockings and high heels. She was billed as the Mighty Mannequin.

Joan was abandoned by her parents when she was three. After some time in a workhouse and a convent, she was taken in by an aunt who hated her. So, at the age of 14, she ran away with eight pence [70p] in her pocket. Outside the National Gallery, she saw a strong man entertaining passers-by and offered to collect money for him. Joan learned his tricks and, in 1949, she spotted an advertisement from the impresario, Pete Collins, in *The Stage* that read: Freaks Wanted. Joan applied. Pete told her she did not look like a freak, whereupon she tore up his phone books and lifted him up and carried him round his office. She got the job and found herself in a show called *Would You Believe It?* Also on the bill were:

- Elroy, the Armless Wonder, who painted, fired guns at targets and threaded needles
- Captain Jack Harvey and Mushie, the Forest-Bred Lion, who ate steaks off a woman's forehead
- Johnny Vree, who threw what appeared to be a large golliwog round the stage. At the end of his act, the golliwog removed its mask, revealing itself to be a beautiful girl

Joan, who by now had developed a 15-minute act, was a hit and was immediately booked by Moss Empires to tour their leading theatres. Her routine took her all over the world. She appeared with Marlene Dietrich, Fred Astaire and Sammy Davis Junior. In a Christmas show in Iceland, she picked up Bob Hope, but fell backwards and broke her heel. Almost immediately, she received a telegram from Bing Crosby saying: 'It should have happened sooner and harder.'

Once famous, she found she was getting different reactions from men:

The more intelligent men tend to think 'She's stronger than I am' and leave it at that. For others, I become instantly not a woman, but someone they're in opposition to and they try to prove something. The obvious thing is to try to get me into a bedroom … and I'm a sitting room girl! … It put me on my guard. I don't mind them asking my measurements, but, when they ask me 'What are your biceps measurements flexed?' that's when I start to worry.[136]

Joan became accustomed to all sorts of approaches by all sorts of men. After a matinee in Southport, she was invited to tea by a fan, the notorious British Fascist, James Larratt Battersby, who treated Hitler like a God. He told her she would marry him and become the mother of the strongest Aryan children in the world. Joan dropped her teacup and fled. Her most famous suitor was ex-King Farouk of Egypt, who every night filled her dressing room in Rome with flowers and perfume. He told her he had 29 beds: 'Would you like to break one for me?' Her riposte on this occasion was: 'Not tonight, Josephine.'

After travelling abroad, she always returned to her small flat in Belsize Park, which was her base for more than 60 years. It was jammed full of her costumes, pictures from her cabaret days, albums of newspaper cuttings, many of her drawings [she was a talented artist], figurines, collages and a portrait of her painted by Dame Laura Knight. On some afternoons, she played Scrabble with her life-long friend, another one-off, Quentin Crisp. In 2004, she was presented with a Lifetime Achievement Award by the British Music Hall Society.

CHAPTER EIGHT

Infinite Variety

Memory Man, Quick Change Artiste, Grumbling Juggler and the Chimps

Joan Rhodes became a big star because she had no competitor. Strongwomen, particularly beautiful strongwomen, are rare. Strongmen are less rare. So, they have to over-compensate. Murray, an Australian who came to Britain in 1926 [you have really made it if you are known by only a single name], was a case in point. Within weeks of his arrival, he contrived to free himself from a strait jacket while suspended upside down from a crane 150 feet [50 metres] in the air over Piccadilly Circus. In 1927, Samson, similarly mono-titled, topped the bill at the London Coliseum, enthralling his followers by lifting a platform with nine men on it, by raising a girder with his teeth and by lying on the stage while a lorry, full of passengers, was driven across his back.

The speciality acts, many and multifarious, were beautifully typified by Mrs Shufflewick's [see Chapter 20] invention, Bubbles Latrine and Her Educated Sheepdogs. They died out as the variety theatre neared its end. Eric Morecambe remembered some of them:

Balancing acts like Jacky, the Dutch boy, who would balance on his hands on wooden blocks on a pedestal, building up his pile of bricks until he was practically out of sight; tableau acts with men and girls in white, riding white horses with white dogs; knife- and axe-throwing acts; trampoline and tightrope acts; speciality dance acts with acrobatic dancers, rag doll dancers, Egyptian hieroglyphic dancers, sand dancers and mechanical dancers; illusionists like Lionel King, who would get three people on the stage, then

HIPPODROME
IPSWICH   Phone : 2447
Lessee : A. A. Shenburn   Licensee and Manager : R. A. Sims

6.0 COM. MONDAY, APRIL 19TH 1948 **8.10**

Pete Collins' **WELL, I NEVER!**

SEE — THE ONLY PERFORMING CATS IN THE WORLD!

MEKKO

THE HUMAN AQUARIUM! HE SWALLOWS LIVE FISH WITHOUT HARMING THEM AND CAN DRINK 100 GLASSES OF BEER IN 10 MINUTES!

HELLO THERE!

A GENUINE ROBOT WORKED BY PHOTO-ELECTRIC CELLS! MOVES! TALKS!

THE TALKING GUITAR! (IT REALLY DOES TALK!)

SPECIAL MATINEE SATURDAY AT 2.30

SEE THE ARMLESS PIANIST — THE LIVING BATTERY — THE NOISIEST MAN ON EARTH — THE HUMAN AQUARIUM — THE PERFORMING CATS — THE ELECTRONIC ROBOT — THE TALKING GUITAR Etc., Etc.

THE MODERN MIRACLE SHOW

THIS IS MORE THAN A SHOW—IT IS AN EXPERIENCE

go into the audience and play them in a game of poker from the auditorium and win every time.[137]

The chimps' famous TV advert.

W.C. Fields is credited with saying 'Never work with animals and children.' He knew how to handle the latter. He plied one with gin to make him behave. Animals are even less predictable and yet some variety entertainers owed their careers to the animals they trained: dogs, cats, chickens, goats, rabbits and, most famously of all, chimpanzees.

Gene Detroy,[138] born, more prosaically, Samuel Wood, began his showbiz career at the age of 12 in an acrobatic act with his father. He dreamed up the act that made him internationally famous after buying a chimpanzee for £300. He was best known for his appearances with his favourite chimp, Marquis. By the 1950s, he and Marquis travelled the world. His only appearances in Britain were at the London Palladium:

Marquis and Family [ride] motor-cycles and bicycles made for three. [It] seems easy enough for them, but their great asset is their natural comedy, the presentation being considerably enhanced by Mr Detroy's wisecracks [eg. "If you do this trick, I'll take you to the zoo on Sunday … If you don't, you'll be there tonight."[139]

Detroy's chimpanzees starred in Britain's first successful television advertisement. At Christmas 1956, they were seen extolling Brooke Bond tea on Britain's fledgling independent television channel. A further series of commercials followed using chimps recruited from Billy Smart's circus. Voice-overs were provided by Peter Sellers, Bob Monkhouse and Bruce Forsyth.

Detroy's act appeared in a show at the London Palladium that was attended by the Queen. George Black was worried about a part of the act, in which Marquis was seen preparing to go to bed, saying its prayers and then reaching under its cot for a chamber pot to sit on. George told Detroy to omit anything that might offend the Queen. Detroy promised George he would tell Marquis to cut that part of the act. George was not convinced and, during the performance, stood nervously in the wings alongside the comedian, Charlie Chester:

When Marquis knelt down to say his prayers, all went well, but then suddenly the little brown, hairy hand shot under the bed and pulled out the potty. GB closed his eyes. Gene hissed at Marquis, 'Don't you dare sit on it.' The monkey looked at him with brown questioning eyes. Suddenly, he moved as if he was going to sit as usual, then he picked up the chamber pot and rammed it on his head. George Black breathed the biggest sigh of relief I have ever heard.[140]

Leslie Welch was billed as the Memory Man and his speciality was sport. He memorised FA Cup and Derby winners. In fact, it was hard to catch him out on the statistics and details of any one of 37 sports. He was seen or heard in dozens of radio and television programmes; he even appeared at the Palladium; and yet he reckoned he was doing only what most people could do. 'Every one of us is born with a perfectly functioning memory. The fatal mistake of most people is to allow 70 to 80 per cent of it to lie dormant, mainly due to the invention of pen, pencil and paper.'[141]

Leslie[142] worked first as an accounts clerk in the Civil Service. In the Second World War, while serving with the Eighth Army in the Western Desert, he overheard two officers arguing about the result of a football match. Leslie put them right and, before long, he began working for ENSA. By day, he used his accountancy skills in balancing the performers' books. By night, he entertained the troops. After he was demobbed, his wife wanted him to return to the Civil Service, but she soon realised the importance of his love of performing. Sheila Van Damm remembered his appearances at the Windmill [see Chapter 16]:

> Six times a day, he faced our audience while they fired questions at him, poring over reference books in the semi-darkness of the auditorium and trying hard to catch him out. In all, he answered 4,600 questions from the Windmill stage [and] failed only 200, most of which were frivolously impossible, such as 'When was I born?' We were in awe of Leslie's ability.[143]

It was BBC radio that made Leslie's name, particularly *Calling All Forces*, in which he appeared for 127 consecutive weeks. He once said he had trained his memory to work like a card index system. One of the show's scriptwriters, Bob Monkhouse, bore witness to that as he watched him standing to attention on stage, his fingers flickering as though he was counting off page numbers.

Leslie Welch toured in variety shows, but began to weary of them. He found he could spend only a few hours on a Sunday with his wife before he set off for the next theatre. So, he relinquished his fame and took a job at a Labour Exchange in north London. Oddly, his colleagues there remembered him as a somewhat forgetful man.

In music hall, quick-change artistes liked to refer to themselves as 'protean' to try to prove that, in spite of being rogues and vagabonds, they had acquired a little learning. In Greek mythology, Proteus was a sea-god capable of

---

Owen McGiveney [Owen Joseph McGiveney]

- Born Preston, Lancashire, 4 May 1884
- Married Elizabeth Louise Hughes [professionally known as Betty Earl] in Paddington, London, 1 November 1936
- Died Los Angeles 31 July 1967

The fastest Novelty act in Variety!

OWEN McGIVENEY

NOT ONE ACTOR BUT FIVE
NOT FIVE PEOPLE BUT ONE MAN!

changing shape, which, on occasions, must have been handy. In variety, the greatest quick-change artist was Owen McGiveney, who presented an act based on Dickens' *Oliver Twist*. He played Fagin, Bill Sikes and Nancy, changing costumes and his voice in a matter of seconds.

Inevitably, there was some trickery. Owen's fully-grown son, Michael, sometimes took his place on stage while he was changing in the wings. The act earned Owen international fame. After appearances at the Palladium and the Coliseum, he toured America.

You gotta have a gimmick, as the song reminds us. A gimmick sets you apart from your peers. So, if you are a good juggler, what can make you different? Rob Murray found a simple answer, but a brilliant one too. While performing all manner of complicated feats, he maintained a mumbled commentary about the inadequacy of his private life. He arrived in Britain from his native Australia in 1948. Within a year, he was supporting Danny Kaye at the London Palladium.

It was Murray's comic patter that was all important: 'unhappy mutterings about the wife and six children he has to support',[144] as one paper put it, while another spoke of him as 'a fellow who doesn't trust his inanimate assistants … He's constantly on guard lest they betray him and go skittering out of reach.'[145]

His end was sad. In 1988, an American friend went to see him at his flat in Croydon only to be told by his landlady that he had died of bronchitis a few months previously. He was 62. No word of his death reached any news agency or any of the papers.

CHAPTER NINE

When Harry wrote *Sally*

Toe-tapping Tunesmiths

For the most part, the songwriters of the variety theatre were as eccentric as their music hall counterparts. The chief difference was money. The music hall songsmiths sold their compositions outright for a guinea [£50] or two a time. Many died in poverty. The Performing Right Society [now the MCPS-PRS Alliance], the organisation that collects royalty payments on behalf of composers and lyricists, changed all that. Even so, some Twentieth Century songwriters still saw small fortunes slip from their fingers. Harry Leon was one of three men who wrote Gracie Fields' signature tune, *Sally* [1931]. Over the years, it made tens of thousands of pounds. But Harry sold his share for just £30.

An East End Jew, Harry could be seen most lunchtimes in a pub near Denmark Street, the short road that became London's Tin Pan Alley. He wore a cloth cap, a muffler and smoked Woodbines from a gold cigarette case. As a young man, he spent 12 years as a merchant seaman.

On his return, he found a job playing the piano at a pub in the Whitechapel Road. He could not read a note of music and played exclusively in the key of D natural. One night, after six months at the pub, he played a tune that had just come to him. He worked on it and decided to call it *Gypsy Sweetheart* in memory of a girl he had met in Cuba. He took it to a friend, Leo Towers, who had spent most of his twenties playing sax and clarinet in various bands before switching to songwriting. After Leo had written a lyric, a publisher was found, Will Haines, of Cameo Music. Haines, however, felt the lyric was wrong. The song did not have a gypsy flavour. He wanted a girl's name in the title. Working in the Cameo office, Harry and Leo at first tried 'Mary': 'Mary, Mary, don't be contrary. Say that you love me, please do.' Then, they substituted 'Sally' but got stuck on the word 'smiling'. At that point, another songwriter, Percy Edgar, put

The World famous Theme Song

SALLY

Words & Music by   HAINES, LEON & TOWERS

Sung & Recorded by

GRACIE FIELDS

KEITH PROWSE MUSIC PUBLISHING CO · LTD · LONDON · W · 1
Made in England

2'6

Harry Leon [Aaron Sugarman]

- Born Stepney, east London, 18 August 1901
- Died Hampstead, north-west London, 18 February 1970

---

his head around the door. 'What rhymes with smiling?' Leo asked. 'What about beguiling?' Percy replied.

With the lyric complete, Harry, Leo and Will went to see Gracie in her dressing room at the Metropolitan, Edgware Road. Gracie heard the song, but politely turned it down. Her phone rang and the three men left. When they were only a short way down the street, a messenger caught up with them and said Gracie wanted to see them immediately. They returned. The phone call had been from Gracie's agent, who told her he had just drawn up the contract for her first movie, *Sally In Our Alley*. The song was written into the film, but Harry could not be persuaded that the song would sell. It was then that he sold his share. Gracie was never allowed to perform in public without singing *Sally*, but no one questioned that the song should really have been sung by a man:

> Sally, Sally, don't ever wander
>
> Away from the alley and me.
>
> Sally, Sally, marry me Sally
>
> And happy forever I'll be.
>
> When skies are blue,
>
> You're beguiling
>
> And, when they're grey,
>
> You're still smiling, smiling.
>
> Sally, Sally, pride of our alley,
>
> You're more than the whole world to me.

Haines collaborated with Jimmy Harper and Tommie Connor on one of Gracie's best-known comic songs, *The Biggest Aspidistra in the World* [1938]. Tommie, who began his working life as a callboy at the Theatre Royal, Drury Lane, also collaborated with Eddie Lisbona on *It's My Mother's Birthday Today* [1935], which was a best-selling record for the Street Singer, Arthur Tracy [see Chapter 12].

At the height of her fame, Gracie Fields was constantly pursued by songwriters trying to sell her their work. When she appeared at variety theatres, there was a strict rule that no one would be allowed past the stage door. One slipped through: a tall, thin lad of 17, who looked like a messenger boy. Gracie let him play one of his tunes on the piano in her dressing room. She liked it and told him to go away and finish it.

Harry Parr Davies

- Born Briton Ferry, Glamorganshire, 24 May 1914
- Died Chelsea, London, 14 October 1955
- Left £7,633 [£135,000]

He was a cobbler's son, Harry Parr Davies, and, as well as writing some of Gracie's greatest hits, he became her accompanist for nine years. In 1934, Gracie's movie, *Sing As We Go*, the story of mill hands thrown out of work by the Depression, needed a rousing march for the finale. Harry remembered a song he had written for a school play, changed the words and quickened its tempo. It became the film's title song. Five years later, he worked with the lyricist, Phil Park, on *Wish Me Luck [As You Wave Me Goodbye]* for *Shipyard Sally*.

Harry was an odd man. Pale, effeminate and wearing extremely thick spectacles, he was often on the set of George Formby's films, *I See Ice* [1938] and *It's In The Air* [1939] as he supplied songs for both. He and George became unlikely friends. George's virago of a wife, Beryl, was happier to see him in the company of 'that grumpy nancy boy' than with any of the girls in the cast. Harry apparently attributed his bad moods to constipation.

His big ambition was to write a musical and he achieved it. With lyrics by Harold Purcell, *The Lisbon Story*, which centred on the wartime exploits of a French singer and a British spy, opened at the London Hippodrome in June 1943 and ran until July 1944. Its hit song was *Pedro the Fisherman*.

Harry cared little for socialising and lived on his own. Feeling unwell at his mews flat in Chelsea one night, he took aspirin. He was suffering from a severe stomach ulcer. The aspirin caused the ulcer to burst and Harry died from internal haemorrhaging at the age of 41.

Women were well represented in variety, but only one became a songwriter. [That figure would rise to three if you included Emily Bedell and Nellie Tollerton, who played in an orchestra at a restaurant. They wrote *Cruising Down the River [On a Sunday Afternoon]* {1945}, but that was just one song]. For our purposes, Annette Mills, the older sister of the actor, Sir John Mills, was the only female songwriter in variety.

Annette had three careers. First, she was a dancer. She teamed up with Robert Sielle, whom she married. They became so famous across the world that they were rated as second only to Fred and Adele Astaire. One critic said Annette

---

Annette Mills [Edith Mabel Mills]

- Born Clapham, London, 10 September 1894
- Married [1] Henry William Douglas McClenaghan in Devonport 13 January 1917
- Married [2] Cecil Leon Roberts [professionally known as Robert Sielle] in London 28 November 1925
- Died 10 January 1955
- Left £20,916 [£350,000]

---

had the prettiest legs in Paris, but in Cape Town in 1930, she broke a leg and resolved to become a songwriter instead.

She came up with *Hands, Knees and Boomps-a-Daisy* to accompany a new dance; *Lizzie, the Pre-War Flivver*[146] for the risqué revue and cabaret entertainer, Douglas Byng [see Chapter 20]; and a version of *Little Red Riding Hood*, called *Oh Grandma*, which was recorded by an unlikely duo, Hermione Gingold and Gilbert Harding. Most notably, however, Annette wrote *We Want, Muffin! [Muffin, the Mule]*, the signature tune of the popular puppet with whom she appeared on television from 1946 until her early death from a brain tumour in 1955.

Reginald Armitage was the organist at Wakefield Cathedral and later St Anne's, Soho. He started writing songs for revues and, not wanting to embarrass the church, he opted for a nom de theatre. Passing a theatre on his way to sign a contract at the BBC, he saw the names of the two stars appearing there. One was Noel Coward, the other, Maisie Gay, one of Coward's favourite actresses. Armitage took the first name of one and the surname of the other and, as Noel Gay, became one of the most lyrical songwriters of his generation.

Noel Gay [Reginald Moxon Armitage]

- Born Wakefield, west Yorkshire, 15 July 1898 [Moxon was his mother's maiden name]
- Married Amy Marshall 26 April 1927
- Son, Richard[147] [12 August 1928–17 November 1986] Married [1] Caroline Hay [dissolved] Two sons, Charles and Alex [2] Gabrielle Lloyd [dissolved]
- Noel Gay died London 4 March 1954
- Left £6,471 [£115,000]

Noel was described as 'looking less like a successful songwriter than a doctor or a lawyer'[148] and, according to his son, Richard, 'there lurked beneath a deceptively … smiling exterior a volcanic wrath that usually struck those he best liked whenever they disappointed him.'[149]

The revue producer, Andre Charlot, first spotted his talents and hired him to write songs for *The Charlot Revue of 1926*, starring Jessie Matthews. The following year, he contributed to the revue, *Clowns in Clover*, with a cast led by Jack Hulbert and Cicely Courtneidge.

Noel, working with the lyricist, Harry Graham, wrote his first hit in 1930, *The King's Horses*, which was sung in another Charlot revue, *Folly to be Wise*. From that moment, there followed a torrent of successful songs and shows. As far as the variety theatre is concerned, he was responsible for three enormous hits. For Gracie Fields, he collaborated with Desmond Carter on one of her best comedy songs, *I Took My Harp to a Party [But Nobody Asked Me to Play]* [1933].

In 1935, Noel wrote *Leaning on a Lamppost*, which George Formby sang in his movie, *Feather Your Nest*. The critic, Harold Hobson, was ecstatic, calling the song 'the true theatre, the real thing, the golden coin and the gates of pearl.'[150] Unfortunately, Noel had to contend with George's wife, Beryl. She demanded that George's name was added to the song-writing credits, something that his regular writers, Harry Gifford[151] and Fred E. Cliffe,[152] had had to agree to. She also threatened that, if he refused, she would sue him. Noel told her that, if she did, he would reveal that George's musicianship did not even extend to him being able to tune his own ukuleles. He won.

Noel's third variety hit was *Run, Rabbit, Run [Don't Give the Farmer His Fun]*, which Bud Flanagan sang in *The Little Dog Laughed*. No one is now sure of its provenance. Was it based on a German air raid whose only casualty was a rabbit or was it in response to a remark by Hitler that he would invade Britain and dine on rabbit?

The crowning glory of Noel's career was the musical, *Me and My Girl*, [1937], which he wrote with Douglas Furber and L. Arthur Rose. Its hit song, *The Lambeth Walk*, set London alight. Staged at the Victoria Palace, it ran for 1,646 performances.[153]

There was the occasional oddity about Noel's behaviour. He once phoned his wife and was told she was in bed and too ill to come to the phone. Noel insisted he had something important to discuss. Under protest, his wife made her way from the bedroom and, with a weary and husky voice, asked him what he wanted. 'What the hell are you doing out of bed with a voice like that?' he demanded. 'Get back at once!'

Another of George Formby's songwriters, Jack Cotterell, also had to deal with Beryl Formby's demands. Jack wrote the song that became George's signature tune, *Chinese Laundry Blues*, as well as all the songs for his first film, *Boots! Boots!* Beryl tried to buy his songs outright for £5 each to stop him earning royalties. Jack always took the £5, but made sure he got the royalties too. Jack had offered *Chinese Laundry Blues* to George in 1922, but was told it was too jazzy. Later, George said he would never have recorded the song were it not for the bandleader, Jack Hylton, who heard him sing it at a party.

Jack and his wife, Dorothy, started out as a comic double act. When they appeared with George in a show in Blackpool, Jack tried to spend as much time as he could with his young daughter, who was in hospital suffering from a tubercular abscess. When Beryl found out, she told him that, if he continued seeing the girl, he would never work for George again. When Jack died of cancer in 1947, Beryl refused to send flowers to the funeral.

The song-writing partnership of Jimmy Kennedy and Michael Carr lasted only five years, but it was nonetheless highly productive. Jimmy and Michael wrote two enormous hits for Flanagan and Allen, *Home Town* [1937] and *We're Gonna Hang Out the Washing on the Siegfried Line*[154] [1939] as well as *South of the Border* [also 1939], which was recorded by more than 100 singers, including Frank Sinatra and Bing Crosby.

After working for some time in the Colonial Service, Jimmy Kennedy turned to song-writing in the late 1920s. His first success was *The Barmaid's Song* [1930], better known as *Time, Gentlemen, Please*, which was recorded by Florrie Forde. Three years later, he supplied the lyric of a song based on a picnic organised by the former American president, Theodore [Teddy] Roosevelt. It was *The Teddy Bears' Picnic*. The recording by Henry Hall sold more than four million copies.

As a youngster, Michael Carr, the son of a featherweight boxer, known as 'Cockney' Cohen, lived in Dublin, where his father ran a restaurant. In his teens, he ran away to sea and spent six years in America, where he had a variety of jobs, including that of a stagehand and a newspaper reporter. He also played small roles in movies and, for nine months, he was even a cowhand in Montana.

Jimmy Kennedy [James Kennedy]

- Born Omagh, County Tyrone, 20 July 1902.
- Married [1] ---
- Married [2] Margaret Elizabeth Winifred Galpin in Tooting, south London, 11 June 1932
- Three children, Derek, Janet and James
- Married [3] Elaine ----
- Died Cheltenham 6 April 1984
- Left £177,625 [£350,000]

Michael Carr [Maurice Alfred Cohen]

- Born Leeds 11 March 1905
- Married [1] Rachel Eifer in London 12 September 1929 [dissolved]
- Married [2] Gertrude Carr in London 19 July 1961
- Died Maida Vale, London, 16 September 1968

On his return to Dublin, he wrote a tune for a song contest that so impressed a local bandleader that he gave him a letter of introduction to Jimmy Kennedy. At first, the two men worked well together and, on occasions, incredibly quickly. They wrote *Home Town* in seven minutes while taking a taxi to the London Palladium, where a song was required that night for the Crazy Gang show, *London Rhapsody*.[155]

During the Second World War, Jimmy was in the army and stationed a few miles out of London. One day, he saw a cartoon that he thought was ideal material for a song. It showed a young British soldier writing home from France and saying 'Dear Mum, I'm sending you the Siegfried Line to hang your washing on.'

Jimmy summoned Michael who found him walking up and down on guard inside the perimeter fence of a water pumping station in the pouring rain. There and then, they worked out the structure of what was to become one of the biggest morale-boosting songs of the war.

Two other song-writing partners, Jimmy Campbell and Reg Connelly, were very different men. Jimmy was a flamboyant, larger than life character, while Reg was a quiet and reserved man, and, as time proved, an astute businessman. With the bandleader, Ray Noble, they wrote *Goodnight, Sweetheart* [1931], first sung by Rudy Vallee, and, with Harry Woods, *Try a Little Tenderness* [1932].

In 1925, the two men had founded a publishing company, Campbell Connelly, but Jimmy was more interested in spending money than making it. He was extravagant, over-generous and almost dismissive of financial security. After a few years, he sold his stake in the firm and organised a tour of Australia with the dance bands led by Roy Fox and Jay Whidden. It flopped because the halls he had booked were not large enough. He returned home to face a tax bill of £6,000 [£200,000]. He went to Hollywood to write film music and came home to find

---

Jimmy Campbell [James Alexander Balfour Campbell Tyrie]

- Born ---
- Married [1] Betty Balfour, a star of Britain's silent movie era, in France 1932 [dissolved 1941] [She died in Weybridge, Surrey, 4 November 1978]
- Son, David, born 2 March 1937
- Married [2] Mitzi ----
- Jimmy Campbell was reported by *The Times* to have died in Tangier 19 August 1967, but no record of his death has been found by the British Consul in Rabat.

Reg Connelly [Reginald John Connelly, also known as Conoley]

- Born 1896 [?]
- Reg Connelly died Poole, Dorset, 23 September 1963

his marriage in ruins. For a time, he worked for Noel Gay as a song 'plugger' and then rejoined Campbell Connelly. By then, Reg Connelly had built the firm up into a powerful publishing company with 14 associated companies and branches in Europe, America and Australia. Campbell Connelly was bought by Music Sales Ltd. in 1982.

It is questionable as to whether Lawrence Wright was a better songwriter than he was a publicist or the other way round. He was certainly skilled as both. Under the nom de plume, Horatio Nicholls, he wrote *Among My Souvenirs* and *Shepherd of the Hills* [both with Edgar Leslie] [1927] and, using another pseudonym, Betsy O'Hogan, *Old Father Thames* [with Raymond Wallace] [1933].

As a publisher, his PR stunts were legendary. When the comedy songwriter, Ted Waite, wrote *I've Never Seen a Straight Banana* [1926], Lawrie offered £1,000 [£30,000] to anyone who could produce a straight banana. Parcels containing dozens of bananas arrived at his office. No banana was completely straight and so Lawrie awarded the money to the person with the least curly one. To promote *Me and Jane in a Plane* [1927], he hired an aircraft from Croydon airport, persuaded the Jack Hylton band to play the song on board, flew low over Blackpool and dropped thousands of copies of sheet music onto the resort's crowded beaches.

Lawrie's father, a violin teacher, ran a stall in Leicester market selling sheet music and musical instruments. At the age of 12, Lawrie left school and became apprenticed to a printer's firm. But two years later, he decided he wanted a job connected with music and so he joined a concert party at Eastbourne as a violinist and singer. He went on to work with a number of concert parties before returning home at the age of 18 to run a stall selling music in the same market as his father.

On each piece of music costing sixpence [£1.40], he made a profit of twopence halfpenny [about 50p]. He soon saw he would earn more if he wrote and published his own songs. His first was *Down by the Stream*. It cost him a halfpenny to print each copy and he charged his customers sixpence a time. He sold 5,000 copies.

In 1910, he heard a busker singing a tear-jerking song he had written entitled *Don't Go Down the Mine, Daddy*. Lawrie liked it and paid the man £5 [£250]

Lawrence Wright [Frederick Lawrence Wright]

- Born Leicester 15 February 1888
- Married [1] Edna May Prentice in Leicester 19 January 1911 [dissolved]
- Married [2] [dissolved]
- Married [3] [dissolved]
- Wright's private life was tempestuous. On his death-bed, he was tended by Lillian Jackson, a singer and pianist who had been his close friend for 25 years
- Lawrence Wright died 16 March 1964
- Left £366,297 [£4.25 million]

for it. In a twist of fate, 136 men and boys lost their lives in a mining disaster at Whitehaven in Cumbria a few weeks later. Lawrie pubished the song and within three weeks, he had sold a million copies.

The following year, he decided to try his luck as a writer-publisher in London. Arriving at St Pancras station, he hired a barrow and pushed his stock of music to a basement he had rented in Denmark Street. It was Lawrie who was responsible for turning Denmark Street into Britain's answer to Tin Pan Alley. From then on, it seemed he could do no wrong. He moved to larger premises and, at one time or another, nearly every British songwriter worked for him.

In 1914, working with his favourite British lyricist, Worton David,[156] he produced *Are We Downhearted? No!* which became one of the great marching songs of the First World War. One day in 1919, he and Worton overheard an argument between two women. As they walked by, they heard one of the women say, 'She may be old-fashioned, but, after all, she is my mother.' In that remark, Lawrie and Worton saw the seeds of a song. They wrote *That Old Fashioned Mother of Mine* which became the biggest success of the variety singer, Talbot O'Farrell, who specialised in Irish ballads.

At first, it made no impact at all. Lawrie forgot all about it and concentrated on another song, *The Kingdom Within Your Eyes*, which he persuaded John Tiller, of the Tiller Girls dancing troupe, to include in his next show at the Winter Gardens, Blackpool. Lawrie was convinced it would be an enormous hit and had posters advertising it put up all over Blackpool. The show opened and the song flopped. But an unknown Welsh tenor, who made a brief front-cloth appearance while scenery was being shifted, sang *That Old-Fashioned Mother of Mine*. The audience would not let him leave the stage, Lawrie worked hard at ordering as many copies of the song sheet as he could and it eventually sold 3,000,000 copies.

Away from the piano, Lawrie directed his own summer show, *On With the Show*, which started on the Isle of Man in 1924 and transferred the following year to Blackpool, where it ran for 32 years. He also founded the weekly musical paper, *The Melody Maker*, which was published from 1926 to 2000. In 1940, Lawrie's home in the Maida Vale area of London was bombed. He moved into the Park Lane Hotel and never moved out. Three years later, he suffered a stroke, which confined him to a wheelchair for the rest of his life. He carried on working, though, arriving at his office at 8.15 each morning and writing at least one new tune every day, continuing to stand by the slogan he had coined for his company: You Can't Go Wrong With a Wright Song.

In 1969, the Wright catalogue was bought by the Beatles' company, Northern Songs, for £812,500.

CHAPTER TEN

George and the Dragon

George and Beryl Formby

The name, George Formby, was central to music hall and variety for more than 150 years. First, there was the illegitimate son of a drunken prostitute, George Formby senior. He billed himself as the Wigan Nightingale and, by constantly exaggerating the status of a jetty at Wigan, invented Wigan Pier, amusing George Orwell sufficiently to use it in the title of his study of Northern working class life in the 1930s, *The Road to Wigan Pier*. Within music hall, George senior was so highly regarded that Marie Lloyd chose to watch only two acts from the wings, Formby and Dan Leno.

George, whose real name was James Booth, wanted his son to have nothing to do with the stage and even refused to allow the boy to watch his act. He sent George junior to work as a stable boy, hoping that one day he would be a jockey. George junior became an apprentice jockey, but never rode a winner. After his father died in 1921, aged only 45, his mother suggested that, before he returned to the stables, he should spend a few days in London to try to get over the shock. While there, so the story goes, he went to a music hall and saw a Tyneside comedian singing the songs of George senior and even adopting his gestures and mannerisms.

George was so angered by the impersonation that he decided that, if anyone were going to imitate his father, it would be him. Back home in Warrington, his mother, who, besides George, had six children under the age of 16 to support, agreed and enlisted the help of George senior's pianist, Harry Duckenfield. Dressed in his father's stage clothes, a small bowler hat, a tight jacket, ill-fitting trousers and a pair of heavy shoes worn on the wrong feet, he learned to put over his father's greatest successes, including *One of the Boys*, *Since I've Parted My Hair in the Middle*, and *Playing the Game in the West*.

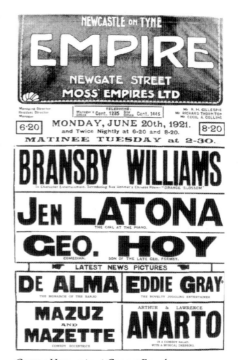

George Hoy, not yet George Formby.

George senior's stage persona was John Willie, a slow-witted but likeable Lancashire lad. Ten weeks after his father died, George made his debut at a cinema in Earlestown, not far from St Helens. Seized with nerves, he dried up halfway through his first song and would have given up completely were it not for shouts of encouragement from his father's supporters. In spite of his failure, one of his father's best friends, Danny Clarke, the far-sighted manager of the Argyle, Birkenhead, offered him a ten-minute spot there, but no one could hear him. He was drowned out by barracking from the gallery. The next two years continued in much the same way. He toured northern halls and cinemas, still playing John Willie, but earning little money. It was a mistake to try to build his career purely by emulating his father. His mother liked the idea because she wanted to keep the memory of her late husband alive, but George needed to prove he had a talent of his own. Unfortunately, he was lazy and would have been happy to have pottered on for years, making some money, but never becoming well known.

In 1923, two things changed his life: meeting Beryl Ingham and buying a ukulele. There was only one reason for trying to learn how to play the uke: it solved the problem of finding something to do with his hands. [A ukulele or a banjulele? Formby fans still argue about it]. At the Alhambra in Barnsley, he played it on stage for the first time, accompanying himself singing *Going Back to Tennessee* and was startled to hear audiences cheering him to the rafters. He met Beryl, a clog dancer and one half of an act called the Two Violets, when they shared a bill at Castleford in West Yorkshire. George fell in love with her and pursued her in the face of several rebuffs. He finally broke her resolve and the couple married in September 1924.

Beryl was then earning more than George. She was getting £10 [£300] a week against his £5 [£150], but she was astute enough to appreciate that clog

---

George Formby [George Hoy Booth]

- Born Wigan, Lancashire, 26 May 1904
- Married Beryl Ingham in Wigan 13 September 1924 [died 25 December 1960]
- George Formby died in Preston 6 March 1961
- Left 135,162 [£1,900,000]

dancing was going out of fashion and that, properly nurtured, George's homely gormlessness could have enormous appeal. Without Beryl, there would have been no George Formby. She abandoned her career and stopped at nothing to further his. She never left his side. She told him what to do and how to do it. She handled the money he earned and gave him pocket money to spend.

Their marriage was, in fact, more of a business relationship than a union of souls. From the outset, she made it clear that she did not want children. Indeed, for most of their lives, they slept in separate beds. Throughout the world of variety, she was seen as a termagant, but that was of no concern to her. 'Wherever George had to go, Beryl had to go too,' she once said. 'I just used to say all the time: if you want George, you've got to have me. They always wanted George. So they had to put up with me.'[157]

Beryl first ordered George to learn to play the ukulele properly.[158] It is not a difficult instrument to master, but George became adept at strumming it with an infectious rhythm. In spite of finding a prop that set him apart from his father, he traded on the popularity of John Willie for some years. He played the part in his first gramophone records in 1926,[159] but began to establish his own style, regularly singing saucy lyrics when he signed a three-year contract with Decca in 1932. Even when he made his first two films,[160] *Boots! Boots!* [1934] and *Off the Dole* [1935],[161] he appeared as John Willie, although the uke had become his trademark by then.

It was the success of those early recordings that made Beryl decide the time was right for George to make movies. At first, she approached ATP [Associated Talking Pictures], where she met her match in Basil Dean. He told her he was keen to have George on his books, but not her, suggesting in colourful language that she trapped her tongue in the door on the way out. [Later, Dean did employ George, but he let slip his contempt for popular entertainment when he described George as 'a simple uncomplicated person of limited talent {like many music hall personalities of that day}.'][162] Irving Asher, the British representative

Inevitably, many of George's saucy songs were not approved by the BBC. In 1944, Beryl told the Corporation that its censorship had become so silly that it was not worth the trouble trying to put a programme together. But not everyone at the BBC knew which songs were banned. When George appeared on *Henry Hall's Guest Night* in June 1946, one producer had not heard that one of George's most risqué lyrics, *With My Little Stick of Blackpool Rock*, had been marked NTBB [Not to be broadcast]. On transmission, the producer faded the song out three times and later said he thought it would be better if George were not booked for any further Henry Hall programmes. [The producer must have had a very unsullied mind. Part of the lyric reads: 'With my little stick of Blackpool rock, along the promenade I stroll. It may be sticky, but I never complain. It's nice to have a nibble at it now and again.']

of Warner Brothers, told Beryl that George would never make films because he was too stupid to play the bad guy and too ugly to play the hero. Finally, John Blakeley of Mancunian Films suggested a movie for which there would be a 15-day shooting schedule and a budget of £3,000 [£100,000], which included a £200 [£7,000] salary for George and ten per cent of the profits.

George Formby's Filmography

The movies; the studios; the directors, well-known songs and other variety performers. From 1937 to 1943, George Formby was Britain's top box office attraction.

1934   *Boots! Boots!* [Blakeley Productions]. *Chinese Laundry Blues*, written by Jack Cotterell. Only the melody of this song, which became George's signature tune, is heard. It is part of the opening music and accompanies a very able tap dance by Beryl.

1935   *Off the Dole* [Blakeley Productions]. *With My Little Ukulele in my Hand*, written by Jack Cotterell.

1936   *No Limit* [Associated Talking Pictures]. Director, Monty Banks. Sir Michael Balcon, who began working at Ealing in the early 1940s, described George as an odd and not particularly lovable character. He also made the point that, although George's British audience was enormous, the West End of London was not interested. 'We rarely got a booking for a Formby film in one of the major West End cinemas, but, when we did, you could have shot a cannon-ball through the theatre without hurting anyone.'[163]

George and his co-star, the impressionist, Florence Desmond [see Chapter 21], disliked each other from the start. She became angry that, while filming on the Isle of Man, large studio vans transporting cameras and lights also carried advertising boards that read: 'Associated Talking Pictures, now making *No Limit*, starring George Formby.' As her contract named her as co-star, she complained, but nothing was done. So, she told Monty Banks that, unless the boards were changed, she was walking out. To save trouble, the boards were simply removed. That infuriated George and, from then on, the couple spoke to each other only when they had to. Basil Dean wrote: 'George was jealous of opportunities given to other members of the cast. Putting it bluntly and vulgarly, he wanted the lot. Dessie knew her own value and had no intention of being put upon. There were violent quarrels.'[164]

1936   *Keep Your Seats, Please* [ATP]. Director Monty Banks. *When I'm Cleaning Windows*, written by Harry Gifford and Fred E. Cliffe.[165]
         In spite of the problems with *No Limit*, Basil Dean wanted Florence Desmond for this film too. He broke the news to her over lunch at the Savoy. She flatly refused, but Dean told her that *No*

Limit had been a great success and the distributors were keen to have the same team again. 'Foolishly, against my better judgment, I was talked into doing another film with George Formby. This one ... was again an unhappy experience for me. I was even more relieved when the cameras stopped turning.'[166]

1937 *Keep Fit* [ATP]. Director Anthony Kimmins. George tried to flirt with all his leading ladies. As Beryl denied him sex, that is not surprising, but she jealously refused him contact with any actress who appeared with him. She also tried to impose her will on the direction of the film. Anthony Kimmins was simply scared of her. She thought nothing of storming onto the set in the middle of a scene and telling Kimmins how incompetent she thought he was.

1937 *Feather Your Nest* [ATP]. Director William Beaudine. *Leaning on a Lamppost*, written by Noel Gay.

1938 *I See Ice* [ATP]. Director Anthony Kimmins.

1938 *It's in the Air* [ATP]. Director Anthony Kimmins.

1939 *Trouble Brewing* – George was supposed to kiss his leading lady, but, when he did, his eyes rolled. 'There was pandemonium. Beryl gave a loud cry, collapsed into a sea of tears and left the set sobbing heavily.'[167]

1939 *Come on, George!* [ATP] Director Anthony Kimmins. This time, George's leading lady was the glamorous Patricia Kirkwood, who was playing a policeman's daughter. First, her hair was cut short. Then, she was disallowed make-up. Beryl apparently thought that her hair was too sexy for a policeman's daughter and that her make-up was too theatrical. In addition, Pat said her costume could have been bought at a country jumble sale. She was not allowed a song of her own or even to share a duet with George. '[He] never addressed a remark to me during the entire film nor even come near me ... Anthony Kimmins ... assured me that GF had probably been warned off me by ... Beryl, who was apparently very jealous.'[168]

1940 *Let George Do It* [ATP]. Director Marcel Varnel. *Mr Wu is a Window Cleaner Now*, written by Harry Gifford and Fred E. Cliffe, and *Granddad's Flannelette Nightshirt*, written by Eddie Latta. Phyllis Calvert, who found George boring, at least admired his timing. 'There's a scene ... where he goes to five doors in a nightclub [and finds] his way blocked by ... villains. He's singing and playing his uke all the time. The song ends when he gets to the last door. He had to do this several times during shooting and on each occasion he finished the song at the exact moment he reached the final door. He was just as effective in another scene in which he gets out of bed singing, shaves, brushes his hair, dresses ... and hits the last note as he buttons his coat. This was absolute perfect timing – all in one camera take.'[169]

1941 *Spare a Copper* [ATP]. Director, John Paddy Carstairs. Beryl Reid.

1941 *Turned Out Nice Again* [ATP]. Director, John Paddy Carstairs. *Auntie Maggie's Remedy*, written by Eddie Latta. *South American George*

[1941], *Much Too Shy* [1942], *Get Cracking* [1943], *He Snoops to Conquer* and *Bell Bottom George* [both 1944], *I Didn't Do It!* [1945] and *George in Civvy Street* [1946] were all made at Columbia and directed by Marcel Varnel. The script of *Much Too Shy* was written by Ronald Frankau; Billy Caryll and Hilda Mundy appeared in *I Didn't Do It!*; and the scriptwriters of *George in Civvy Street* included Ted Kavanagh, who wrote ITMA, Max Kester and Gale Pedrick.

By the end of the Second World War, George's brand of morale-boosting lightweight comedy had gone out of fashion. He reacted badly to the change of circumstances, suffered a nervous breakdown and was admitted to a psychiatric hospital in York. Incredibly, Beryl told the doctors that he should stay there until he was completely better, but that, if he failed to recover, he should be committed to a mental institution. A month later, though, she signed a contract for him to tour Scandinavia, where hardly anyone knew him. She went to the hospital to collect him, but, as a doctor refused to discharge him, George had to sign the discharge papers himself.

Increasingly, George suffered from both physical and mental illness and worked less and less. But in 1951, he was booked for his first West End musical, *Zip Goes a Million*, at the Palace Theatre. It was based on *Brewster's Millions*, an old farce in which a man has to spend £1 million by midnight on New Year's Eve in order to inherit a further £7 million. When the impresario, Emile Littler, decided to turn it into a musical, he discovered the rights belonged to Eric Maschwitz. The two men met for a rather argumentative lunch. By the end, though, they agreed that Littler would stage the show and that it would be adapted by Maschwitz and Eric Posford, with whom he had written *Good-night Vienna*. For months, Maschwitz worked on an outline of the show while keeping in close contact with Littler and Charles Hickman, who was to direct it.

In fact, so much time was spent on the outline that, a month before rehearsals were due to start, no dialogue or songs had been written. For a whole week, which included Maschwitz's fiftieth birthday, he was locked in a room at Littler's home, bashing away on his typewriter. The only concession to his birthday was that he was allowed a different drink every hour, beginning with a Pernod at 10am and finishing with a weak whisky and soda at midnight. At the end of the week, the show was ready.

Hickman had a little trouble from Beryl, although, as in the films, she refused to allow George to kiss his leading lady, Sara Gregory. She also insisted on something that had become a habit: taking a curtain call with George. Most audiences were perplexed to see a woman on stage at the end of a show in which she had not appeared. Most reviewers liked *Zip Goes a Million*, but not the doyen of theatre critics, Kenneth Tynan:

> I concede George Formby's piercing, sunny little singing voice to be one of the pleasantest in London ... [But] I cannot laugh as he fidgets and gapes and fusses flat-footed across the stage ... and I am unable to accept the theory that

a banality or a catch-phrase acquires wit or 'philosophy' when delivered in a North country accent.[170]

George, Littler and Maschwitz had little to fear from Tynan. For many weeks, there was not a seat to be had at the Palace, but then George suffered a heart attack and his part was taken by the comic, Reg Dixon. In 1953, George was well enough to join a Palladium show, *Fun and the Fair*, with Terry-Thomas. The eminent critic, Harold Hobson, was better disposed towards him than Tynan:

With a carp-like face, a mouth outrageously full of teeth … and a smile of perpetual wonder of the joyous incomprehensibility of the universe and the people in it, Mr Formby has that foolish simplicity which one would like to think is a better protection from harm than all the wisdom of the worldly.[171]

George cancelled a 1953/54 pantomime on his doctor's advice, but opened in a summer show in Blackpool the following June. Here again, he had to pull out after six weeks because of dysentery and depression. In 1955, Beryl fell seriously ill. Hospital tests showed she had inoperable cancer of the womb. George was told she had no more than two years to live. To cope with the pain, Beryl began drinking heavily. For the next five years, George continued to play the round of summer shows and pantomimes, but the pace was slowing.

At Christmas 1960, he starred in *Aladdin* at the Bristol Hippodrome. A few days before opening, he was told that Beryl had lapsed into a coma. Two hours before curtain up on the first night, there was another call to say that she might not survive the night. The show went ahead. As soon as it finished, George drove to the home of two old friends in Warrington. He was not with Beryl when she died. George battled on with *Aladdin*, but quit halfway through January 1961 with a heavy cold. His condition worsened and two days later he was admitted to a hospital in Blackpool.

Every day, he was visited by the daughter of long-standing friends, Ada Patricia [Pat] Howson, a 35-year-old teacher. In February, he discharged himself and, to the astonishment of the variety world, he announced that he and Pat were to marry the following May. It was not to be. Before the end of the month, George suffered another heart attack and died a few days later. In only three months, George had made three wills. In the last of them, he left £5,000 [£75,000] to his valet, Harry Scott,[172] and the rest to Pat Howson. On the day of his funeral, 150,000 people lined the route. One nice touch was that the undertaker was Bruce Williams, who, as Eddie Latta, had written *Auntie Maggie's Remedy* and *Granddad's Flannelette Nightshirt*.

A legal row about the last will dragged on interminably, but Pat Howson was to see none of the money. She died of cancer in November 1971 at the age of 46. Eliza Booth, the wife of one outstanding comic, George Formby senior, and the mother of another, George Formby junior, died in 1981 at the age of 102.

Will Hay, another northern comic who made highly popular movies in the 1930s, could not have been more different from George. Whereas George was dumb, Will was a polymath, the sort of man who would have made a success of any career. He was fluent in French, German, Spanish, Italian and Afrikaans.

Will Hay [William Thomson Hay]

- Born Stockton-on-Tees 6 December 1888
- Married Gladys Perkins in Salford 7 October 1907. [Died in Dover, Kent, 1982] [The marriage broke up in 1935, but Gladys refused Will a divorce as she was a Catholic. Thereafter, Will spent many years with a much younger Norwegian woman, Randi Kopstadt.]
- Daughters, Gladys and Joan. [Gladys, who died in 1979, became a comedienne, most notably in BBC Radio's *Ignorance is Bliss*.]
- Son, Will
- Died Chelsea, west London, 18 April 1949
- Left £27,155 [£625,000]

In fact, like Enoch Powell, he learned a new language just for the fun of it. He played the piano and the violin and he was an expert astronomer. When he discovered a white spot on Saturn, he made front-page news.

Although largely associated with the cinema, Will had his roots in variety. The son of an engineer,[173] he developed his own comic character, a hopeless incompetent, who always pretended to know more than he really did. He was at his best playing schoolmasters largely because he looked scholarly.

At first, he got his ideas from his sister, Eppie,[174] a teacher, who amused the family with stories of pranks her pupils played. He composed a musical sketch about schoolboy mischief, in which he appeared in a mortar board and gown. From this, there developed Will's best-known routine, the Fourth Form at St Michael's.

Will Hay's Filmography

The movies; the studios; the directors. Will was at his best when teamed with Moore Marriott, playing a toothless old fool, called Harbottle, and Graham Moffatt as Albert, a plump and idle schoolboy.

1934   *Those Were the Days* [BIP]. Director, Thomas Bentley. An adaptation of *The Magistrate* by Arthur Wing Pinero. Will played the title role and the part of his son was taken by John Mills: 'The film's success was almost entirely due to Will's subtle and peculiar brand of comedy.'[175]

1934   *Radio Parade of 1935* [BIP]. Director, Arthur B. Woods. A glorious send-up of the bureaucratic BBC, in which Will, playing the Director

General, is up-staged by a plethora of variety stars, Billy Bennett, Claude Dampier, Ronald Frankau, Lily Morris, Beryl Orde, Ted Ray, Stanelli, Nellie Wallace and the Western Brothers.

1935   *Dandy Dick* [BIP]. Director, William Beaudine. Another Pinero adaptation.

1935   *Boys will be Boys* [Gainsborough]. Director, William Beaudine. Will plays a schoolmaster, but not at St Michael's. This is Narkover College, featured in Beachcomber's column, *By the Way*, in the *Daily Express*. Hay was one of the screenwriters. J.B. Morton, who wrote Beachcomber, provided additional material. Claude Dampier was also in this film and attracted excellent reviews. In 1978, Dampier's widow, Billie Carlyle, wrote: 'When I saw a re-showing of *Boys Will Be Boys* a year or two ago, I found most of Claude's best scenes had been cut out. Will Hay was a friend of ours and we liked him very much, but he refused to do any more films with Claude, saying he was a "picture stealer"!'[176]

1936   *Where There's A Will* [Gainsborough]. Director, William Beaudine. Will was one of the writers.

1936   *Windbag the Sailor* [Gainsborough] Director, William Beaudine. The first film to feature Moore Marriott and Graham Moffatt. Again, Will was one of the writers. *Good Morning, Boys* and *Oh, Mr Porter!* [both 1937], *Old Bones of the River*, *Convict 99*, *Ask a Policeman* and *Hey! Hey! USA* [all 1938] and *Where's That Fire?* [1939] were all made by Gainsborough and directed by Marcel Varnel. *Where's That Fire?* was the last film to feature Moore Marriott and Graham Moffatt.

1938   *The Big Blockade* [Ealing] Director, Charles Frend. Michael Redgrave and Robert Morley were also in the cast.

1941   *The Ghost of St Michael's* [Ealing]. Director, Marcel Varnel.[177]

1942   *Go to Blazes* [Ealing]. Director, Walter Forde. A short government-sponsored film about how to deal with incendiary bombs. *The Black Sheep of Whitehall* and *The Goose Steps Out* [both 1942] and *My Learned Friend* [1943] were all made at Ealing and directed by Will and Basil Dearden.

Will's decision to dissolve his partnership with Marriott and Moffatt marked the start of his decline. Then, in 1943, he contracted cancer. Four years later, he suffered a stroke and was told that only six months in South Africa would give him a chance of recovery. In fact, it gave him another two years of life. On his death, *The Times*, in circumlocutory mood, wrote of him:

The pedagogue was never more typically himself than at the moment his essential ignorance was about to be exposed, but there was a saving pugnacity about the man and fortune, relenting at the last moment, would save his face and launch him into yet further adventures which would try to the utmost that mixture of blustering effrontery and threadbare capacity of which his character was composed.[178]

CHAPTER ELEVEN

By 'Eck

Up North: Albert Burdon, Norman Evans, Albert Modley, Sandy Powell, Al Read, and Frank Randle

Among the very best Northern comics, Norman Evans was first among equals, but as a young man, he had no intention of going on the stage. His father worked for the Borough Treasurer in Rochdale and Norman started his working life in a local solicitor's office and was later a salesman. He became involved in amateur dramatics and was soon a regular speaker at concerts and dinners.

Norman was at his best playing Fanny Fairbottom who enjoyed gossipy chats with her neighbour; hence his bill matter: 'Over the Garden Wall.' Norman modelled Fanny on his mother and introduced the caricature at a Sunday school concert when he was only 17.

Fanny had to stand on a bucket to make herself heard, at one point slipping and bruising her ample bosom: 'Ooh, that's the third time this week on the same brick.' More recently, the sketch was performed by Les Dawson not as an act of plagiarism, but in homage to a brilliant character study:

You mean her at number seven. Oh, I won't say a word. I never talk. Mind you, I'm not a bit surprised … I knew what she was the first time I saw her. Oh, yes. The coalman was never far away, you know. I mean – don't tell me it

---

Norman Evans

- Born Rochdale, Greater Manchester, 11 June 1901
- Married Annie -----
- Daughter, Norma, born 1933 [?] [Married --- Wittenberg. Died 24 July 2007]
- Norman Evans died Blackpool 25 November 1962

takes 35 minutes to deliver two bags of nuts. Oh, yes. I knew what was going on when I saw him shout 'Whoa!' to his horse from her bedroom window. Oh and you know Ethel Higginbottom, don't you. She had her face lifted. It's not safe to leave anything lying about these days, is it?[179]

When Norman reached London in 1934, publicists made out that he had been discovered by Gracie Fields. The papers liked the story, but the truth was that Oswald Stoll had recognised his talent and quickly promoted him to the top of the bill at the Alhambra, where he was hailed 'as the vaudeville find of his generation … I anticipate his going from success to success.'[180]

Surprisingly for a dialect comedian, Norman enjoyed some of that success in America, where he made a coast-to-coast tour and appeared on Ed Sullivan's television show. In 1955, he had a bad car accident, swerving to avoid a cat and careering into a lamppost. He lost an eye and broke his nose, but bounced back to star in *The Norman Evans Show* on BBC Television the following year. His choice of guests showed he also recognised talent. They included the sublime Mrs Shufflewick [see Chapter 20] and the eccentric dancers, Wilson, Keppel and Betty [see Chapter 26].

The phrase 'much loved' is often found in resumes of showbiz careers. No one earned the sobriquet more than Sandy Powell, a comedian who never dressed in funny clothes and who never told a risqué joke. He was, according to one reviewer, 'an original with a friendly approach and a manner that is childlike and bland.'[181] Val Parnell described his road shows as tin-pot little affairs. George Black was equally mystified as to how Sandy could fill a theatre with what he called a sixpenny-worth of a show. Visiting Sandy at the Newcastle Empire, Black appeared envious:

> The shows I put on cost me thousands. Top stars, lavish scenery and dresses, expensive producers, trap doors, revolving stages, trick lighting and all that. It costs me a fortune. I come up and find your … show with two black cloths packs them in and you play to capacity.[182]

Sandy was only seven when he first appeared on stage as a boy soprano. His father had left home when he was four and his mother, who had been on the halls as a singer and dancer, exotically named Lily Le Main, had to work to support herself. When she appeared at the Hippodrome, Keighley, the charlatan, Walford Bodie, a ridiculous figure with mesmeric eyes and waxed mustachios, was also on the bill. He claimed he could cure disabled people by using electricity. During the week, Sandy was one of his volunteers, in other words, a stooge. He pretended to go into a trance and jumped about in Bodie's 'electric chair' as though he had received a shock. He was sufficiently convincing for Bodie to slip a few coins into his hand at the end of the week.

Sandy toured as part of his mother's act, but eventually established himself on his own, telling stories and impersonating music hall stars, including Harry Lauder, George Formby senior, Wilkie Bard and his hero, Harry Weldon. While still in his teens, he played the Empire, Dewsbury, where he received a note

Sandy Powell [Albert Arthur Powell]

- Born Rotherham, 30/31 January 1900
- Married [1] Dorothy May Whitty 3 May 1929 London [dissolved 1940]
- Daughter, Peggy; Son, Peter
- Married [2] Kate Powell in London, 20 January 1944 [She died 7 December 1947]
- Married [3] Kathleen Marion White in London 19 March 1951
- Sandy Powell died in Eastbourne 26 June 1982
- Left £102,116 [£230,000]

from a London agent, Bertram Montague, asking him to arrange a meeting. The following morning, Montague told Sandy that, if he became his agent, he would arrange an immediate two weeks' trial at Stoll's theatres. Sandy agreed. He played the first week at the Shepherds Bush Empire, where Stoll saw him and offered him work at his other music halls. It was the break Sandy had been praying for.

His popularity grew in both the variety theatre and pantomime and in 1928 he starred in *Sandy's Hour*, the BBC's first regular variety show. During one broadcast, he dropped his script. While trying to find his place, he kept repeating 'Can you hear me, mother?' five words that became an irritating catch phrase for the rest of his life.

The following year, Sandy recorded his first 78, a sketch called *The Lost Policeman*, in which a cheeky young boy gets the better of Sandy playing the policeman. [Sandy's daughter, Peggy, was the boy]. The recording company gave Sandy a choice: he could receive either £60 [£1,800] as a one-off payment or £30 [£900] plus three-farthings [about 15P] for every record that was sold. Wisely, Sandy chose the latter. In all, seven million copies were bought. From then on, Sandy made a record almost every month: Sandy the Magistrate, the Zookeeper, the Convict and so on. In 1942, he made his last 78, *Sandy Joins the Home Guard*. By then, his royalties were earning him more than £12,000 [£300,000] a year.

Sandy also starred in eight full-length feature films, the most successful of which was *I've Got A Horse* [1938].[183] In his most popular stage act, he played an incompetent ventriloquist, but he went on performing it until it became very stale and embarrassingly unfunny.

Unfortunately, Sandy's private life was also far from funny. His first wife took to drink and threatened to cause a commotion at theatres where he was appearing. After nine years' marriage, he walked out, taking their two children with him. Not long afterwards, he hired three private detectives to keep watch from a flat across the road. One day, when she was entertaining a man with whom she was having an affair, Sandy and the investigators burst in. Sandy hit the man. Although his wife alleged cruelty by him, the judge found in his favour.

To appease Black and Parnell, who never lost an opportunity to mock Sandy over the lack of star names in his shows, he did book two big names, but not from the world of show business. The first was one of England's greatest flyweight boxers, Peter Kane, who built an act around skipping, ball punching and shadow boxing, and finished with three rounds with a sparring partner. The second was Commander A.B. Campbell, one of the team on BBC Radio's *Brains Trust*.[184] In spite of initial misgivings, he eventually joined the show for a six-week run. He spoke about the *Brains Trust*, recited Rudyard Kipling's *If*, described his time in the Navy and ended with a poem he had written himself. After a while, Sandy followed the act with one in which he lampooned Commander Campbell.

As his career progressed, Sandy found he was another Northern comic who could be just as popular in the south, particularly Eastbourne, where he played 21 consecutive summer seasons. The one place where he failed to draw crowds was his home town of Rotherham. At the height of his fame, he was due to appear there, but pulled out in favour of a better date. When he returned later in his career, a local paper published an article saying that, if Rotherham was not good enough for him while he was topping bills, it did not want him when he was on his way down.

In the variety theatre, Al Read was unusual in several respects. He was in his forties when he made his professional debut as a comedian; he was already a successful businessman and so did not need show business to provide him with him a living; and he developed a style that was unique: he performed sketches in which he played all the parts, even that of a dog, if necessary. Among his peers, he attracted some envy. Mostly, though, they were amused by his overweening conceit.

Most variety entertainers were ambitious, but Al seemed to have plotted his career well in advance. He was a sausage manufacturer. That is to say, the family

Al Read [Alfred Read]

- Born Salford, Lancashire, 3 March 1909
- Married [1] Joyce Entwistle 18 April 1938 [dissolved 1970]
- Two sons, one daughter
- Married [2] Elizabeth Ann Read 13 June 1970
- Al Read died Northallerton, North Yorkshire, 9 September 1987

firm ran a meat products factory in Salford. Al proved to be a talented salesman and, at the age of 23, he was made a director of the firm. The job allowed him enough free time to play golf, usually at a course in Blackpool, some miles from his home, but where dozens of entertainers were to be seen during the summer season.

For many years, Al was an amateur comedian, appearing as an after-dinner speaker playing a gallery of characters in an entertainment he called Pages from Life. In the late 1940s, he offered to pay the Blackpool impresario, Jack Taylor, for a spot at a Sunday concert on the South Pier. By his own admission, he was a flop. All the time, he was trying to get on the radio. Bowker Andrews, a producer in the BBC's Light Entertainment department in Manchester, saw him perform one of his monologues, *The Decorator*, at an after-dinner entertainment at a hotel in the city in 1950. As a result, he was booked to do the same piece in an edition of *Variety Fanfare*. The sketch was all about finding someone to decorate a small bedroom:

> 'Is it bad?' 'Bad? Well, I've seen nothing like it.' 'Can you do it?' 'I can do it. It might take 12 months. It might take two years. There are seven or eight papers on here. All have to be stripped. You'll want six or seven men with blowlamps. Your ceiling's gone in that corner. That means re-roofing, re-guttering. I don't know. I can't tell. I'll tell you better when we get the scaffolding up.'[185]

This was the start. Andrews introduced Al to a talented scriptwriter, Ronnie Taylor, and, after a series of appearances in *Variety Fanfare*, Al was given his own show, *Such is Life*. By now, Al's gallery included a loud-mouthed football fan, a henpecked husband, a boy having his hair cut, a car park attendant, a holidaymaker locked out of his boarding-house, an embarrassingly inquisitive child and many more. In no time at all, Al was a radio star, listened to by no fewer than 35 million people. His catchphrases, Right Monkey and You'll Be Lucky, were repeated across the land:

> Read was a radio original, relying for his laughs not on a stream of gags and funny voices, but on the skilful observation of everyday life. He drew particularly on his own experience of working-class Lancashire, but the humour was universal, put across with beaming, winking bonhomie.[186]

Al's radio shows ran until 1983. He tried television, but did not feel comfortable. There was no reason to see Al. Hearing him was enough. That said, two shows in which he appeared at London's Adelphi Theatre, *You'll Be Lucky* and *Such is Life*, enjoyed long runs. In addition to the wealth he accrued through sausages, Al enjoyed all the trappings of showbiz success and let everyone know how well he was doing. At news conferences, he appeared in expensive clothes and told the bored hacks where he had bought his shirt, his tie, his hat and so on.

For the 1964 summer show on Blackpool's Central Pier, Al was booked alongside three Irish lads, the Bachelors. They were to be paid £150 a week on the strength of three moderately successful songs. By the time the show opened, however, they had topped the charts with *Diane*, which sold a million copies, and followed it up with *I Believe*, which sold 600,000 copies in Britain and another 300,000 in America. They honoured their contract and the theatre was besieged by fans, journalists, radio and TV crews. Al thought the attention was all for him. Such is life.

More than once, Albert Burdon seemed to be on the point of becoming a star. He was a big name in the provinces, but, in spite of several forays into London, he never quite established himself there, although there were many plaudits from the press: one paper called him 'a knockabout genius with a sense of humour and a quaint, taking personality.'[187]

Albert Burdon

- Born South Shields 4 July 1900
- Married Violet Spurgin in London 29 March 1933
- One son, Bryan; one daughter
- Albert Burdon died South Shields 13 April 1981
- Left £115,380 [£300,000]

For four-and-a-half years, Albert was the lead comic in a touring revue, *On the Dole*, followed by a similar show, *League of Neighbours*. C.B. Cochran recognised his talent and in 1930 gave him a part in the Rodgers and Hart musical, *Ever Green*, Jessie Matthews' greatest success at London's Adelphi Theatre. But, according to Clarkson Rose, who appeared in pantomimes with Albert at the Lyceum, Cochran's efforts to turn him into a posh West End comedian did not work. He made nine movies, including *It's A Boy* [1934], which won him more fans. His sketches are lovingly remembered too: the Lightning Shave, in which he played a non-stop barber, and the World's Worst Wizard, in which he tried to demonstrate his magic cabinet with a maniacal volunteer from the audience, his son, Bryan. Then, there was the Means Test Committee:

> 'Are you married?' 'Sixteen wives and no children.' 'You can't have sixteen wives.' 'Oh, yes, you can. It says so in the Marriage Service. Four richer. Four poorer. Four better. Four worse. Sixteen.' 'When did you last work?' 'He's been out of work so long he thinks manual labour is a Spaniard.' 'I'll find you a job at your own trade and, when I find you a job, I'll see that you accept it. By the way, what is your trade?' 'I'm a Coronation programme seller.'[188]

Albert Modley, with his trademark peaked cap, was billed as Lancashire's favourite Yorkshireman. He worked first as a grocer's boy, then as a butcher's deliveryman and after that as a railway porter. It was not what his father,

Professor Modley, had in mind. The 'professor', who ran a gym in Ilkley and who had worked on the halls as a strong man, wanted him to be a fitness instructor. He would have been proud, though, to see Albert become a resident compère of BBC Radio's *Variety Bandbox* with a regular audience of between ten and 14 million.

Albert Modley [Albert Frederick Modley]

- Born Liverpool 3 March 1901
- Married Doris Cox, also known as Doris Readshaw, in Ilkley 27 January 1927
- Son, Peter
- Albert Modley died in Morecambe 23 February 1979
- Left £17,604 [£55,000]

As a porter, Albert used to entertain his colleagues. This led to him doing a turn in pubs to earn beer money. He gave up his job on the railways to join a concert party. In a pantomime in Bradford, he conceived his most famous act, in which he played a drum kit decorated as a tram. The drums and the cymbals produced the tram's noise and Albert provided a running commentary. It sounds like a simple idea, but Albert, responding to shouts from the audience, was still performing the sketch 40 years later.

He teamed up with another comic, Harry Korris, in a double act. Albert appeared as Enoch and Harry as Mr Lovejoy. [Later, when Albert was replaced by Robbie Vincent and a third comic was taken on {Cecil Frederick as Ramsbottom}, the act became the mainstay of another hugely successful BBC Radio show, *Happidrome*, which was broadcast for most of the 1940s]. By then, Albert was touring with his road show, *On With the Modley*. He joined *Variety Bandbox* in 1949, replacing Derek Roy. On his first appearance, he was faded out, not the result of questionable jokes, but because he was overrunning and the Ten O'Clock News had to start on time.

After Albert had retired, the director, Stephen Frears, cast him as one of two old men chatting outside a hut on an allotment in Alan Bennett's TV play, *Sunset Across the Bay* [1974]. When filming started, Albert appeared to be unsure of his lines and covered up his forgetfulness with stock phrases from his variety days: By! It's a beggar, is this. Or: By shots, this is a funny do. Modley's wife, who was on the set, was unhappy about the cap he had been given to wear. She produced a hatbox containing the much larger cap he had worn on the halls. He has to wear his own cap, she insisted. Folks won't recognise him in that fiddling thing.

It was a delicate moment, but the cameraman found a solution. Albert would rehearse with the smaller cap and wear the larger one once filming started.

That was agreed. But it was the rehearsal that was filmed and, when Albert performed the scene with the big cap, there was no film in the camera.

The most notorious of the northern comics was Frank Randle, who always played a hard-drinking lecherous buffoon. In real life, he was no buffoon. Nor was he lecherous although, away from his long-suffering wife, he had girlfriends.[189] But hard-drinking he was. There was always a crate of Guinness in his dressing room and, at one stage, he was drinking a bottle and a half of whisky a day. He sometimes disappeared for days on end for a spree with his drinking partner, Josef Locke. Even his catchphrase underlined his interest in drink: I've supped some stuff toneet. Frank trashed his dressing room years before rock stars came along. As an entertainer, what made Frank magical was a sense of danger. What would he do this time? How far would he go?

Frank Randle [Arthur Hughes, the illegitimate son of Rhoda Hughes]

- Born Wigan 20 January 1901 [Rhoda Hughes married Richard McEvoy, a mechanic, in Blackpool on 7 May 1913; Frank assumed his surname]
- Married May Annie Victoria Douglas [known as Queenie] in Greenwich, south-east London, 5 May 1928 [Frank had a son, the artist, Arthur Delaney [1927–1987] by Genevieve Delaney, also known as Willis]
- Frank Randle died Blackpool 7 July 1957

Randle was rabidly anti-Establishment. In Blackpool, his arch-enemy was the Chief Constable, Harry Barnes, a staunch Methodist. It particularly irked Barnes that Frank could appear on stage, minus his teeth, seemingly drunk, certainly with a bottle in his hand and could belch and fart as much as he wanted. But, provided he stuck to an agreed script, there was nothing the authorities could do. Barnes ensured that there were police officers in the audience at each of Frank's shows checking on whether he was deviating from the script. He frequently did; Barnes would then threaten to close the theatre; and the manager had to try to persuade Frank to stick to the script.

Offstage, Frank could be wild. His antics have been well documented. Three will suffice here:

BUTCHER'S FILM SERVICE LTD. *present*

Harry
KORRIS · **RANDLE**
Frank

in

*S*omewhere in England

ROBBY VINCENT *(Enoch)* and **DAN YOUNG**

TRADE SHOW—RIALTO (Coventry St.), Friday, March 31, at 11 a.m

- Angered by a drinks bill at the Hulme Hippodrome, Frank vandalised the theatre's bar with a fireman's axe
- At Barrow-in-Furness, his company, Randle's Scandals, gave a charity performance in aid of the NSPCC. Frank was so disgusted at the food provided that he hurled sausage rolls at the portraits of past mayors lining the walls
- At a mayoral banquet, the Lord Mayor introduced his Lady Mayoress to Frank with the words 'Mr Randle, this is my wife.' The reply: 'Well, that's your fucking fault, old pal.'

At the height of his fame, Frank was earning £1,000 a week. He played three characters: a boatman, a grandfather and an elderly hiker, dressed in baggy shorts, wearing oversized boots and carrying a rucksack, a bugle and a flagon of beer. As he swigged from the flagon, the belches grew louder and longer:

> By gum, there's 36 burps to the bottle. Ah'll sup this stuff if it keeps me up all neet. The landlord of the pub where I got this said, 'Ah bet tha's nivver tasted owt like that.' I said, 'Nay, but Ah've paddled in it.'[190]

Eight of Frank's movies were made by the Mancunian Film Corporation [*Somewhere in England*[191] [1940]; *Somewhere in Camp* [1942]; *Somewhere on Leave* [1942]; *Home Sweet Home* [1945]; *Holidays with Pay* [1948]; *Somewhere in Politics*[192] [1948]; *School for Randle* [1949]; and *It's a Grand Life* [1953]. John Blakeley, who founded Mancunian, produced movies primarily aimed at northern audiences. His stable of stars included George Formby, who made two of his earliest films with Mancunian, *Boots! Boots!* [1934] and *Off the Dole* [1935]; Norman Evans: *Demobbed* [1944], *Under New Management* [1946] and *Over the Garden Wall* [1950]; and Jewel and Warriss: *What a Carry On* [1949] and *Let's Have a Murder* [1950]. All Blakeley's films were made on a shoestring. The first were shot in London. Then, in 1947, he startled everyone by opening a studio in Manchester.[193]

A board of directors ran the operating company, Film Studios Manchester, one of them, at his own request, Frank. On the face of it, this might have appeared to be unwise of Blakeley, but he appreciated that Frank was a cinema attraction and that, by becoming a director, Frank was committing himself solely to Mancunian films.

Frank, though, used his newfound status to be more difficult than usual. During the filming of *Holidays with Pay*, he made it clear that he did not like being directed and that he had his own ideas about what he should do. When Blakeley called for a short break in filming, Randle always left the set and returned only when he wanted to. It usually fell to Arthur Mertz, the son of Blakeley's screenwriting partner, to try to persuade him to go back. Mertz would go to Frank's dressing room, where he would be offered a Guinness. The two men would chat amiably and Mertz would eventually ask Frank if he was ready to return. Frank would say he was, but as soon was on the set, Blakeley announced a break for lunch, game-playing that allowed him some sort of revenge. Frank then stormed back to his dressing room, where he kept a punch ball, which he pretended was Blakeley. People passing his door would hear him saying: You bloody, Blakeley, you. You bloody so-and-so.

In *It's A Grand Life*, Frank was teamed with the 1950s sex symbol, Diana Dors. It was now the job of Blakeley's assistant, Bert Marrotta, to make sure actors were on the set when they were needed. Marrotta often had to go to Randle's hotel to get him up and ready for work. Frank took a dislike to Marrotta and eventually declared that he would resume filming only if Marrotta was sacked. So, Marrotta was sacked. But then, the technical crew threatened to strike in protest. So, Blakeley reinstated Marrotta and, to his credit, Frank shook hands with him and apologised.

On another occasion, a woman friend arrived at the studio asking to see him. A receptionist told her that Frank was on the set and, while the red light was showing, no one could go in. A few days later, the receptionist was in the studio canteen when Frank arrived in a crazed mood. Shouting and swearing, he screamed at her: I want you. One of the stagehands calmed him down, but, only a few minutes later, gunfire could be heard in Frank's dressing room. He was shouting: Where is she? I'm going to kill her. Needless to say, little of this appealed to Diana Dors:

> Randle went wild after a few days of shooting, his good behaviour having been strained to the last degree by that time – and daily there were chaotic scenes in his dressing room as he fired gun shots at the wall or at his current girlfriend's foot or got drunk and wrecked the place or refused to work at all for days on end, thus leaving the sets hanging about and incurring great expense all round.[194]

Many of those who worked with Frank said his violent outbursts coincided with a full moon. Others thought that was just an excuse: he was just plain mad.

Contrary to legend, Frank did appear in the south of England. He made his London debut with Jimmy James and Randolph Sutton[195] in 1936 in *The Show That Jack Built*; in 1950 and 1951, *Randle's Scandals* played several dates in London; and in 1952, Jack Hylton, in a fit of misjudgement, presented a revue called *Televariety* at the Adephi Theatre in London. It was made up of variety turns, including Joan Turner, sketches starring Frank and, inexplicably, games from the popular television show, *What's My Line?* Most papers poured scorn on it. In a review, *The Times*[196] referred to Frank's sketches as 'devoid of subtlety, but not of vulgarity', although Ivor Brown, writing in *The Observer*, was more conciliatory:

> Frank Randle, whom I have long admired for his lurid portraiture of toothless antiquity and rude forefathers, seemed to be off his beat at the Adelphi. He needs a warmer audience and one of the cosy homes of proletarian laughter.[197]

Televariety closed after two weeks and Frank was hurriedly booked to appear at the Metropolitan, Edgware Road, where there were House Full notices every night. But as the 1950s slipped by, his popularity was on the wane. A month after appearing on a mediocre bill at the New Theatre, Crewe, in 1957, he died of gastroenteritis. One of his 1953 company, the underrated all-round entertainer, Roy Castle, had plenty of memories, one of them surprising:

> The last time I saw him … he was carrying a Bible under his arm and trying to spread the message to anyone who would listen … It rather seemed like a naughty boy saying 'sorry' to the teacher just before he received his punishment. It reminded me of that well-known saying 'Many people, planning to repent at the eleventh hour, die at ten-thirty'.[198]

CHAPTER TWELVE

A Little Bit of Locke

Balladeers Josef Locke, Cavan O'Connor, Arthur Tracy

F rank Randle's drinking partner, the Irish tenor, Josef Locke, had a life every bit as colourful. He was a man of enormous contradictions: a one-time policeman who fled Britain to avoid the taxman and an international star who became a recluse. A powerfully built man, he sang such light quasi-operatic material as *I'll Take You Home Again, Kathleen;*[199] *Goodbye [Goodbye. I wish you all a last Goodbye];*[200] and his signature tune, *Hear My Song, Violetta,*[201] all performed with a twinkle in his eye that confirmed him as an Irish broth of a boy. Towards the end of his life, *Hear My Song* lent its name to a movie, which earned Josef a late burst of stardom and a frenetic interest in his old recordings. When an LP of part of his repertoire was issued, it reached the Top Ten, making Josef the oldest 'pop' star to enjoy such acclaim.

His real name was Joseph McLaughlin. Jack Hylton abbreviated it so that it would fit on billboards better. He was one of nine [or possibly ten] children born to the wife of a butcher and cattle dealer in Londonderry. At the age of seven, he started singing in churches in the Bogside and, as a teenager he lied about his age so that he could enlist in the Irish Guards. He served in the Middle East, rose to the rank of sergeant and took part in many troop concerts. Back home in

---

Josef Locke [Joseph McLaughlin]

- Born Londonderry 23 March 1917 [His private life was erratic. It is thought he was married four times, but his second marriage was bigamous as he had not by then divorced his first wife. There were a number of children born out of wedlock. In 1957, a former housekeeper successfully brought a paternity suit against him. He was later ordered to pay for the upkeep of three other children. Josef's last wife was Carmel].
- Josef Locke died in Clane, County Kildare, 15 October 1999

Londonderry, he joined the Royal Ulster Constabulary, sang at charity functions and became known as Ireland's Singing Policeman.

Josef first went to London in 1945 to join the Crazy Gang show, *Together Again*. The following summer, he played the first of 19 summer seasons in Blackpool. The venue was the Opera House. He made a good friend of George Formby, who was topping the bill, and they toured Australia together in 1947.

That was also the year that Josef's recording career began. He made about 100 78s for Columbia and, by the end of the decade he had sold more than 1,000,000 records. His film career began in 1948 with *Holidays with Pay* for Mancunian. That was followed by *Somewhere in Politics* [also 1948] and *What a Carry On* [1949] with Jewel and Warriss.

Although Josef exuded Irish charm in public, Jimmy Jewel saw a tougher side of him. During one summer season in Blackpool, a girlfriend of Donald Peers [see Chapter 27] asked Ben Warriss for a lift home. When she refused a similar offer from Josef, he thought nothing of socking Ben in the jaw. Ben told Jimmy about it the next day. Jimmy immediately picked up a knife and confronted Josef in his dressing room:

'I'm warning you. If you clout anyone else, I will personally cut your bloody head off.' I showed him the knife and glared at him, though actually I was terrified. I had no intention of using it and, if had decided to, he could have wiped the floor with me. But he just sat there and looked at me in the mirror. 'You know something,' he said. 'I believe you would too.'[202]

By the 1950s, Josef was able to command up to £2,000 [£40,000] a night. Conscious of his status, he flew into a rage when he was left out of a Royal Variety show in his adopted home town, Blackpool, in 1955. He sold his home and moved to America, vowing never to return. He did return, but fled when Inland Revenue demanded tax arrears from him. As policemen scoured Blackpool for him, he scarpered to the Irish Republic where he bought a farm, some racehorses and a pub he named the White Horse Inn.

In 1967, his love of the good life and his addiction to gambling led to him being declared bankrupt with debts of £20,000 [£200,000]. The following year, he was sentenced to four months' imprisonment for stealing documents from the Companies' Registration Office in Dublin, but, on appeal, he was made to pay a fine instead. During this time, he was, as they say, well known to the Irish police, but, as he grew older, he contented himself with a pint of stout and a crossword puzzle.

Then came the movie. *Hear My Song*, brilliantly directed by Peter Chelsom, centred on one of the more bizarre episodes in Josef's life. During his exile, he was impersonated on television by a so-called Mr X. It was a stunt dreamed up by Hughie Green, the unctuous compère of the talent show, *Opportunity Knocks*. Viewers were asked to guess whether he was, in fact, Josef, even though he denied it himself. His protestations, however, were not enough for Josef's female fans, who crowded around stage doors for a glimpse of him. Police officers and tax inspectors had to be convinced as well. The episode was further complicated by a man impersonating Mr X.

Josef attended the premiere in London, serenaded Diana, Princess of Wales, with *Danny Boy* and cheekily complimented her on her shapely legs. Michael Aspel then confronted him with the famous red book and he was whisked away to record *This is Your Life*.

The career of Cavan O'Connor needs some unravelling too, largely because he recorded under countless pseudonyms: Harry Carlton, Shaun Cassidy, Peter Coleman, Cliff Conelly, Con Conway, Patrick Ernest, Ray Filme, Billy Hayman, Pat Hugh, Patrick Moore, Pat O'Brian, Pat O'Brien, Pat O'Dell, Francesco Odoli, Patrick O'Moore, Terry O'Neil, Alan O'Sullivan, Earl Parry, Jack Smithson, Jack Vaughn and quite a few others.

Cavan was born in Nottingham, but he claimed Irish provenance, insisting that his parents, William and Lydia, were as Irish as they come. Wearing an open-necked shirt and a battered trilby, his sleeves rolled up and an old sports jacket carried over his shoulder, Cavan strolled onto stages up and down Britain and sang about the Lakes of Killarney and the Mountains of Mourne.

Cavan O'Connor began his working life as an apprentice to a printer. On the outbreak of the First World War, he, too, lied about his age and became a soldier at the age of 15. At one point, he served on the Western Front, but emerged unscathed. After the war, he could not get his old job back and began singing at local concerts and in working men's clubs. He was fortunate enough to win an open operatic scholarship to the Royal College of Music, where he met his wife, Rita Tate, the niece of the diva, Dame Maggie Teyte, herself the sister of the music hall songwriter, James W. Tate.

Although Cavan found work at the Old Vic and Sadler's Wells, he became better known as a dance band vocalist, singing *What Does It Matter?* with Harry Bidgood's Orchestra in 1927 and following that with *A Dear Little Irish Mother*. In all, he worked for about 15 different record labels and, over the next few years, he made hundreds of records, once cutting 40 in five days. The 1930s saw the heyday of the comic song and, before Cavan's style was firmly established, he found himself singing such favourites as *Riding on a Camel in the Desert*, *I'm Happy When I'm Hiking*, and *Once Aboard the Lugger [and the Girl is Mine]* .

In 1935, Eric Maschwitz gave Cavan a new pseudonym, the Vagabond Lover, in a radio series, in which he sang, but never spoke. Its signature tune was borrowed from the American crooner, Rudy Vallee, *I'm Just a Vagabond Lover*, but

---

Cavan O'Connor [Clarence Patrick O'Connor]

- Born Nottingham 1 July 1899
- Married Margherita Ninetta Odoli [professionally known as Rita Tate] in Kensington, London, 15 June 1929
- Three sons
- Died London 11 January 1997
- Left £503,000 [£550,000]

Cavan wanted his own song. He remembered one he had heard in Berlin, *Only a Strolling Vagabond*[203] *[So Goodnight, Pretty Maiden, Goodnight]* and began singing that. Newspapers enjoyed the gimmick of the anonymous Vagabond; millions of listeners were intrigued to know who he was; and, when Cavan's identity was finally revealed, he became one of Britain's highest paid broadcasters. Variety tours confirmed him as a headliner, as everyone wanted to know what the vagabond looked like. From 1946, his Sunday lunchtime radio series, *The Strolling Vagabond*, was heard by up to 14 million people. He was still making LPs and performing regularly in the 1970s. Even in the 1980s, he joined Old Time Music Hall bills. Cavan O'Connor died at the age of 97.

Another balladeer shared characteristics with Cavan. He too had considered calling himself the Singing Vagabond; he too used the mystery of anonymity to further his career; and, late in life, he too made records with Harry Bidgood, who became better known as Primo Scala. There, the similarities end as this singer, Arthur Tracy, was not a tenor, but a baritone, and he was not Irish, but Jewish.

Arthur Tracy [Harold Rosenberg]

Born Russia 25 June 1899
Married and divorced three times
Died New York 5 October 1997

Some accounts say Arthur was born in Eastern Europe, but quickly fled to America with his parents and eight brothers and sisters to escape the pogroms. Arthur himself said he was born in Philadelphia, but the truth is that he came from Russia.

The disputed part of his career ends there. From then on, everyone agreed that he won a singing competition and was booked to appear in touring productions of the operettas, *Blossom Time* and *The Student Prince*. His big break came in 1931 when CBS offered him a 15-minute programme to be broadcast three times a week. He decided to appear anonymously and first chose to be the Singing Vagabond, but, as with Cavan, he felt that Rudy Vallee's associations with the title were too great.

He chose instead another nom de theatre, the Street Singer, possibly because Frederick Lonsdale's play of that title was on Broadway at the time. The element of mystery was heightened by the CBS announcer assuring listeners that the Street Singer was just around the corner and would soon be singing to them. The imagination of radio audiences was gripped in the same way as Cavan's had been in Britain. CBS received thousands of letters a week, mostly from women, wanting to know who the Street Singer was. During his two-year contract, his salary increased tenfold. When he appeared at theatres, police had to control the crowds; traffic jammed the streets; and he set new box office records.

At that time, Arthur also found a signature tune, *Marta [Rambling Rose of the Wild Wood]*, after hearing it played by the composer Moises Simons at a music publisher's office. Arthur recorded it in the same year, the first of hundreds of records he was to make until the 1960s.

In 1932, he appeared in the movie *The Big Broadcast* with Bing Crosby, whom he rivalled for popularity for some years. Other films followed: *Limelight* [1936] with Anna Neagle; *The Street Singer* [1937] with Margaret Lockwood; *Command Performance* [1937] with Lilli Palmer; and *Follow Your Star* [1938]. In 1935 he topped the bill at the London Palladium, a date that was to prove a turning point in his career. He was given bookings at variety theatres all over Britain. Audiences here liked his style. Appearing at the side of the stage under a street lamp and dressed in an overcoat with a turned up collar and a broad-brimmed hat, he sang [to the accompaniment of a piano accordion] songs from a diverse repertoire, Viennese operetta, cowboy songs, love songs and others in various languages.

When he returned to America at the start of the Second World War, he was shocked to find that his popularity had waned, but, when he next came to London in 1948, he saw that he still had an army of loyal fans here. He made two LPs in Britain in the 1960s.

In 1995, when he was, by any reckoning, a very old man, he took part in a live BBC Radio show. The previous day, the BBC had announced that he was to appear and, when he arrived at Broadcasting House in London, a crowd of fans was waiting for him, taking photographs and requesting autographs.

Arthur Tracy died at the age of 98.

CHAPTER THIRTEEN

Musical Mayhem

Melodists Teddy Brown, Kay Cavendish, Dr Crock, Sid Millward, Stanelli, Three Monarchs, Albert and Les Ward

Variety boasted many instrumental groups, the most successful of which introduced comedy into their acts. Sid Millward and his Nitwits, a ten-piece band that offered zany arrangements of popular songs and well-known classical pieces, became famous around the world, particularly at the Paris Lido and the Stardust Inn, Las Vegas. Roy Hudd was a fan:

> The tabs would open to reveal an idiot conductor in an ill-fitting tail suit with mad hair and a Hitler moustache. He would introduce the members of his orchestra individually and a bunch of idiot-looking senile delinquents would take their places on the stand. From then on musical mayhem would rule, wild versions of classical lollipops were the order of the day, interspersed with lots of great visual gags.[204]

A recurrent joke involved Cyril Lagey, a black musician who appeared to be wearing a bowler hat. In fact, it was only a brim. When he raised the brim, it was clear he was bald. The band owed something to America's Spike Jones and his City Slickers. After their version of *You Always Hurt the One You Love*, complete with screams and gunshot, no one could take it seriously again.

Sid Millward, who studied woodwind at the Royal College of Music, worked in the dance bands of Jack Hylton, Jack Payne and Lew Stone. He was already an established bandleader himself when the Nitwits made their first appearance on BBC Radio's *Ignorance is Bliss* [1946–53] and became very big names indeed. Pathe News called them

Sid Millward and his Nitwits.

'breezy broadcasting bandsters'[205] and a news clipping filed at the University of Nevada referred to them as 'ten wonderful, nonsensical, motley musical entertainers'.[206]

Engagements in Las Vegas were highly lucrative. The Stardust, although now a model of corporate probity, was then bankrolled by the Mafia. So strong were the Nitwits' links with Las Vegas that three of them set up home there. Sid was asked once about the qualities he sought in a new band member:

> That he is a first class musician. I wouldn't expect him to be a comedian ... After he had been with the band a short time, he would soon find his level of fun. Most people can be nitwits.[207]

Sid was found dead in a hotel room in Puerto Rico in 1972. His widow, Bonita,[208] who had heard tales of his philandering, refused to pay for his body to be repatriated and he was buried in a pauper's grave.

When the Nitwits broke up, a smaller group, Nuts and Bolts, took their place and proved equally popular. Cyril Lagey[209] joined Nuts and Bolts, as did Tony Traversi, whose rendition of *Post Horn Gallop* earned him standing ovations in Las Vegas. He joined the Nitwits as a pianist, but was soon playing his own invention, the exhaustophone, made from a car exhaust, as well as the watering can and the saw. Nuts and Bolts toured working men's clubs, played at European casinos and undertook a voyage on the *QE2* to the Far East. Toni Traversi[210] was married for 35 years, but saw his wife only rarely.

When the Nitwits left *Ignorance is Bliss* in 1947, their place was taken by a new fouteen-piece band, Dr Crock and his Crackpots. Dr Crock was Harry Hines, a clarinet and sax player, who had worked with Ambrose and Maurice Winnick. The Crackpots sounded like a cross between a small symphony orchestra and a Dixieland jazz band. They had two spots in *Ignorance is Bliss*, usually mangling well-known classical themes by playing them rather too fast and introducing the odd cowbell and hooter.

Ignorance is Bliss, which ran until 1953, was based on an American show, *It Pays to be Ignorant*. By 1947, Winnick had abandoned it in favour of working as an impresario, specialising in buying the rights of American series and adapting them for British tastes. When he invited Hines to succeed Sid Millward, he chose the name, Dr Crock. Hines was not keen as he had enjoyed almost 20 years as a leading musician under his own name. But, as *Ignorance is Bliss* was a

Morton Fraser's Harmonica Gang.

prime-time show, he capitulated. Not long after, paradoxically, he took Winnick to court as he felt he had built up a reputation as Dr Crock whereas Winnick believed he held the copyright to the name. Hines won the case.

Another madcap musician was Sid Plummer, who appeared in Pete Collins' show, *Would You Believe It?* He had built a xylophone with bellows that were worked by a foot pedal. The bellows blew up a balloon, which, on bursting, let loose a shower of confetti.

Morton Fraser[211] had a solo harmonica act before forming his Harmonica Gang just after the Second World War. The band performed all over the world and repeatedly played the London Palladium. It was closely based on an American outfit, Borrah Minevitch's Harmonica Rascals. The Rascals' main clown was the tiny Johnny Puelo, who scrambled around the edges of the band, trying to find a gap he could squeeze into and play. His British counterpart was Tiny Ross.[212]

The harmonica was a favourite instrument with instrumentalists in the variety theatre. The Three Monarchs had 600 of them, one of them only an inch long, another measuring five feet that all three played at the same time. The original members, Jimmy Prescott,[213] Les Henry[214] and Eric Yorke,[215] teamed up in 1945. At first, they were a serious instrumental act, but in 1950, when they went to entertain troops in Germany and Austria, Henry developed a character called Cedric with a tiny black beard and a squeaky voice. The comic element made them international stars, who toured in more than 30 countries.

When the act broke up in 1981, Henry, who now called himself Cedric Monarch, went solo, his act combining brilliant harmonica playing, visual comedy and one-liners [he had a data base of 17,000 jokes]:

> Via landlady jokes ['It's £15 a week and I don't want any children.' 'You're in luck. I've got a bad back'] and Tommy Cooperish magic, he eventually issued a threat to perform a striptease. 'I'm not a pretty sight. The last time I did it, there were two old ladies in the audience and one of them had a stroke. The other couldn't quite reach.'[216]

In 2005, Cedric Monarch was given a Lifetime Achievement Award by the British Music Hall Society and would have been better received had he not made racist jokes.

Teddy Brown could play practically every instrument in the orchestra, but he specialised in the xylophone as he felt it failed to win the attention it deserved. His xylophone had six octaves, two more than usual, and it was instructive to watch him move nimbly from one end of the instrument to the other, his agility made all the more remarkable in that,

The great Teddy Brown.

Kay Cavendish on the Keys.

at five feet [150 cms], he weighed 24 stone [336 lbs]. But Teddy Brown was no freak. A New Yorker, born Abraham Himmelbrand, he was an excellent musician. His girth, though, led to his early death in 1946 at the age of 45 while appearing in Lew and Leslie Grade's road show *Road to Laughter* at the Hippodrome, Wolverhampton.

A first-rate sportswoman, Kay Cavendish was educated at the Royal Academy of Music, but enjoyed lighter music too. Kay was recruited as an announcer, first for the BBC Television Service and, when that closed at the start of the Second World War, for Forces programmes on radio. During one broadcast, she was asked by an engineer struggling with a defective tape recorder to play or sing while he tested the machine. Kay gave an impromptu show of songs and piano solos. The next morning, she was offered her own series, *Kay on the Keys*, which ran for more than 400 editions.

Albert and Les Ward were a welcome addition to any variety bill. They were either musical comics or comical musicians. Whichever they were, they posed no threat to any of the dedicated instrumentalists or comedians they worked with. Unusually, they lived in the same house in Cardiff all their lives. It was their parents' home and, after they had died, Albert lived upstairs with a nurse he had married: Les lived downstairs on his own.

Long before skiffle[217] had been invented, Albert and Les played guitars, washboards, bicycle pumps, anything that could accompany their Country and Western songs. 'I was the mechanic,' said Les 'and Albert was the brains.'[218] They were often on the radio and, in the late 1950s, they supported American stars at the London Palladium. After Albert died, Les was regularly invited to show business luncheons, but he always refused, saying he was not in the same league as those who would be there. He considered himself a figure from the past. Nobody realised how depressed he was about life without his brother. He hanged himself.

Stanelli found fame with his 'hornchestra', a large steel frame on which were fitted all manner of motor horns, each emitting a different note. Stanelli had a classical education, having studied the violin at the Royal Academy of Music and the Royal College of Music. For a time, he was one half of a double act, Stanelli and Edgar, two violinists who played and danced. He devised Stanelli's Stag Party, which the BBC insisted should be known as *Stanelli's Bachelor Party*, more sexually dubious than the original. The Hornchestra can be seen at its best in the *Radio Parade of 1935*.

By naming his invention the Hornchestra, Stanelli must have been aware of another meaning of 'horn'; an erection. It was well known throughout the variety world that Stanelli was extraordinarily well-endowed: 'a legend among landladies from Scunthorpe to Cockermouth,' as Bob Monkhouse has recalled. 'Every time old Stan gets pissed, out it comes,' chuckled Ted [Ray]. 'Like a child's arm holding an apple.'[219] As a youngster, Bob was at a charity night as the guest of the bandleader, Sidney Lipton. Also appearing was Ted 'Kid' Lewis, who, in matters penile, was similarly blessed. Before the end of the evening, bets were placed on which man had the bigger cock. Everyone interested in the outcome crowded into an ante-room, but not Bob, who was told he was too young to attend.

CHAPTER FOURTEEN

Hutch – Too Much

Talented and Troubled: Leslie Hutchinson

L eslie Hutchinson, universally known as Hutch, was sensational: a handsome West Indian who accompanied himself at the piano. He sang in a rich baritone voice; had an unerring ear for songs of quality, favouring the sophisticated work of Cole Porter, Richard Rodgers and Lorenz Hart and the Gershwins,[220] and his jazz-based piano style was both intricate and inventive. Hutch worked in cabaret and variety. At some theatres, police had to control the crowds that gathered to see him and, during his act, women screamed, wept or fainted.

In his private life, he was a relentless social climber who affected the airs and graces of the aristocracy whose company he craved. His sexual life was both diverse and exhausting. Massively endowed, he had a lengthy affair with Lady [Edwina] Mountbatten, who ordered Cartier to make a jewel-encrusted cast of his penis. In addition, he enjoyed relationships with Cole Porter and Ivor Novello, the composer of the musicals *Glamorous Night*, *The Dancing Years* and *King's Rhapsody*. Although married, he treated his wife appallingly, seeing her only when it suited him. He fathered at least six illegitimate children by different women.

Hutch's father, who was born in Barbados, settled in Grenada where he imported cloth and sold stylish hats. His mother was a wealthy Scottish woman. At the age of eight, Hutch started taking piano lessons. Aged 12, he won a scholarship to the Grenada Boys' Secondary School. Hutch's father wanted him to study medicine and, when Hutch was sisxteen, he was sent to a college in Nashville. After nine months, he dropped out and made his way to New York. His father was so angry that he stopped his allowance. In turn, the withdrawal of support so angered Hutch that he neither saw, nor spoke to, his father again.

In later years, he displayed a similar disregard for his mother. When he was rich

Ivor Novello, one of Hutch's lovers.

Leslie Hutchinson [Leslie Arthur Julien Hutchinson]

- Born Grenada 7 March 1900
- Married Ella Byrd in United States 1923/24 [Died London 1 April 1958]
- One daughter, Lesley Bagley Yvonne, born 9 April 1926 [Illegitimate children: Gordon, born Liverpool August 1926; Gabrielle, born 1930; Gerald, born 1948; Christopher, born 1948; Graham, born 1953; Emma, born 1965]
- Died London 18 August 1969
- Left £1,949 [£20,000]

and famous, his mother, by then widowed, contracted an eye infection, which made her blind. She sent frequent letters to Hutch asking for help. Although he expressed concern for her, he had no intention of going to Grenada to see her or bringing her to London, where she might cramp his social life. She also died without being reunited with him.

In New York, Hutch faced racial bigotry on all sides. Penniless, cold and unknown, he felt most at ease in Harlem and was resourceful enough to exploit his musical talent. Through studying piano rolls made by the likes of Scott Joplin and Jelly Roll Morton, he learned the rudiments of jazz. He found work playing in clubs, including the Bamville, which was frequented by the society heiress, Edwina Ashley, who was later to marry Louis Mountbatten. He started making friends, among them a black singer and dancer, known as Bricktop, and Layton and Johnstone, who sang duets to his accompaniment.

After six years in New York, he was ready for London, but first he went to France and then to Spain, where he gave piano lessons to the children of Queen Ena, the wife of King Alfonso XIII and a cousin of Mountbatten. Back in France, he again met Bricktop and began playing for dancing lessons she was giving. Their pupils included the Prince of Wales [the future Edward VIII], the Aga Khan and the doyenne of gossip columnists, Elsa Maxwell. Bricktop, who had recently met Cole Porter, opened a nightclub, the Music Box. Cole and Hutch were there every night, guaranteeing that the place was always packed.

Cole, who had a penchant for black men, began his affair with Hutch in 1925. He was then 34 and had still to write his immortal shows, *Anything Goes, Kiss Me, Kate* and *Can-Can*. Even so he had a lot to teach Hutch, who was nine years his junior: how to dress, how to enjoy good food and wine, and how to behave in society. Seated at two pianos, they worked for hours on Cole's songs. Cole showed Hutch exactly how he wanted his work performed. In time, Hutch was to record three of Cole's hits and frequently included them in his act: *Let's Do It* [1928], *Night and Day* [1932] and *Begin the Beguine* [1935].

When Hutch arrived in London in 1926, Edwina Mountbatten threw a party

Lady Mountbatten, another of Hutch's lovers.

for him. One of the guests, C.B. Cochran, heard him play and asked him to join the orchestra for his show, *One Dam Thing after Another*, starring his latest protégée, Jessie Matthews, the saucy Douglas Byng [see Chapter 20] and a young Max Wall [see Chapter 25]. During the interval, Hutch played alone under a single spotlight. On the opening night at the London Pavilion, the Mountbattens took a box and showered him with sweets.

In spite of the recognition Hutch enjoyed in London society, he suffered the same prejudice as in New York. He had to play in the pit because it would have been deemed improper for a black man to appear on stage with a white woman; when he was asked to entertain at sumptuous parties in large homes, he was expected to arrive and leave via the servants' entrance; hotels sometimes refused to allow him to stay; and, when he appeared at the Chatham Empire, he was booed. The manager appealed to the audience to give him a fair hearing and he quickly won them over.

In 1928, Hutch took part in another Cochran show, *This Year of Grace*, written by Noel Coward and again starring Jessie Matthews and Dougie Byng. But once more he was confined to the pit.

Hutch finally broke through in 1929. His records were selling well, he had another Cochran show, *Wake Up and Dream*, and he consolidated his role as a star of the cabaret circuit. He also began working in variety. Not only was he on stage now, but he topped the bill.[221] Seated at a grand piano with his trademark large white handkerchief,[222] which he used to mop his brow, he presented his 18-minute act at the London Palladium, the Coliseum, the Victoria Palace and his favourite theatre, the Holborn Empire. Hutch changed his style for his variety appearances. He dropped all his Coward and Porter songs and even sang differently:

[He] abandoned his crisp and careful delivery in favour of a maudlin tremolo and other oppressively theatrical touches. Hutch was fully aware of what he was doing. His variety audiences applauded these effusions; and Hutch was simply giving them what they wanted. However, by demeaning his talents in this way, he coarsened himself as an artist and, eventually … the purity of his music was irretrievably lost and he gradually became a parody of himself.[223]

In 1932, *The People* published an article suggesting that a woman who was 'highly connected and immensely rich' had been associating with 'a coloured man' and had been advised to leave London for a time 'to let the affair blow over'. No one was named, but the Mountbattens sued for libel and won. *The People* published an apology and awarded Edwina damages which she gave to charity. As a result, Lord Beaverbrook forbade mention of Hutch in his newspapers, Buckingham Palace made it clear that he was not to appear in any Royal Variety Show, and the BBC gave him less work.

Later, Edwina admitted privately that she had lied in court and, amazing though it may seem, she accompanied Hutch on his variety tours whenever she could. One night at Quaglino's, a drunken Louis Mountbatten complained, 'That nigger, Hutch, has a prick like a tree trunk and he's fucking my wife right now.'

By the middle of the 1930s, Hutch was earning £500 [£17,500] a week in variety. He was at the peak of his career in 1935, but, by the late 1930s, he was putting on weight. In

Cole Porter, yet another of Hutch's lovers.

1937, he booked himself into a Swiss sanatorium to try to combat the effects of heavy drinking. It did not work and, in a memo later that year, a BBC official noted that 'this artist is … unable to perform without alcoholic stimulant'.

By the end of the Second World War, Hutch's drinking was out of control. HMV Records dropped him and he was no longer at the top of the bill. There were further visits to clinics, but he was now well past his best. Towards the end of his life, his sexual predilections turned sordid. He hung around Paddington trying to pick up young girls and boys.

Hutch died in 1969 and was buried in Highgate cemetery. His poor wife had died 11 years previously. Her body lies in an unmarked grave in Hampstead cemetery.

CHAPTER FIFTEEN

The Day War Broke Out

Every Night Something Awful

On the outbreak of the Second World War, government departments moved quickly. Conscription was introduced immediately; children were evacuated from cities to rural areas; and all theatres, cinemas and dance halls were closed, a decision viewed by Shaw as a master-stroke of unimaginative stupidity:

> During the last war, we had 80,000 soldiers on leave to amuse every night. There were not enough theatres for them and theatre rents rose to fabulous figures. Are there to be no theatres for them this time? We have hundreds of thousands of evacuated children to be kept out of mischief and traffic dangers. Are there to be no pictures for them? The authorities, now all-powerful, should at once set to work to provide new theatres and picture-houses where these are lacking. All actors, variety artists, musicians and entertainers of all sorts should be exempted from every form of service except their own important professional one. What agent of Chancellor Hitler is it who has suggested that we should all cower in darkness and terror?[224]

In the event, the government was seen to have moved too quickly.[225] This was the start of the 'phoney war' that was to last for a year, but, in readiness for protracted hostilities, plans were made to keep troops amused both at home and overseas. Basil Dean, who had been made an MBE for his services to national entertainment during the First World War, was put in charge and given the Theatre Royal, Drury Lane, as his headquarters. He was not an ideal choice. Although he had directed movies starring Gracie Fields, he regarded the variety theatre as inferior to the so-called legitimate stage. To George Black and Oswald Stoll, he was no more than a dilettante. He headed ENSA, the Entertainments National Service Association, but comically referred to as 'Every Night Something Awful'.

The war turned nasty in September 1940, the start of the Blitz,[226] which continued until May 1941. London was bombed night after night. Forty-three thousand people were killed and more than a million homes were damaged. In March 1941, a direct hit on the Café de Paris, dubbed London's safest restaurant, claimed more than 30 lives, including that of Ken 'Snake Hips' Johnson, the leader of the resident West Indian Dance Orchestra. A few weeks later, the crooner, Al Bowlly, was killed when a Luftwaffe parachute mine exploded outside his flat in Jermyn Street. Areas central to the war effort, Merseyside, Tyneside, Belfast, Glasgow, Hull, Bristol, Plymouth, Birmingham and the industrial Midlands were also targeted.

By the start of the Blitz, some theatres had reopened. Performances began in the afternoon and very early evening so that both audiences and entertainers could get home before the bombing started. The rule was that, once a raid began, everyone remained where they were until the 'all clear' was given. On the worst nights, some theatres kept their patrons entertained until four in the morning. Hutch changed his act and sang *Land of Hope and Glory* and *There'll Always Be an England*. His fans sang along with him and loudly applauded his patriotism.

Jewel and Warriss were playing the East End of London during the Blitz:

> For over a month, we barely slept and never had a bath. The sirens would go when we were in the theatre and we simply carried on the act till four or five in the morning, dredging up all the old material and improvising: anything to keep the audiences' minds away from the bombing. Once the 'all clear' sounded, we would get back to our digs in Chelsea – a terrible place. We slept at daybreak.[227]

To keep the entertainment going, casts dashed from one theatre to another to help out; Tommy Trinder set a record by appearing at 27 theatres in one night; and if members of the audience wanted to go on stage and perform their party piece, they were more than welcome. The revue artiste, Hermione Gingold, found some theatregoers well prepared:

> It got to the point when most of the audience arrived with their accompanists, longing for an air raid so they could get up on stage and do their stuff. I'll never forget a particularly bad raid one night. We might have been seconds from death, but we stood in the wings trying to suppress our laughter as an enthusiastic lady, who was old enough to know better, sang *Lo! Hear the Gentle Lark* with bomb obbligato.[228]

Some variety stars also went down into the London Underground to entertain people who believed it was the safest place to spend the night. At first, London transport officials barred everyone except bona fide travellers,[229] but, when thousands of civilians invaded the Tube on 7 September 1940, they had to give in. At the height of

Tommy Trinder at a showbiz auction.

the Blitz, 177,000 people crowded into London Underground stations every night. Hutch sang unaccompanied. It was easier for George Formby, who had only his ukulele [or would it have been his banjulele?] to carry. He sang to 3,000 people accommodated on a short branch line on the Aldwych section of the Piccadilly line. The rails had been removed, the walls of the tunnel cleaned, bunks installed and lavatory facilities improved. Alterations there served as a model for adapting a further 79 stations.[230]

At the height of the Blitz, all London's theatres were closed, except the Windmill. The bombing closed some of them for good. On 7 September 1940, the Holborn Empire, where Max Miller and Vera Lynn had just opened in *Apple Sauce*, was reduced to a pile of rubble and on 26 September 1940 the stage and back stage areas of one of the most important provincial music halls, the Argyle in Birkenhead, were almost completely destroyed, although the façade remained intact.

Other variety theatres that were bombed, some so badly that they never reopened, included the Gaiety, Bexhill; the Birmingham Empire; the Bow Palace; the Crouch End Hippodrome; the Devonport Empire and Hippodrome and the Alhambra, Devonport; the Phoenix, Dover; the Tivoli, Grimsby; Gatti's-in-the-Road in Lambeth; the Poplar Hippodrome; the Rotunda, Liverpool; the Sheffield Empire; the Southampton Hippodrome and the Palace, Southampton; the Stratford Empire and the Willesden Hippodrome.

Just before midnight on 15 October 1940, a 500-pound bomb fell through the roof, gallery, upper circle and grand circle of the Theatre Royal, ENSA's headquarters, and exploded at the back of the stalls. The safety curtain took the full force of the blast, preventing the stage from being damaged. But half an hour later, several incendiary bombs destroyed most of the orchestra stalls. In the morning, the theatre was a sorry sight with broken chandeliers and woodwork and thick plaster dust everywhere.

ENSA's work, however, proceeded without interruption. By the end of 1940, 7,000,000 troops had seen 40,000 shows. But the criticism of Dean continued. His detractors accused him of spreading the talent at his disposal too thinly and, although some good shows were staged, there were terrible ones too:

Audiences saw a lot of rubbish, only one removed from barrack room horseplay, but they also watched people who were destined to become stars and performances by some of the greatest artists of the century. Cultural barriers came tumbling down as opera, ballet, classical music and drama were discovered to be as enjoyable as variety or a band show.[231]

There was some cavilling between stars over who was doing most. In North Africa in 1943, George Formby gave a controversial interview to *Union Jack*, a Forces paper published in Algiers:

Most of the stars are where we left them – in the West End. Some of them give concerts to the troops provided such concerts are not in some dreadfully remote camp where there is a shortage of red carpet and cocktails. Some of them appear at an occasional Sunday concert in London. At least one of them, a healthy young man of military age has had his calling-up deferred provided he gives a certain number of shows to the troops. He gives the shows, but sees to it that they are all in or near London and the suburbs.[232]

The following week, Bud Flanagan responded:

To the people not in show business it is difficult to understand why all the stars are not in the Middle East or in Italy. But when you have a contract to fulfil, you have to carry it out … And if you are lucky enough to have a hit – well, you stay in the show as long as the public want you. It is nice to think there is still a laugh in the West End for the boys and girls of the Services and the war workers to come to when they get a little relaxation.[233]

Come the end of the war, ENSA reckoned that it had employed more than 4,000 actors and entertainers and had played to more than 500 million people. But the general assessment was that, although there was quantity, the quality had fallen short. The actor, Nigel Patrick, felt that ENSA was an easy target:

It was terribly easy to say that the shows stank and were no good … Some … were appalling, but the vast majority were in the 'all right, not too bad at all' bracket. The remainder were absolutely first class whether they had stars or not.[234]

During the early days of ENSA, the novelist, Richard Llewellyn, was Basil Dean's right-hand man: 'Without Basil Dean, it would never have been. He was a martinet, a son-of-a-bitch bastard, a monolith, a kindly – sometimes – tyrant, a bully, but he knew what he wanted and others didn't.'[235]

Many of those who entertained the troops sought a career in show business once the war was over. Others who had just begun in showbiz in 1939 perfected their skills during the war. A large number of them, particularly such comedians as Sir Harry Secombe, Sir Norman Wisdom, Benny Hill, Peter Sellers, Tony Hancock, Tommy Cooper and Terry-Thomas, went on to be stars of light entertainment until almost the end of the century.

On 8 November 1945, a bronze tablet, presented by the Variety Clubs of America, was unveiled on an outside of wall of the London Hippodrome. It read:

To the everlasting honour of those British and American performers who, during the darkest days of the London Blitz – when steadfastness and sheer courage counted as weapons of war – remembered the slogan of their profession … 'Tonight and every night, the show must go on.'

When the Hippodrome became a cabaret theatre-cum-restaurant, the 'Talk of the Town', the tablet disappeared. It has not been seen since.

CHAPTER SIXTEEN

Bare-Faced Chic

Windmill Nudes, Fan Dancer Phyllis Dixey, Boys in Drag

The Windmill Theatre managed to stay open during the worst atrocities of the war as a result of an amazing display of loyalty by cast and staff alike. The Windmill had become one of the most famous theatres in the world. Since 1932, it had staged non-stop revue, the special attraction being the dimly lit appearance of naked, curvaceous girls. The Lord Chamberlain,[236] who controlled censorship in the theatre between 1737 and 1968, surprisingly allowed the innovation, providing the girls did not move.

At the start of the Battle of Britain, many of those involved in the shows, called Revudeville, moved into the theatre. They worked by day and slept on mattresses on the floor at night. Their allegiance was largely the result of the way the Windmill's owner, Laura Henderson, a surgeon's daughter, and her general manager, Vivian Van Damm, looked after them. The girls, all chosen for their beauty, youth and personality, were paid more than Equity's minimum rate of pay; they were taught how to sing and dance; they were groomed by the best West End hairdressers and beauty salons; the Windmill's non-stop canteen sold them meals cheaper than in nearby cafes; and the theatre had its own doctor and dentist, as well an accountant who sorted out their tax problems. In the summer, a canvas swimming pool was installed on the roof and, if it was cloudy, sunray lamps could be used in the rehearsal room.

To set up home in the theatre in the thick of the war seemed natural. Van Damm himself slept in a small dressing room, but annoyed everyone by snoring loudly. His daughter, Sheila, who was the Windmill's press officer and a close

---

Laura Forster

- Born Southwark, South London, 6 December 1863
- Married Robert Stewart Henderson in central London 26 April 1884 [He died 8 August 1916, aged 65, leaving £82,914 {£4.25 million}]
- Son [killed in the First World War]
- Laura Henderson died London 29 November 1944
- Left £246,191 [£5.5 million]

friend of the newspaper and magazine columnist, Nancy Spain, and her lover, Joan Werner Laurie, usually slept with the showgirls.

They were all enormously brave. During a raid in October 1940, one girl, Valerie Tandy, waited for a lull in the bombing before dashing across the road to a café to get a sandwich. After a brief chat with a girl behind the counter, she raced back. Before she reached the stage door, she was blasted into the theatre. The café had taken a direct hit and everyone inside was killed.

On another occasion, a dancer, Joan Jay, slipped out to buy a coffee. A few minutes later, her dancing partner, Nugent Marshall, heard a bomb explode. He rushed out and pulled Joan from a heap of smoking rubble. After she had been taken to a casualty centre, he went back to the Windmill, re-applied his make-up and returned to the show.

After the worst raids, Mrs Henderson arrived early the next morning to see that everyone was all right. That was natural to her. She had always made a point of going from dressing room to dressing room to make sure the girls were happy. By all accounts, she was an extraordinary woman. Standing just 4'11" [150 cms], she had prodigious energy and lived in some style, employing a butler, a footman, a cook, a chauffeur and a lady's maid. As a girl, she had never been allowed to go to the theatre. After she married a wealthy jute merchant, he took her to see a West End show. When the curtain rose on a woman in tights, she burst into tears.

When her husband died, she inherited a small fortune and bought the Windmill, then a small cinema, to give herself something to do. She spent £15,000 [£500,000] converting it into a modern theatre that sat just 312 people. Plays were staged, but they were not a success and the Windmill reverted to movies. When Mrs Henderson met Van Damm, he had just been offered £80 [£1,500] a week to manage the then small chain of Granada cinemas. In contrast, Mrs Henderson offered him £8 a week to be the Windmill's general manager. Something about the Windmill intrigued him and, to the consternation of Granada's owner, Sidney [later Lord] Bernstein, he chose the Windmill.

Vivian Van Damm [Vivian Talbot Vandamm {sic}]

- Born Willesden, London, 28 June1889
- Married Natalie Lyons [a niece of the caterer Joe Lyons] in Hampstead, London, 30 June 1914
- Daughters including Sheila [Born Paddington, London, 17 January 1922. Died Paddington, London, 23 August 1987]
- Vivian Van Damm died London 14 December 1960

Van Damm continued showing films, but then met a French producer, Lucien Samett, who had made a big success staging non-stop variety in France. Van Damm thought it would work in London. So did Mrs Henderson, who agreed to put up £10,000, the first of a number of payouts she made to bail the theatre out. Sheila estimated that between 1932 and 1940, she lost about £60,000 [£2 million] at the Windmill.

The first Revudeville opened in February 1932. Samett booked 42 performers for this edition and 118 for the next three. Five shows ran back-to-back from lunchtime until late in the evening with no act lasting more than seven minutes. The girls, whose average age was 19, worked in two troupes, each appearing every other day.

Van Damm was against Revudeville having a star, but Mrs Henderson was not so sure. As the first night approached, a lugubrious-looking salesman with downcast eyes and a drooping mouth went to see Van Damm to try to persuade him to place advertisements in a financial newspaper. He spoke with great pomposity for about 20 minutes. When he finished, Van Damm declined his offer, but said that, if he could be as funny on stage as he was in an office, he would book him. This was John Tilley,[237] who, without any previous theatrical experience, was given a solo spot at the Windmill playing a salesman trying to sell a tobacco pouch to a foreigner and getting hopelessly confused. It was the start of a career that took him to Broadcasting House and the London Palladium. Described by one reviewer as a seedy-looking individual with a public school accent and a public house face, he specialised in delivering burlesque lectures on all manner of subjects: scouting, the League of Nations, tuning a piano, the gold standard and so on. A promising career was cut short when he died in 1935 at the age of 36.

At the first performance of Revudeville, Mrs Henderson sat in her private box, her black lace gown covered by a coat of Chinese brocade and diamonds blazing on her corsage. The newspapers panned the show, but it was good enough for other theatres to copy the format. By Mrs Henderson's reckoning, non-stop variety was filling eight theatres in the West End within six months of its inception at the Windmill: '[Our show] set the non-stop ball rolling. We had given the public something new and the public liked it.'[238]

Naturally, the competition from other theatres posed new problems for the Windmill. So, later in 1932, Van Damm introduced tableaux vivants, living statues, featuring girls in the nude. At first, his girls did not like the idea. Doris Barry became their spokeswoman:

When we first heard, we all decided no way were we going to do that. But in his very ... persuasive way, [Van Damm] said "Now, look. You have all been to the National Gallery and seen those beautiful paintings. It's going to be like that.""[239]

In his autobiography, Van Damm intriguingly made only one reference to the tableaux, omitting to mention that the girls were naked. It took the Sapphic Sheila to give a straightforward explanation of Revudeville's sensational popularity:

The idea of a wholesome young girl – English at that – posing naked for everyone to see sent a thrill of excitement or stunning shock ... through the nervous system of the nation. The whole thing smacked of Continental wickedness at its worst and most delicious.[240]

After the war, the Windmill played a major part in the re-birth of variety. That was because Van Damm wanted stand-up comics to fill the gaps between the musical scenes. Many would-be entertainers returned to civilian life in Britain after the war looking for a way of breaking into show business. They were faced with an impossible situation. They all wanted agents, who asked where their acts could be seen. Inevitably, they said they could not secure work unless they had an agent.

Some star comedians got their earliest work at the Windmill. Peter Sellers, whose act was based on his talent for mimicry, so impressed Van Damm that he was hired to start work immediately. Harry Secombe had an act in which he impersonated how different men shaved. Tony Hancock was then one half of a double act, Hank and Scott. They did an imitation of a scruffy end-of-season seaside concert party. Morecambe and Wise were hired, but were sacked before the end of their first week.

Van Damm passed other talent by. After telling the first joke of his audition, Benny Hill heard Van Damm's familiar cry of 'Next, please' from the darkened auditorium; Norman Wisdom told one joke, fell over and, before he could get up, was told 'Thank you. That will be all'; and Kenneth Tynan was dismissed with 'You're much too queer for our audience.'

Van Damm conceived a ploy to keep the Lord Chamberlain happy. The night before a new show opened, a special performance was staged. The theatre was packed out with friends and families of the cast and the staff. The Lord Chamberlain was the guest of honour and unsurprisingly never delegated the duty. Van Damm kept him liberally supplied with alcohol. The girls were decked out in yards of tulle and flimsy lace and the Lord Chamberlain smilingly gave the show his complete approval. It would be six weeks before he went to the Windmill again and the tulle and lace were packed away until then.

Men were strictly forbidden from using binoculars or opera glasses to get a better look at the nudes. One inventive regular constructed an ultra-short pair of binoculars that made him look as though he was wearing thick glasses. They suited his purpose in the auditorium, but, as he could not see properly when he left, he fell down a flight of stairs and broke a leg. His glasses were confiscated and an ambulance was called.

The men usually read newspapers when a comic was on, but often masturbated under raincoats on their laps once the nudes appeared. It was not uncommon for a girl to leave the stage at the end of an act and tell the stage manager 'Row three, seat six, elderly grey-haired gent. He's at it. Dirty old man.'[241] A commissionaire was then sent into the audience to eject the miscreant.

One of the comics, Arthur English, who used to specialise in playing a spiv, made a joke about it:

> Do you know, I don't think people come in here to see me. For instance, there's two blokes who come in here regularly. Whenever I come on, they get out a packet of cards and start playing. The other day, only one of them came in. He didn't have anyone to play with. So, he sat there and played with himself.[242]

Van Damm carpeted English and the joke was removed.

When anyone left the front row, those sitting further back leapt over the seats to try to get a better view, a practice known to everyone at the Windmill as the Steeplechase. The seats became damaged so frequently that an assistant stage manager regularly had to bolt them back together. One stagehand was offered an extra 30 shillings [£40] a week to speak a line in a sketch. The line was 'Is that your car outside, sir?' – the first words professionally uttered by Kenneth More, who was later to play the war hero, Douglas Bader, in *Reach for the Sky*.

Some comics, among them, Eric Morecambe, found the sight of beautiful naked girls standing in the wings highly disconcerting:

> One said 'Damn it, Eric, give me a cigarette. I need a drag before the curtain goes up. Otherwise, I'll get an uncontrollable urge to scratch my bum in the middle of the scene.' I couldn't hold the lighter steady. 'Oh, you silly Billy,' she said with a flutter of big violet eyes. 'After you've been here six weeks, you won't turn a hair.' 'It will have all fallen out,' I predicted.[243]

From time to time, Mrs Henderson presented herself at the box office in disguise. She was trying to find out whether anything untoward was taking place at the Windmill without her knowing. This was either her idea of fun or a sign of paranoia. Once she arrived as a Chinese woman. On another occasion, she was an elderly businessman. Another time, she was a bearded German. Van Damm was fooled on each occasion.

His method of keeping the Lord Chamberlain at bay began to fail during the Second World War. There were a number of written exchanges:

> In Scene Three, the reclining nude sang two verses of a song. In doing so, the strict rule regarding static nudity was necessarily infringed. The deep breathing necessitated movement of the body and this the Lord Chamberlain will not allow. Cannot you arrange for the verses to be sung 'off'? The two girls with the large balloons were also insufficiently covered about the breasts.[244]

Van Damm replied the following day:

> In the matter of the singing ... this I am having done off stage. Regarding the breast covering of the two girls, I have taken this up with the Wardrobe Master and it appears that, during this exceptionally hot weather, the elastic holding the tops ... is inclined to become slack after a day or two.[245]

When Laura Henderson died in 1944, she bequeathed the theatre to Van Damm. When he died in 1960, Sheila took over, but the Windmill lasted for only another four years. Striptease clubs had established themselves in London in the 1950s and the raincoat brigade decided they liked them better.

Before the last performance, Sir Norman Gwatkin, at one time the Comptroller to the Lord Chamberlain, wrote to Sheila:

> 'I am so sorry and I know you will all be quite miserable about it. What will the London Morality Council do for their spare evenings? I shudder to think.'[246]

The Council and other self-appointed moral guardians also scrutinised the variety theatre's best-known stripper, Phyllis Dixey. She was not variety's first and she was not really a stripper, at least, not in today's parlance. Her speciality was the fan dance, in which she undressed behind an enormous fan made of ostrich feathers. As she danced, she carefully manoeuvred herself, always promising a glimpse of nudity. For that, her followers had to wait until the very end of her act. She was naked for a split second before the stage was blacked out.

For a woman whose career was based on the erotic, Phyllis was a curious mixture. Privately, most people found her shy and reserved; she frequently read the Bible; and yet, when angered, she could be ferocious. On one occasion, screaming hysterically, she hauled one of her husband's mistresses off a stage. Perhaps most curious of all, physical intimacy with her husband did not begin until he asked her to cut his toenails. As there was not a pair of clippers close by, she bit his toenails short.

Phyllis's father, Ernest, a ship's steward, disapproved of her interest in the stage, but she was encouraged by her mother, Selina, who worked as a cashier

---

Phyllis Dixey [Phyllis Selina Dixey]

- Born Raynes Park, south-west London 10 February 1914
- Married John James Tracey [born Irish Republic 8 April 1897] [professionally known as Jack or Snuffy Tracey] at Raynes Park 8 December 1938 [Died Kingston-upon-Thames 11 October 1978. On his death, his surname was given as Tracy. Throughout his life, the two surnames were interchangeable]
- Phyllis Dixey died in Surrey 2 June 1964

at the Karsino pleasuredrome, run by the showman, Fred Karno, on Tagg's island near Hampton Court. It was here that Phyllis first performed in public, dancing a hornpipe. At the age of eight, she won a children's talent contest singing *Ain't She Sweet?* She had dancing lessons, became a chorus girl and, at the age of 15, joined a show produced by the impresario, Wallace Parnell,[247] and became his mistress. Many told her that he had a string of girlfriends, known as the Wallace Collection, but she paid no attention until she was shown a photograph of his wife, a soubrette known as Queenie May, who closely resembled Phyllis.

She left Parnell and became Ernie Lotinga's leading lady in plays and revues for three years. Then, she met Jack Tracey,[248] a diminutive comedian and trombonist, and they formed a double act, billed as the Sap and the Swell Dame. In 1938, they married, but life was hard. They earned little money until Jack persuaded Phyllis to strip. Jack wrote a monologue for her, which she performed for the first time at the Hull Tivoli in November 1938. That night, the theatre was poorly attended:

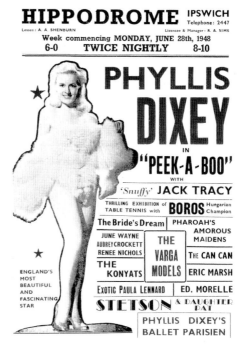

> As the act progressed, the house was completely hushed. That hush is still what I work for, a silence of mingled shock and expectancy that is rarely followed by applause simply because the impact is too mixed … There were no snags. To my running commentary, the dress slid off smoothly. So did the petticoats. I fumbled a bit with the brassiere, holding my fan grimly as I smiled tauntingly at the audience, now thoroughly startled. After that – my panties, hastily altered so that they could unwrap from around me. Then, the crucial moment, the swirl of the fan – and blackout.[249]

For the rest of the week, the Tivoli was packed. A short time later, Phyllis and Jack were in Cardiff. Members of the local Watch Committee had read about the new act. Someone pointed out that, as Phyllis was performing a sketch, it should be approved by the Lord Chamberlain. A call was put through to London, but the Lord Chamberlain was not there and his two principal aides were serving in the armed forces. A relatively minor official, the appropriately named George Titman, not knowing what to do, sent a telegram to Cardiff asking the theatre manager to cancel the act. Jack saw the potential for publicity. Phyllis's bill matter immediately became The Girl the Lord Chamberlain Banned. This was the breakthrough she and Jack had been waiting for.

Within two years, they were at the Whitehall Theatre in London in a string of shows built round Phyllis's act: *Piccadilly to Dixie*; *All's Fair*; *Step Out with Phyllis*; and *Good Night, Ladies*. In May 1944, Phyllis took over the theatre herself and staged *Peek-a-Boo!* followed by *Peek-a-Boo Again!* Each part of every show had to be approved by the Lord Chamberlain, but his representatives showed they clearly liked her: 'She is a mixture of charming simplicity and subtle audacity. Possession of these qualities enables her to transform vulgarity into artistry.'[250]

The rules were hard to follow. The London County Council, the forerunner of the Greater London Council, was tougher than the Lord Chamberlain and local Watch Committees differed in what they would allow Phyllis to do. She was successfully prosecuted only once. Magistrates in Skegness fined her for indecency.

In 1942, she was invited to appear on BBC radio's *Shipmates Ashore*. The producer, Howard Thomas, thought men at sea would be tantalised, but his only show with Phyllis earned him a rebuke from his bosses:

She was demure and had a small, meek voice, which gave her a whispering
     style over the stage microphone:
'I'm not like lovely Frances Day[251]
Who can sing and dance and play.
I have the boys in my dressing room
And give them tea and crumpet.'

The script and recording [were] duly passed by the two censors [for security and taste]. But I did not get away with it … I had a telephone call from the Controller in person, who asked me if he had heard aright. 'Crumpet? You know what that means.' 'Of course,' I answered. 'Something you have for tea.' … Some weeks later, I received one of those memos which goes into the offender's dossier … I was to consider myself censured for an error of taste in broadcasting the word "crumpet." Then followed a second paragraph … 'If, however, the word had been used in the plural, there would have been no objection.'[252]

As with the Windmill, the strip clubs of the 1950s marked the end of Phyllis's career. She became a cook at a guesthouse and Jack found work as a steward at a golf club. As Phyllis looked back at her career, she regretted the day she decided to strip:

Always and ever, I've been a reluctant stripper … I am convinced that it is a lowering of womanhood. I only wish girls who plan to go on the stage will remember the lessons I have learnt. The first lesson is never to do anything that betrays your sex; the price you pay is too high.[253]

At one point, Paul Raymond, who opened his Revuebar in Soho in 1958, thought he might make Phyllis the centrepiece of a show, but he abandoned the idea, finding her difficult to get on with:

She stayed awfully correct and didn't give as much to the boys as they could get elsewhere. Everyone had to call her 'Miss Dixey' and she had to have her own way. I couldn't get her to change her act.[254]

However, Raymond did produce a roadshow starring Christabel Leighton-Porter, who at one point posed a threat to Phyllis's career. She was the real-life personification of Jane, a *Daily Mirror* cartoon. Jane's Journal or the Diary of a Bright Young Thing, the creation of a freelance cartoonist, Norman Pett, first appeared in the *Mirror* in 1932. Jane, a leggy blonde, wore very few clothes and often managed to lose those. Her risqué adventures made her the most daring of the Forces' sweethearts during the Second World War.

Christabel Drewry

- Born Eastleigh, Hampshire, 11 April 1913
- Married Arthur Leighton-Porter 1934
- One daughter, Jane [died after 14 hours]
- One son, Simon, born 1957
- Christabel Leighton-Porter died Horsham, West Sussex, 6 December 2000

When Raymond made Jane come to life, he paid Christabel a salary that astonished his rivals. They all predicted financial disaster, but Raymond proved them wrong. When he opened his Revuebar, he was able to ignore the ban on the movement of nudes because clubs fell outside the Lord Chamberlain's jurisdiction.

The international doyenne of strippers, Gypsy Rose Lee, came to Britain more than once. In 1951, she topped the bill at the London Palladium, but failed to impress the critics:

From her honky-tonkily exotic name and somewhat bizarre profession, we naturally expected a sultry, sexy, hip-swinging hoyden of the diamonds-are-a-girl's-best-friend school … But … Gypsy Rose turned out to be a self-possessed, charming and witty matron who would grace any drawing-room and, when she got down to bare essentials, the effect was as shattering as if the hostess at some sedate cocktail party had slipped out of her dress while passing the olives.[255]

While the girls were taking their clothes off, the boys were putting them on. Men in drag were popular from the First World War onwards. The all-male

Reg Stone.

concert party, *Rouges et Noirs*, was formed in the early days of the Great War. Female entertainers were not allowed to work on the front line. So a show was put together in which soldiers took women's roles. It was the work of Captain Eliot Makeham of the Sportsmen's Battalion. Before the war, he had spent a year in *Pelissier's Revue*[256] at London's Alhambra. *Rouges et Noirs* launched the careers of many well-known female impersonators, including Reg Stone,[257] who had appeared in the Irving Berlin revue, *Watch Your Step*.

After the war, the troupe reformed itself as *Splinters*. The show was staged in London and every major provincial centre for nearly 20 years. The Palace Pier Theatre in Brighton played host to *Splinters* in May 1919:

> They throw the average professional pierrot troupe hopelessly into the shade … Every soldier is an artist. These elegant damsels, outward embodiments of feminine grace and vivacity indisputable, are clever.[258]

When *Splinters* reached London's Savoy Theatre in August 1919, the *Daily Express* suggested that Stone could write a textbook of hints to actresses.[259] Over the years, many young men who were to make their mark in drag joined *Splinters*.[260] Jimmy Slater[261] joined in 1920 and toured with the show for ten years. After his wife died in 1975, he retired and ran a business hiring out fancy dress. His collection included gowns once owned by Florrie Forde and Sophie Tucker. He died at the age of 100.

Another member of *Splinters* was Chris Sheen,[262] who in 1936 formed a double act with Vic Ford. For most of the year, they were glamorous ladies, but, during the pantomime season, they turned themselves into a grotesque pair of Ugly Sisters. They appeared in the all-male shows of the late 1940s and 1950s, including *Soldiers in Skirts* and *Misleading Ladies*, in which a young female impersonator, Daniel Carroll, was given his first speaking role. Carroll, who later changed his name to Danny La Rue, became Britain's most celebrated female impersonator. His greatest achievement was to turn drag shows from entertainment aimed at gay men to good, clean fun for the whole family.

Like Vivian Van Damm and Phyllis Dixey, the drag revues of the 1940s and 1950s had to be approved by the Lord Chamberlain. One of his officials went to see *We're No Ladies*, even though the show had already been licensed. He was disturbed to find that the audience was familiar with what he called the phraseology of the perverted. He recommended the closure of the show as it was likely to become [in his words] a focal point for pederasts.

CHAPTER SEVENTEEN

From The Heart of My Bottom

They Know Not What They Say:
Milton Hayes, Oliver Wakefield

We English love nonsense: the verse of Edward Lear, the infelicities of Mrs Malaprop, the speeches of George Bush and John Prescott – and that love dates back many years. Victorian music hall devotees thronged to the Oxford to see one James Unsworth, known as the Stump Orator with his catchphrase 'Am I right or any other man?' With a rickety table, a pewter tankard and an old umbrella for props, he lectured his audience: 'My dear friends, if I may call you so without the risk of danger, allow me to remark that we are here today and gone yesterday. But where are we now?' At this point, he banged his umbrella on the stage. 'Am I right or any other man? Talking of Man reminds me that all you men except myself are made wrong and I will prove it with the proofiest proof.'[263] Another bang of the umbrella.

Soon, all music hall fans – on making a statement of fact – were adding 'Am I right or any other man?' Unsworth, a devout Catholic, became so famous that in 1868 he set off for America on a tour that lasted six years. But, by the time he died in Liverpool in 1875, at the age of 40, he was virtually forgotten.

It was some years before the public took to another Stump Orator ['stump oratory' being an outmoded description of making speeches during a tour of towns and cities, the sort of activity politicians used to undertake during election campaigns]. While serving in the First World War, Milton Hayes listened to an inane young officer trying to explain how to read maps. The officer made such a hash of it that Hayes, who had already begun a career on the halls, seized on the comic potential, invented a character called Monty and issued, in all, 12 78 rpm records entitled *The Ramblings of Monty*. The first was called *The General Outlook*:

> What we have to do is to make a bold … to get right down to rock bottom and bring everything into work all the … every sort of … make it into a common pool and then we can make … because, if we don't, the whole thing … that's what will happen.[264]

Hayes' first steps in music hall earned him a review from a *Sunday Chronicle* columnist called Bayard, the pen name of W. Buchanan-Taylor, who later came an agent. Buchanan-Taylor described Hayes' Monty as a 'diverting study of a stylish modern youth trying to philosophise, but never reaching the end of the thought or the sentence.'[265]

Milton Hayes [James Milton Hayes]

- Born Manchester 13 August 1884
- Married Germaine van Hoecks in central London 10 May 1925 [dissolved]
- Milton Hayes died Antibes, France, 15 December 1940

Shortly after the First World War, Buchanan-Taylor fixed Hayes a place on the bill of the Palace, Blackpool. Within two years, Hayes was a star, earning between £100 and £120 a week [£20,000 and £24,000]. He never worked in variety for more than six months a year for fear that he might grow stale: 'What I do then … is to throw the whole thing up … I generally go abroad and devote myself to something [other] than my stage work.'[266] Then, suddenly, one of those breaks became permanent. Hayes moved to the south of France, running away from success, as Buchanan-Taylor put it:

He had strong views about the iniquity of income tax and he chose Nice [as his home] as much for its remoteness from the Inland Revenue authorities as for its climate. Anyhow, he stayed on with his French wife and joined a coterie of litterateurs of a rather gingerbread[267] quality.[268]

Hayes had earlier had another side to his career: writing and performing dramatic monologues, the best known of which is *The Green Eye of the Little Yellow God*. Many people still remember at least its first line: 'There's a one-eyed yellow idol to the north of Katmandu …' Hayes wrote it in about five hours in 1911. The character actor, Bransby Williams,[269] who specialised in readings from Dickens, maintained he was the first to declaim it. He said Hayes went to see him when he was appearing at the Palace, Manchester. Hayes showed him the monologue, but Williams felt it was too long and suggested ways to make it more powerful. Hayes accommodated the suggestions and returned to the theatre with the improved manuscript the following night. Williams decided it should form part of his repertoire and, from then on, he was expected to recite *The Green Eye of the Little Yellow God* wherever he went.

Then, Hayes became resentful at Williams' success and Williams took umbrage:

I was both hurt and surprised when informed by the BBC that I must not use the poem on the air … Not a very grateful return! [Hayes] even said that he had made me popular, forgetting that the name of Charles Dickens had done that some years before.[270]

The piece was ripe for lampoonery, most notably by Billy Bennett. His version began: 'There's a cock-eyed yellow poodle to the north of Waterloo …' Hayes tried to take legal action against Bennett, alleging breach of copyright, but the matter was settled out of court.

Oliver Wakefield

- Born Natal, South Africa, 29 May 1909
- Married [1] Mary Alice Collins
- Married [2] Barbara ----
- Two sons, Christopher and David; one daughter, Susan
- Oliver Wakefield died Rye, New York State, 30 June 1956

The nonsense monologue was next taken up by Oliver Wakefield, who arrived in Britain from his native South Africa in 1936. A startlingly handsome man with perfect diction, he appeared before American audiences as Lord Oliver Wakefield – and they believed him: 'For some considerable time, millions of people thought I was a peer of the realm and I was afforded many privileges of a lord – droit de savoir faire and all that.'[271]

Wakefield was billed as the Voice of Inexperience:

There are many, many ways of spending Christmas, but I think the best way is to spend it is on or about the twenty-fifth of Septober, Octember ... no wonder we make such a fuss about it. After all, Christmas is just one of those days and, when you come out of the daze about four o'clock in the afternoon having stuffed yourself with everything that ... I think the all-important question arises at that time of how to abuse ... amuse the kiddies.[272]

In print, the work of both Hayes and Wakefield looks nothing. The cleverness lay in the performance. At first, the BBC loved Wakefield. He was frequently on the radio, but, before long, he contravened the Beeb's strict rules on vulgarity.

In a 1941 edition of *Music Hall*, he had the line: I thought mine were big until I saw Clark Gable's. The producer suggested he added the word 'ears'. Wakefield agreed, but then paused after 'Gable's' before continuing with 'ears, I mean', earning him a bigger laugh than he might have got otherwise. The BBC knew how to deal with such transgression. Wakefield was banned from broadcasting for six months.

CHAPTER EIGHTEEN

Nothing Up My Sleeve

How Did They Do That? Sawing a Woman in Half and Doves Everywhere

As long as people want to be entertained, there will always be an interest in magic. We are enthralled by tricks that baffle us, but, with new technology making movies and computer games more and more spectacular, younger audiences are demanding ever more startling illusions. Magicians have one thing in their favour. An ingenious act can be staged in silence. It is an art that has no language barrier.

Ghoulish though it may be, the best-known trick [or illusion, as magicians prefer it to be called] is Sawing a Woman in Half. But who invented it? It could be Selbit, an English magician who was born Percy Tibbles. Aware that his real name would make him sound more like a kitten than a man of mystery, he [more or less] reversed it. Or could it be a Polish Jew, Horace Goldin, who began his career in America and went on to pioneer quick-fire presentation? He routinely performed 45 tricks in 17 minutes, leaving audiences no time to ask how one trick was done before the next begins.

Selbit, a tall, slender, fair-haired man, first built a box for Sawing a Woman in Half at his London apartment in 1920. By the end of the year, he had rehearsed it well enough to try it out in front of Nevil Maskelyne, of the Maskelyne dynasty of magicians, and several managers of Moss Empire theatres at St George's Hall opposite Broadcasting House. Maskelyne was not impressed, but the men from Moss Empires thought it good enough to arrange its first performance at the Finsbury Park Empire in North London on 17 January 1921.

P.T. Selbit [Percy Thomas Tibbles]

- Born Hampstead, London, 17 November 1881
- Married Edith Mabel Short in Paddington, London, 17 August 1901
- Son born in Nottingham
- P.T. Selbit died Sonning, Berkshire, 19 November 1938

The hapless woman assistant first had five ropes tied around her neck, wrists and ankles. The ropes were threaded through holes in the sides of the box and the woman got into it. A few members of the audience were told to hold the ends of the ropes tightly so that they could tell whether she changed her

position once fastened inside. The lid was closed; padlocks secured it; and the box was laid lengthwise on a wooden support two feet above the stage. Selbit then pushed three panes of glass and two steel blades through the box and began dramatically sawing it in two. When he had finished, the glass and steel

were removed, the padlocks were opened, the lid was lifted and the woman walked out smiling – and intact.

The trick caused a sensation. In New York, Goldin read reports of it and told reporters that he had first thought of the idea in 1909. He had offered to stage it in 1917, 1919 and 1920, but no one was interested. Quickly, he arranged to present his version of the trick at the annual banquet of the Society of American Magicians in New York on 3 June 1921.

Horace Goldin [Hyman Elias Goldstein]

- Born Vilna, Poland [now Vilnius, Lithuania] 17 December 1873
- Married Helen Leighton ----
- Horace Goldin died north London 22 August 1939
- Left £587 [£175,000]

In America at least, Goldin was in the lead. By the time Selbit arrived in New York, several of Goldin's companies were already on tour. In each city Selbit was due to play, Goldin or one of his staff appeared a week beforehand and sawed a woman in half. The craze did not last long. Theatregoers had lost interest in it by the autumn of 1922, although George V and Queen Mary asked to see it at the Royal Variety Show at the end of that year.

Goldin had become famous in Britain 20 years before the furore that surrounded the trick. Eleven days before the outbreak of the Second World War, he was playing the Wood Green Empire in north London, where one of the most famous practitioners of magic, Chung Ling Soo, was shot dead on stage. After the first night, Goldin returned to his apartment, went to bed and died in his sleep. Selbit's career had ended the previous year. He became a chronic alcoholic and drank himself to death.

Cardini was a one-off. He made playing cards and other objects appear and disappear and no one seemed more surprised than him when it happened. A model of sophistication, he was billed as The Suave Deceiver. His parents separated before he was five and his mother opened theatrical digs. Here, he watched in awe as magicians who stayed there rehearsed their tricks. At the age of nine, he ran away from home and found work first in a butcher's shop and then as a pageboy at a hotel. He became a good billiards player, made friends of card sharps who used to hang around billiards halls and learned some of their tricks.

Richard saw service in the First World War. Soldiers were allowed to carry packs of cards with them but, in the trenches, it was so cold that he was unable to practise manipulating them without wearing gloves. From then on, he could not work without gloves, but that meant he could never produce just one card from a pack. They always came out in bunches or small fans. Today, that is common practice among magicians, but Richard pioneered the technique.

After the war, Richard decided to make magic his profession. He worked under several pseudonyms until a booker suggested he adopted a name like Houdini. The obvious choice was Cardini. On a tour of Australia, he frequently appeared at a theatre for many weeks at a stretch and he felt the need to change his act every week. So, during the first week, he worked with cards and billiards balls, for example; during the second, with cigarettes and silk scarves; the third, rabbits and flags; and so on.

In 1925, Cardini arrived in America and proved so successful that the following year he appeared at the Palace, New York. During this period, he became a seasoned professional. A top hat, a cane and a monocle became his trademarks and he found an excellent gimmick: to appear very slightly drunk.

Cardini [Richard Valentine Pitchford]

- Born Swansea 24 November 1895
- Married Swan Sunshine Walker at Portland, Maine, 23 April 1927 [She was born 20 February 1903 and died 27 November 1993]
- Son, Richard, born 18 August 1927
- Daughter, Carole, 13 July 1939
- Cardini died New York, 11 November 1973

To the tune of *Three O'Clock in the Morning*, he arrived on stage looking like a reveller on his way home after a night on the town. A pageboy takes a newspaper off him and he is surprised to see a fan of cards appear in its place. He throws the cards into the newspaper only to find another fan appear, then another and then more. Finally free of the cards, he hands his hat and cape to the boy only to find ping-pong balls appear in his hands. As he bounces them offstage, more and more materialise. To relax from this, Cardini decides to place a cigarette in a holder held between his teeth, but the cigarette keeps disappearing before he is able to light it. He eventually succeeds, but then, dozens of lit cigarettes appear from everywhere. Finally, the cigarettes give way to a lighted cigar, which, in turn, is replaced by a lit pipe. Smoking the pipe, Cardini totters off stage.

George Black saw Cardini in New York and immediately booked him for the Palladium.

The most outstanding illusion performed by Maurice Fogel was the bullet catch, in which he appeared to catch in his mouth a bullet fired directly at him. It was this trick that killed Chung Ling Soo, at the Wood Green Empire in 1918. Unsurprisingly, the bullet catch was rarely performed for many years after that incident, but Maurice was determined to perfect it after learning that Houdini was fearful of including it in his act. He succeeded in making the illusion his own.

Maurice had an impoverished childhood. His parents emigrated from Poland to Britain in 1910. They settled in the east end of London, where Maurice's father, Nathan, found a job in a small factory making women's clothes. At their lodgings, they slept on the floor. Maurice made friends, but was too embarrassed to play with him as he wore baggy second-hand clothes. Instead, he went to public libraries and found books about magic, which captivated

Maurice Fogel

- Born East London 7 July 1911
- Married
- Daughter, Nadine [married Christopher Woodward]
- Maurice Fogel died 30 October 1981

him. He learned some card tricks and, at the end of each school term, he was asked to stage an act.

Nathan wanted Maurice to follow him in the rag trade, but knew of his passion for magic and so introduced him to a Jewish magician, Albert Marchinski, whose stage name was Rameses, the Eastern mystic. Maurice worked for Marchinski at the Kursaal amusement park in Southend and learned all he needed to know about showmanship.

When he started out on his own, he worked for a while as Moish Fogel and his Performing Fleas, but then presented an act, in which he impersonated other magicians, such as Cardini doing a few card tricks, Jasper Maskelyne making a glass disappear into a paper bag and Horace Goldin changing a chair into a suitcase.

Maurice Fogel is remembered for many stunning illusions. He presented the Headline Hunter, in which he read out a line of print that someone in the audience had chosen from a small cutting culled from several different newspapers. One of his most sensational exploits was his presentation of Russian roulette in which he had to determine whether a bullet about to be fired was live ammunition or a blank.

Fogel was a quick thinker. At one show in the Midlands, the local Mayoress went to the cloakroom in the interval, removed a ring while she washed her hands and forgot to put it back on again when she left. By the time she realised her mistake and returned to the cloakroom, the ring had gone. She reported the theft to the theatre manager, who asked Fogel to make some sort of announcement at the start of the second half.

When Fogel told the audience what had happened, he announced that he knew the identity of the thief. He also said a collection for charity would be made. A cloth bag would be passed up and down each row. When it reached the thief, he was to put the ring in the bag instead of a coin. If the ring was not in the bag by the time the collection was over, the police would be called and the identity of the thief revealed. Needless to say, when the bag was emptied, there was the ring. Of course, Fogel had absolutely no idea who the thief was.

Sometimes embarrassingly billed as the Most Beautiful Man in the World, Channing Pollock was a commanding figure on stage. Tall, handsome and immaculately dressed, he smiled only briefly at the end of his act. His charisma, he explained, was based on fear.

Channing Pollock's speciality was doves, producing them from nowhere and, just as inexplicably, making a large cage full of birds vanish. Indeed, he invented the trick in which doves disappear and reappear, a routine that has been widely copied since.

Channing Pollock [Channing West Pollock]

- Born Cement, near Sacramento, California [a small town that disappeared after the Depression of 1929] 16 August 1926
- Married [1] Naomi ------ [dissolved]
- Son, Russell
- Married [2] Josie Boulton [dissolved]
- Married [3] Corinne Shoong 1967 [died 2000]
- Died Las Vegas 18 March 2006

The son of a manager with the Portland Cement Company, he became interested in magic while serving with the American Navy at the end of the Second World War. He studied forestry at the University of Sacramento, but left to take a course at the engagingly named Chavez College of Manual Dexterity and Prestidigitation. From there, he emerged with an act, which involved billiard balls, coins and cigarettes. He got his big break when the agent, Mark Liddy, one of the most influential men in American show business, agreed to represent him. Liddy secured bookings for him at New York's top night clubs and won him an appearance on the immensely popular *Ed Sullivan Show* on American television in 1954.

The beautiful Channing Pollock.

Lew Grade, who was in America, immediately booked him for two weeks at the London Palladium and a further two at the Savoy Hotel.

By 1958, Pollock was one of the highest paid magicians in America and Europe. Then, at the peak of his career, he abandoned magic to become a movie actor and gave his entire act to his chauffeur as a present. A further career followed. As a gentleman farmer, he created one of the first organic farms in northern California, supplying vegetables to the most exclusive restaurants of San Francisco.

Pollock evidently believed that theatrical skills were at the root of a magician's talents. He once said that, if he had had a son who wanted to take up magic, he would have sent him to a drama school for four years before he taught him his first trick.

Robert Harbin was a great inventor of illusions. He did not have an act as such, because he changed his tricks from night to night. Harbin, who was born in South Africa, was attracted to magic as a child when a conjuring show was put on at his school. He scoured the *Boys' Own Paper* for adverts for London stores that sold tricks and, while still in his teens, he was able to see Clive Maskelyne, another member of the Maskelyne dynasty, during an appearance in Durban. Harbin managed to speak to Maskelyne after the show and confided in him that he wanted to be a magician too. Maskelyne did all he could to deter him, but Harbin, then still known as Ned Williams, the name he was born with, set off for London.

Robert Harbin [Edward Richard Charles Williams]

- Born Johannesburg 12 February 1909
- Married Edith Lilian Philp [professionally known as Dorothy Hall] 22 March 1932
- Died 12 January 1978

By then, Harbin had cobbled an act together and found some work at music halls and in concert parties before he was booked for a trial week in *Maskelyne's Mysteries* at St George's Hall. At the end of the week, he was booked again and eventually gave 3,000 performances there. It was at St George's that he adopted his stage name: Harbin was his mother's maiden name and Robert was part of the name of his idol, Jean Robert-Houdin, the Nineteenth Century magician known as the Father of Modern Magic.

After the Second World War, Harbin toured with Jasper Maskelyne's show, *Hey Presto*. Not every magician was able to find work after the war, but Harbin was in a class of his own:

Just consider how his fertile mind worked. He would produce some silk scarves from a tiny box ... Walking right down to the footlights, he would produce from the cluster of scarves hanging from his hand bouquets of flowers. Superb – but Harbin was not finished; suddenly he would whip away the scarves and reveal not one, but a whole stack of goldfish bowls, all filled with water and all with live goldfish swimming in them.[273]

Harbin next appeared as Merlin in the stage musical, *Wizard of Oz*, proving Channing Pollock's point that a magician must first be an actor. The role gave him a new billing: A Wizard If Ever There Was.

In the 1960s, he perfected his best-known illusion, The Zig Zag Girl, in which a woman was sawn not into two parts, but three. It was quickly pirated by an American magician; copyright on magic is as complicated as copyright law. Harbin was so upset that he decided to divulge the secrets behind Zig-Zag and many of his other presentations in a book, *The Magic of Robert Harbin*. He allowed only 500 copies to be printed, he supervised its publication and he sold every book himself to make sure they were bought only by other magicians. Afterwards, in a discreet ceremony at the Magic Circle's headquarters, the plates used for illustrations were broken up to ensure there would not be a reprint.

More evidence that the BBC was making stars for theatres to employ emerged with the arrival in Britain in 1949 of the mind-readers, Sydney Piddington, and his wife, Lesley Pope, a former actress, from their native Australia. They had already appeared in 57 of their own shows in Australia, but the BBC at first showed no interest in them. They were eventually commissioned to make eight radio shows. Their following grew so rapidly that, by the third show, no fewer than 22 million listeners were tuning in; national newspapers featured their activities on their front pages; and the couple had to deal with between 400 and 500 letters from fans each week.

Sydney Piddington

- Born Australia, 14 May 1918
- Married [1] Lesley Hazlitt [professionally known as Lesley Pope] July 1946 [dissolved 1954]
- Son, Mark, born London
- Married [2] Robyn Craig 1972
- Son Edwin Sydney [initials, ESP]
- Died 1991

Piddington had been interested in magic as a child. He became skilled in tricks involving playing cards and the manipulation of cigarettes. During the Second World War, he was captured and interned at the notorious Japanese prisoner of war camp in Changi, where he met the writer, Russell Braddon. Between them, they devised a routine apparently based on telepathy and extrasensory perception. Barely five years later, Braddon was writing the scripts for their BBC radio programmes. All three realised the need to be bold and outlandish with both the stunts they performed and the settings in which they were enacted.

Once, Lesley, incarcerated in the Tower of London, correctly 'guessed' a phrase written on a blackboard in a BBC studio. During the broadcast, a tug on the Thames sounded its horn and some listeners believed that it must have conveyed some sort of secret signal. It had done no such thing. In fact, no one ever managed to catch them out, although Braddon and their BBC producer knew how they did it.

The Piddingtons toured Britain's variety theatres and, while appearing in Swansea one night, Val Parnell, who had driven from London to see them, booked them to appear at the top of the bill at the London Palladium. Sydney Piddington made no claims about how his stunts worked. He always closed his act with the words: 'Telepathy or not telepathy? You are the judge.'

Another mentalist, as they are known in the business, was Chan Canasta. The son of a Russian émigré, Canasta studied philosophy in his native Poland and then psychology in Jerusalem. After the Second World War, he became a British subject and taught himself a few card tricks to amuse friends. Soon, he concentrated his efforts on improving his memory. Continual exercise gave him the power of immediate recall, enabling him, for example, to give the number of vowels on a randomly chosen page or forecast the sequence of playing cards in a shuffled deck.

Chan Canasta [Chananel Mifelew]

- Born Krakow, Poland, 9 January 1920
- Twice married
- Died London 22 April 1999

In 1951, he appeared on the first of about 350 television programmes in Britain. In one, he said he would use his power of thought to switch off every television set tuned to him. Across the country, screens went blank. Forty seconds later, he reappeared, describing the stunt as a practical joke. A camera focussed on one of the studio's screens had been switched off, then on again. The studio audience applauded, but angry viewers rang the BBC to complain that he had ruined their sets.

David Berglas [David Gert-Heinz Berglas]

- Born Germany 30 July 1926
- Married [1] ---- [dissolved]
- Married [2] Ruth Shiell at Hampstead, North London, 5 October 1956
- Three children, Peter, Marvin, Irena

A stunt David Berglas devised earned him enormous publicity in the popular magazine, *Picture Post*. He was required to find a woman's Chinese slipper, which had been hidden somewhere in London. Wearing a blindfold, he was driven around the streets of London until he reached Battersea Park. He walked, still wearing the blindfold, to a lake in the park, boarded a small boat and found the slipper on an island in the middle of the lake. Similar psychological stunts dreamed up by Berglas for the BBC brought him enough fan mail to allow him a billing from then on as Radio's Man of Magic.

From radio, he moved to television. Appearing on the *Charlie Chester Show* in 1953, he discarded the magician's usual robes in favour of a short-sleeved shirt. Once again, he won himself publicity: here was a magician who worked without sleeves and pockets. Soon, he had his own show, *Meet David Berglas*, in which he appeared to predict the news. At various points in the show, he wrote down the time on a board and made a prediction. For instance, at 9.03pm Berglas might say there had been a car crash in Watford. A member of a panel would then phone a news agency only to be told there was no such report at 9.03pm, but at 9.04pm, it was indeed reported that there had been a collision in Watford.

For once, the magic can be revealed. An assistant of Berglas positioned himself at a London hotel, which took a direct tickertape feed from news agencies. If something interesting happened, the assistant phoned another member of the Berglas team in the studio. By means of a microphone linked to a tiny earpiece Berglas wore, he heard what had happened, picked up his board and made his 'prediction'. As long as the studio clock was kept two minutes fast, Berglas was always ahead.

Another secret can be revealed too. It involves an appearance Maurice Fogel made at the Wood Green Empire in 1951. In great detail, he was apparently able to describe which items members of the audience were holding up while he had his back turned on them. Also on the bill was a little-known Peter Sellers, who was then working as an impressionist. During Fogel's act, Sellers stood in the wings with a pair of binoculars and imitated Fogel's voice with deadly accuracy.

CHAPTER NINETEEN

Use of Cruet: Threepence

On the Road: Some Fearsome Landladies

Cissie Williams of Moss Empires may have been a tartar, but she was brilliant at her job and her judgment was respected throughout the profession. By night, she went from theatre to theatre in search of new talent. By day, she pieced together each weekly programme for every Moss Empires theatre, with the exception of the Palladium: the eternal jigsaw of engagements, as one writer put it. Working with the aid of a complicated card index system, she had to make sure an act did not appear too frequently at any one theatre or at any Moss theatre up to 20 miles away. *The Stage* kept her informed about which acts were appearing at 'opposition' theatres.

In all this planning, she had to consider the rigid form of a variety bill. There were some variations, but, more often than not, it ran along these lines: the opening turn was usually a dance act, two girls tap-dancing, for example. Their act always finished with a very fast display of dancing. They were followed by a ventriloquist or a comedian, who was referred to as a 'second-spot comic'. He worked in front of a backdrop that often carried advertisements for local businesses and had to move about so that no advert was obscured. He was usually allowed seven or eight minutes. There would then be a speciality act [a 'spesh'], a team of acrobats, a juggler, an animal act, a couple on roller skates or a cycling act, for example. They were on for about ten minutes. Another comedian, allowed about 12 minutes, followed and the last turn before the interval was a 'feature act', a pair of adagio dancers perhaps.

After the interval, the first dance act appeared again as stragglers made their way back from the bar. Then, there was another second spot comic, followed by another 'spesh',

A young Frankie Howerd.

such as a paper-tearer. He [or she] was given about five minutes. The next turn depended on who was top of the bill. It might be another comic, possibly a second appearance by the man who had appeared in the fourth spot in the first half, but not if a comedian was the star turn. If that were so, the penultimate act was a straight musical act. Finally, there was the top of the bill, often given 20 minutes, although later in the variety era, the act might fill the whole of the second half.

If this were not complicated enough, Cissie Williams had to balance the programme of an individual theatre with the itinerary of a Moss star on a tour round Britain. Touring was tough. For a start, entertainers on tour rarely saw their homes. There were twice nightly shows from Monday to Saturday and the whole of Sunday was taken up by travelling on to the next place. When planning a tour, thought had obviously to be given to the distance between two theatres in consecutive weeks.

The tour that a 26-year-old Frankie Howerd undertook in 1948 was typical. By then, Frankie had established himself on BBC Radio's *Variety Bandbox*, first as an act, then sharing the role of compère with Derek Roy.[274] *Variety Bandbox* earned Frankie £26 5s [£600] a week.

For the first ten weeks of 1948, he was starring as Simple Simon in the pantomime, *Jack and the Beanstalk,* at the Lyceum Theatre in Sheffield. Then, the tour began:

March 22	Swansea Empire
March 29	Wolverhampton Hippodrome
April 5	Sheffield Empire
April 12	Leeds Empire
April 19	Alhambra, Bradford
April 26	Sunderland Empire
May 3	Edinburgh Empire
May 10	Glasgow Empire

Frankie had played the Glasgow Empire before and knew what to expect:

> By the arrival of the dreaded second house on the climactic Friday night, the customised screwtaps, the sharpened metal tops from bottles of beer, were being hurled at the stage with all of their customary velocity and venom. The conductor, hairless and blameless, was hit on the head and was carried, bleeding profusely, from the orchestra pit, but Howerd survived more or less unscathed.[275]

During 1948, Frankie hired a scriptwriter for the first time: Eric Sykes, who was a year younger. His first contribution cost Frankie £5 [£125], which paid Eric's rent for two weeks. Instead of writing jokes, Eric cast Frankie in ludicrous flights of fancy, such as working as a messenger boy charged with transporting two elephants to Crewe. Back to the tour:

May 17 and 24	Newcastle Empire
May 31	Birmingham Hippodrome
June 7 and 14	Brighton Hippodrome
June 21	Finsbury Park Empire
June 28	Palace, Leicester
July 5 and 12	Nottingham Empire
July 19	Liverpool Empire
July 26	Grand, Derby
August 2	Leeds Empire
August 9	Manchester Hippodrome
August 16	Shepherds Bush Empire
August 23	Birmingham Hippodrome
August 30	Alhambra, Bradford
September 6	Sunderland Empire
September 13	Chatham Hippodrome [350 miles away]
September 20	New, Cardiff [280 miles away]
September 27	Liverpool Empire
October 4	Golders Green Hippodrome
October 11	Wood Green Empire
October 18	Chiswick Empire
October 25	Theatre Royal, Portsmouth
November 1	Derby Hippodrome
November 8	Coventry Hippodrome
November 15	Palace, Leicester
November 22	Lewisham Hippodrome
November 29 and December 2	Hackney Empire

The following week, Frankie started rehearsals for *Jack and the Beanstalk* at Wimbledon. So, not one day off in 1948. Added to which, Frankie had to be in London every other Sunday for *Variety Bandbox*. But it was work. And Frankie described the year as 'super'.

Stars who toured stayed in plush hotels, but most entertainers relied on landladies who specialised in accommodating theatre people. They were a breed unto themselves. The best, who served a roast dinner after the second house, were much sought after. The worst, almost resentful at doing the job, left printed instructions around the house, such as 'Good dogs wipe their paws' in the hall.

The stories about theatrical landladies are legendary. Out of revenge against an inhospitable landlady, a kipper was often tacked under the kitchen table at the end of a stay in the hope that the woman would fail to find the source of the worsening smell for weeks. Another tradition involved the book in which visitors could record their comment. If the words, 'Quoth the Raven', were there, it was a sign that the lodgings were bad. The words are a quotation from Edgar Allen Poe's poem, *The Raven*, the slightly fuller version being 'Quoth the Raven, "never more".'

There was another coded message. If any complimentary comments were followed by the words 'And I shall certainly tell my friends', that meant that the true message was the very opposite of what had been written.

A landlady who ruled through printed announcements devoted one to personal cleanliness:

1. Only one bath per week permitted per person, using no more than five inches of water. 6d [sixpence] for extra bath.
    Do not use bath until permission has been obtained.
    Vim is provided at no extra charge.
    Leave the bath as you would expect to find it
2. Use of cruet 3d extra
3. All foreign coins in gas meter will be prosecuted.
4. No friends in room after 11pm.
5. As there is no light at the bottom of the garden, a torch has been provided. Be sure it's the door on the right. The other belongs to the neighbour and we're not speaking.
6. Payments must be made by Friday lunchtime or Saturday at the latest or luggage will be confiscated.
7. Please leave your comments in the visitors' book.[276]

With reference to Rule Four, one classic story tells of a landlady who suspected that a comedian was bringing a girl home every night. She listened out for him, but it was always only one pair of feet making their way upstairs. One night, she decided to investigate further. She crept into her hallway and found the comic walking upstairs with a chorus girl on his back.

A landlady's lavatory left Tommy Handley covered in embarrassment. It was next door to the kitchen. One night, when the landlady and her family were having supper in the kitchen, Tommy realised he just had to go:

Tommy Handley.

I tried to be as quiet as possible. Then, I pulled the chain. Nothing. I tried again. Nowt. I then tried all sorts of different combinations, you know, two shorts and a long. A pull and a hold-down, a savage jerk, the lot. Just as I was getting totally embarrassed … there was a banging on the door and the landlady shouted "Mr 'Andley, you have to surprise it.[277]

Just after the Second World War, the impresario, Arthur Lane, was staying in digs, where, in spite of rationing, a suspicious amount of meat was served. One morning, he forgot his script and had to go back to his room. On his way in, he found the landlady having sex with the butcher's boy on the kitchen table next to a large tray of chops. The couple did not stop, but, as Arthur tiptoed past, the landlady looked up and said: 'Oh, Mr Lane, you must think I'm an awful flirt.' This anecdote, however, is of dubious provenance. In her autobiography, Julie Walters described how she found her landlady copulating on the kitchen table with one of the lodgers. She too was told: 'You must think I'm a terrible flirt.' Patrick Newley said it was the oldest landlady story in the business.

CHAPTER TWENTY

High Camp, Low Farce

Tres Gai: Douglas Byng and the Supreme Mrs Shufflewick

Noel Coward said he provided the most refined vulgarity in London. On stage for 70 years, he worked in cabaret, variety, pantomime and revue. But more than that, he was an ambassador for camp long before the word had even been invented: Douglas Byng. He billed himself as Bawdy But British, which must have appalled his well-to-do family. When he was eight, he told his mother he wanted to go on stage. Her reply: 'I hope, dear, it will never come to that.'

Dougie, the son of a bank manager, started out as a theatrical costumier in Soho, working six 12-hour days each week. But he achieved his ambition to be an entertainer by the time he was 20 when he joined a concert party in Hastings just before the First World War. In 1921/22, he appeared in his first pantomime as the Grand Vizier in *Aladdin* at the Palladium and then played Dame for the first time in *Dick Whittington and His Cat* at the New Oxford[278] in 1924/25:

> I [played] 26 [Dames] in all and was extremely snobbish about them. They were all ladies … none of the usual charlady types. I used to arrive on a bicycle in a yellow plaid frock and my dames were always extremely well-educated and very gracious. None of your rubbish.[279]

In *Dick Whittington*, Dougie sang the first comic song he wrote, *Oriental Emma of the 'Arem*.

During the 1920s, he established himself as a cabaret entertainer. He opened his own club, The Kinde Dragon, in a yard off St Martin's Lane. On Friday nights, it became the place to go to. Coward, Gertie Lawrence, Jessie Matthews and Gracie Fields not only patronised the club, but sang for free. Florence Desmond tried out her impersonations there for the first time. Dougie himself teamed up with another actor, Lance Lister, and sang songs he had written. One was *The Cabaret Boys*, which he described as 'the first slightly "queer" number to be sprung on the public'.[280]

> We started out in music hall with dear old Dad
> And, though we were put on first, we didn't go too bad
> Till we saw a couple of strong men and we both went mad.[281]

By now, Dougie had come to the attention of two giants of revue, C.B. Cochran, an impresario with a gift of spotting new talent, and Andre Charlot, who introduced intimate revue to London. For Cochran, Dougie appeared in *On With the Dance* [1924/25], in which the magical French star, Alice Delysia, sang Coward's first really big hit, *Poor Little Rich Girl*;[282] *One Dam Thing After Another* [1927]; *This Year of Grace!* [1928]; *Wake Up and Dream* [1929]; and *Cochran's 1930 Revue* [1930] [all at the London Pavilion]. For Charlot, he featured in *How D' You Do?* [Comedy, 1933] and *Hi Diddle Diddle* [Comedy, 1934], in which he was the first to sing Cole Porter's *Miss Otis Regrets*, the haunting tale of a woman cancelling a lunch engagement because she has just killed her former lover.

Douglas Byng [Douglas Coy Byng]

- Born Nottingham 17 March 1893 [Coy was his mother's maiden name]
- Douglas Byng died London 24 August 1987

By the 1930s, Dougie's cabaret career had taken him to the Café de Paris in Leicester Square, where he played eight seasons at £300 a week. Recordings of his own risqué songs were now selling well: *Sex Appeal Sarah*; *Hot Handed Hetty* [*The Vamp of the Jetty*] ; *I'm Millie, a Messy Old Mermaid*; and *I'm a Mummy*:

> I have slept without the aid of soporifics
> In a dim Egyptian grotto
> With a rude Egyptian motto
> Scribbled all across my bust in hieroglyphics.[283]

Dougie caused many problems for the faint-hearted BBC. Its Variety Department agonised over whether he should be allowed to say 'bust', but, in the end, he got his way. One BBC producer said Dougie's lyrics could not be cleaned up, while another maintained that Dougie owed his entire success to double entendres. Whenever he was banned, it meant little to him. His career was progressing nicely without the BBC. The variety theatre had discovered him too and he appeared on many Moss Empires bills, usually performing his one-man pantomime. He kept trying to change the act, but each time Miss Williams demanded the panto, in which he played all the parts, most enjoyably the Dame:

I haven't a thing to wear at the party. I've still got that dreary little three-piece in eau de Nil trimmed with sewer rat. Of course, we girls wear so little nowadays what with open work jumpers and transparent stockings, even a moth's life isn't what it was.[284]

Dougie kept his act clean for Cissie. 'I would say "What a lovely man my late husband was. He had those lovely pale watery blue eyes, like frosted lavatory windows." But that was as far as you could go.'[285]

My rudest joke was one about Nell Gwynne … 'The King would always have his country dance after dinner. I got sick of putting up the maypole. I said "Charles, dear, if you must dance, stick the maypole up yourself and dance round it."' The dear old ladies in the audience would think "How funny, the king dancing around all by himself" and others would think something different. But you were never so rude as to offend anybody.'[286]

At the age of 90, Dougie teamed up with another variety legend, Billy Milton, for a two-man revue, *Those Thirties Memories*, which ran for a fortnight in Bournemouth. Later, in Brighton, they gave a sell-out performance attended by many well-known theatrical personalities. Backstage, the two veterans could cope with each other's celebrity only by constantly talking over each other. The older Dougie grew, the more he became a National Treasure. On his ninetieth birthday, the BBC forgot its past differences and devoted a half-hour radio programme to his career. By now, of course, no one was concerned about his sexuality. So, there was no shock about his disclosure that, behind the scenes at the Café de Paris, he had acted as a gay matchmaker:

George, the Duke of Kent, would come in at about one o'clock in the morning just as I had finished my act and, if he had an eye for a young man, he would have to come round to my dressing room and ask who they were. The manager would have to be sent to the young man with a message to say that 'Mr Byng would like to see you' and the pretty boy would be sent round and I would have to say 'I'm so glad to meet you. Have you met my friend, the Duke of Kent?' Then, the drinks would appear and everyone would disappear. It was all very subtle, very upper class.[287]

Few showbiz memoirs are satisfying, but *The Times* was spot on when it described Dougie's book of reminiscences, *As You Were*, as 'free from pomposity, sentiment, introspection and snobbery.'[288] Other theatre people, please take note.

George Williams was a droll comic whose act was based on his [real or imaginary] ill health.

I was just leaving the cemetery after the funeral when the grave-digger said, 'You're not going, are you? We're stock-taking.'[289]

I said to the doctor, 'Will you give me something for the wind?' So, he gave me a kite.[290]

Looking fatally ashen, George had a catch phrase: 'I'm not well. I'm poorly, proper poorly.' But it was also the catch phrase of Reg Dixon and for years the two men argued about who had said it first.

While still a teenager, George joined concert parties, singing songs and appearing in short sketches; during the Second World War, he took part in about 2,000 shows organised by ENSA; and at the start of 1944, he resumed his variety career, appearing on *Henry Hall's Guest Night*, *Variety Bandbox* and *Workers' Playtime* on BBC Radio.

George Williams [George Smith Williams]

- Born Liverpool 25 May 1910
- George Williams died Lambeth, South London, 23 April 1995

Tragically, George's sexuality ended his career. At Nottinghamshire Assizes in February 1945, he was sentenced to three years' imprisonment for five offences of indecently assaulting a boy. He served only two years and the case, which was not widely reported, did not affect his career.

He was not so lucky in 1953. He was appearing as Simple Simon in *Babes in the Wood* at the Kemble Theatre in Hereford, where he had been praised for bringing 'a fresh conception [to] the role [with] a gentle and whimsical style that makes him a great favourite'.[291] Two weeks into the run, George and another member of the cast, Bryan Lloyd, picked up two boy soldiers, one aged 15, the other 16, and treated them to drinks at a hotel. Later, George admitted indecently assaulting the 15-year-old, but Lloyd denied offences against the other boy. They were immediately sacked from the panto. Charlie 'A Fool If Only He Knew It' Higgins was rushed up from London to take George's place. At Hereford Assizes, George was again sentenced to three years' imprisonment, Lloyd received 18 months and the two boys were sent to an approved school as they had been 'exposed to moral danger and ... in need of care and attention'.

In those less enlightened days, George was dropped by Moss Empires and the BBC, and had very little work for the next ten years. He later wrote his autobiography, *Hang on a Tick*, but made no mention of his criminal record. The French mime artiste, Marcel Marceau, wrote a foreword, in which he described George as Britain's most under-rated comedian, but a publisher was hard to find. Eventually, the manuscript fell into the hands of a fraudster, who sent leaflets to members of the British Music Hall Society announcing that the book was to be published by the previously unheard of British Music Hall Company.

People posted cheques to the firm, but never received the books. One of George's friends, Patrick Newley said the scam had a profound effect on him. 'George went to pieces and … locked himself away, even refusing work.'[292] Not long after, he died.

One of variety's finest comics was Rex Jameson. Except that he was never known as Rex Jameson. He was always Mrs Shufflewick [on stage] and Shuff [in private]. His routines are as funny today as they were in his heyday in the 1950s. Unfortunately, he grew too fond of drink. It affected his act and his career petered out. Many people now remember only his latter days. They should have seen him when he was at his best.

Rex Jameson [Rex Coster]

- Born London 11 June 1924
- Mrs Shufflewick died Camden Town, London 3 March 1983

A diminutive figure, dressed in a scraggy fur ['untouched pussy, practicably unobtainable in the West End of London'],[293] a gaudy necklace, cheap earrings and an extraordinary hat, Mrs Shufflewick was a gin-soaked old tart who constantly found herself at the centre of outrageous situations. Like the evening a sailor chatted her up in a pub:

> He pulled out a packet of picture postcards he'd brought back from the Middle East and, quite honestly, I had never seen anything so disgusting. I mean I'm broadminded to the point of obscenity, but my God, if you'd seen these – and they were in Agfacolor. There was nothing left to the imagination. How they got themselves in those positions – I couldn't do it. So, I gave them back to him after twenty-five minutes. I said I've no wish to look at this type sort of literature, thank you very much. I said, as far as I'm concerned, you can get behind me, Satan. And those were the worst few words …[294]

Shuff was abandoned on the steps of Trinity College Hospital, Greenwich, as a two-week-old baby and was brought up in the rundown Essex seaside town of Southend-on-Sea by foster parents, George and Mabel Coster. Mabel had fostered many children before and Shuff felt he was just the latest in a line. In the RAF, Shuff's Flight Sergeant and drinking partner was Tony Hancock. He went to the Middle East with a Ralph Reader Gang Show and performed an act as a camp vicar. Later, he used the routine at an audition for the BBC, unaware that the Corporation's guidelines banned anything religious as the subject of humour.

Can you do anything else? he was asked. Yes, Shuff said. I do a charlady. He was lying. It was the first character he thought of. He was asked to return the following week, allowing him enough time to write his first Mrs Shufflewick script. At his second audition, he was accepted and he was soon heard on

Variety Bandbox and every other radio variety show. There was, of course, one act for the BBC and another for the clubs, in one of which Shuff recalled the end of a drunken night out, determined not to disturb his 'old man':

Mrs. Shufflewick.

> I thought I'll take all my clothes off downstairs and I'll just sort of slide up and creep in and, if he says anything at all, I'll just say 'I was watching the Epilogue[295] and I nodded off.' So, I got there. I took all my clothes off, all in a bundle under my arm and I was up the staircase, not a sound, and I got to the bit where it bends round the corner at the top. I got the shock of my life. I'm on top of a 29 bus. And all these people turned round – all sober. Oh, I could've hit 'em. As if they'd never seen a woman with no clothes on on top of a bus before.[296]

In the 1960s, offers of work came in less frequently. Shuff had always drunk, but now it took a hold; his brilliant timing disintegrated; and, if he was heckled at a pub or a club, he sometimes broke down in tears. In 1972, Patrick Newley became his manager and was shocked to find that he was being paid £10 [£100] a night at some gay clubs and £15 [£150] at the Black Cap pub in Camden Town, where he was revered. Shuff appeared not to need the money. He ate at 'greasy spoon' cafes, smoked Woodbines and bought his clothes at jumble sales. Even so, Patrick found him better work. Twice, when the alleged singer, Dorothy Squires, hired the Palladium, Shuff was booked as a supporting act. One of his appearances, which was supposed to run for ten minutes, joyfully continued for 18. When he finished, he decided that, rather than listen to Dot in his dressing room, he would go round the front and watch her from the back of the stalls. He changed into his ordinary clothes, told one of the front-of-house staff that he was Mrs Shufflewick and that he wanted to see the rest of the show. He was refused.

> He told me to fuck off and threw me down the steps. I bet that's never happened to anyone who's just played the London Palladium.[297]

CHAPTER TWENTY ONE

Indelible Impressions

Stars in Their Eyes: Afrique, Peter Cavanagh, Florence Desmond, Percy Edwards, Fayne and Evans, Harry Hemsley, Ronnie Ronalde

Most impressionists made famous by television have been brilliant, but the credit should always have been shared with unnamed make-up artists, hairdressers and costumiers. Audio and video cassettes of the impersonator's 'victims' also helped. It was not always so. In her act, Florence Desmond, the most accomplished impressionist of her day, usually imitated eight or ten people, often American film stars. She switched from one to another by merely running her hand through her hair or using the minimum of props, a scarf, a cigarette or a pair of glasses.

Dessie, the daughter of a cobbler, started young. At nursery school, she impersonated friends and teachers. She began training as a dancer and, at the age of ten, she joined a company of children performing pantomimes. Aged 17,

---

Florence Desmond [Florence Elizabeth Dawson]

- Born Islington, north London, 31 May 1905
- Married [1] Tom Campbell Black in central London, 30 March 1935 [He won the London to Melbourne air race in 1934 and was killed when an RAF bomber, landing at Speke Airport, Liverpool, ran into his plane on 19 September 1936]
- Married [2] Charles Frederick Hughesdon, pilot and Lloyd's insurance broker, central London, 23 September 1937
- Adopted son, Michael [After the death of Florence Desmond, Hughesdon married Carole Elizabeth Havers, widow of the former Lord Chancellor, Lord Havers]
- Florence Desmond died Guildford, Surrey, 16 January 1993
- Left £175,525 [£230,000]

she was at the bottom of a bill at the Ilford Hippodrome. At the top of the bill was Marie Lloyd, then a sick woman. In fact, she died only a few weeks later. Dessie studied her performance from the wings. So that, when she was asked to impersonate Marie singing *Don't Dilly Dally on the Way* in *Hi-De-Hi* at the Palace Theatre 21 years later, she felt able to do so.[298] Standing in the wings at the Ilford Hippodrome, Dessie vowed that, if she ever became a star, she would retire before she grew old.

After nearly ten years touring in concert parties, music hall and revues, Dessie became one of C.B. Cochran's Young Ladies in the Coward revue, *On With the Dance* [1925]. Two years later, she joined Coward and Beatrice Lillie in the New York production of another Coward show, *This Year of Grace*. While there, she sought Coward's guidance about her career. He advised her well: 'Specialise, Dessie. Don't try to do too much of everything.'[299]

In 1930, Andre Charlot saw Dessie impersonate the outrageous American actress, Tallulah Bankhead, in her act at the Café Anglais. He had already hired her for *Charlot's Masquerade* at the Cambridge Theatre and now wanted to adapt a skating scene at the end of the first half to accommodate Dessie's impression. She was introduced as Tallulah and, when she swept on stage wearing a white leather coat, a white beret and carrying a large chiffon handkerchief, an exact copy of the costume Tallulah was wearing in a play at the Lyric Theatre, there was a huge round of applause. She then stretched out her arms towards the audience and, adopting Tallulah's husky voice, said 'Bless you, darlings.' The gallery roared its approval.

At the after show party, Tallulah arrived wanting to meet 'the girl who does this divine imitation of me.' On the spot, she gave Dessie some tips: put your colour rather lower on your cheeks, tuck your hair underneath the beret [and] lift up your left shoulder. When Dessie said she was already doing that, Tallulah exclaimed: 'Oh, my God! She speaks like me off the stage – the bitch!'[300]

Two years later, the BBC asked Dessie to broadcast. She quickly wrote a sketch she called *A Hollywood Party*, in which she impersonated, among others, Marlene Dietrich, Greta Garbo, Gracie Fields, Tallulah Bankhead and Jimmy Durante. The following day, HMV phoned her and asked her to make a record of it. She agreed. At rehearsals for *Savoy Follies*, a revue she was to appear in at the Savoy Theatre, one of the writers, Archie de Bear, suggested that she performed the sketch in the show. Dessie was not sure. There was nothing visual about it, she said, but she was persuaded to do it and it stopped the show. *A Hollywood Party* sold hundreds of thousands of records on both sides of the Atlantic.

Dessie was once asked how she went about preparing an impersonation: 'I begin with my subject's face and it is from the shape of the face, mouth and jaw that I produce the voice.'[301] She was admired for tackling not only the easier subjects, such as Dietrich, Garbo and Bette Davis, but also the difficult ones, Claudette Colbert, Barbara Stanwyck and Myrna Loy, for example.

But not all her victims were as helpful as Tallulah. Betty Hutton, who replaced Dorothy Lamour as Paramount Pictures' top female box office attraction, was distinctly piqued. Dessie wanted to sing *Murder, He Says*, which Betty Hutton had performed in the movie, *Happy-Go-Lucky*:

Her attitude towards me froze. She refused to let me have her arrangement copied [and] was not in the least bit helpful. In fact, she was barely polite to me when she learned that I was going on with the imitation. It is the only time in my career that anyone has ever been difficult.[302]

Dessie, not needing the work or the money, was able to honour the vow she made while watching Marie Lloyd 30 years previously. In 1948, her second husband, Charles Hughesdon, the head of the highly successful airline, Tradewinds Airways and an innovator in aviation insurance brokerage, bought a mansion in Surrey, Dunsborough Park. Dessie lived the rest of her days there in great opulence.

Harry Hemsley specialised in impersonating children. He created his own family, Winnie, Elsie, Johnny and the unintelligible Horace. He was so proficient at capturing the voice of children that many people listening to him on the radio understandably believed that these were real children. If he was on at the end of the evening, people phoned the BBC to complain about keeping children up late.

Harry Hemsley [Harry May Hemsley]

- Born Swindon, Wiltshire, 14 December 1878
- Married
- Son, Norman
- Harry Hemsley died Wimbledon, south-west London, 8 April 1951
- Left £14,832 [£300,000]

Harry was the son of a successful scenic painter, W.T. [William Thompson] Hemsley, from whom he inherited a talent for drawing. When he was 16, he began contributing to children's comics, most notably *Ally Sloper's Half Holiday*.[303] His child impressions were first heard at smoking concerts in London a few years later. He then joined H.G. Pelissier's *Follies* and Will C. Pepper's *White Coons*[304] concert party.

Harry was also involved in cinema's earliest days in Britain, making a few films for Will Barker in Ealing before the First World War. He used silent film in his stage act with Winnie and the others. The children were seen on a screen, playing and talking. Harry stood beside the screen, lip-synching what they were saying. If any of them misbehaved, Harry reprimanded them, left the stage and was then seen on the film administering a punishment. A few seconds after he left the screen, he re-appeared on stage.

Harry made his first BBC radio broadcast in 1923 and, from then until 1941, had a prolific recording career. From 1934, he was also heard in the *Ovaltineys' Concert Party*, a programme sponsored by the makers of the malt drink, Ovaltine, on Radio Luxembourg. He even wrote its opening chorus:

We are the Ovaltineys, little girls and boys.
Make your requests. We'll not refuse you.
We are here just to amuse you.
Would you like a song or story?
Will you share our joys?
At games or sports we're more than keen.
No merrier children could be seen.
Because we all drink Ovaltine
We're happy girls and boys.

The show proved so popular that a League of Ovaltineys was formed. Its members had to promise to adopt high morals and show consideration for others. At the height of its popularity, there were no fewer than five million members.

The only impressionist allowed to imitate the Hemsley family was Peter Cavanagh, who billed himself as the Voice of Them All. He started out as a singer, but began developing his talent for mimickry in 1938. He made his first radio appearance on *Variety Bandbox* and was the first impressionist to chop and change between voices, imitating the entire cast of ITMA in quick succession. He found ITMA's star, Tommy Handley, one of the most difficult to mimic. Tommy was born in Liverpool, but, after a few years in London, he had almost lost his Scouse accent. Peter soon realised that, when Tommy spoke quickly, he sounded like a Liverpudlian, but, when he was slow, he was more like a Londoner.

One of Peter's most successful impersonations was Field Marshal Montgomery, who successfully commanded Allied forces at the Battle of El Alamein, a major turning point in the Second World War. It helped in that he resembled Monty. On one of the many occasions he was invited to entertain the Royal Family, George VI was particularly amused at the Monty take-off.

Peter Cavanagh [Peter Cedric Coates]

- Born Croydon, south London, 31 October 1914
- Married
- Son, Roger
- Peter Cavanagh died Chipping Norton, Oxfordshire, 18 February 1981

Peter enjoyed appearing on radio with one of his victims, each of them speaking alternate lines. For instance, he would sing Arthur Askey's *The Bee Song* alongside Arthur and challenge listeners to guess who was singing.

In 1951, he played a clever trick on *What's My Line?* There was always a mystery celebrity guest whom the panel, wearing blindfolds, had to name after asking a limited number of questions. Gilbert Harding was a regular member of the panel and, one week, after the others had to put on their blindfolds, Harding quietly slipped into the celebrity's chair while Peter took his place on the panel. The other panellists, Marghanita Laski, Frances Day and Jerry Desmonde were all fooled.

Percy Edwards left the imitation of people's voices to others while he devoted himself to something he considered far more important. As a noted ornithologist, he could reproduce the song of at least 600 birds; he imitated practically every breed of animal; in fact, he could reproduce practically any sound, if called upon.

Even as a child, he was fascinated by sound. While his baby sister drank from her feeding bottle, he mimicked the sound of the bubbles and, when she finished, he reproduced the burp. Growing up in Suffolk, he absorbed all the sounds of the countryside. No one could catch him out. He knew how the nuthatch warbled and he knew it was different from the song of the tree-creeper.

Percy Edwards

- Born Ipswich, Suffolk, 1 June 1908
- Married Cecily Newby in Ipswich 1 August 1936
- Sons, David and Anthony
- Percy Edwards died Hintlesham, Suffolk, 7 June 1996

Percy began his working life at a firm that made ploughs, but, in his spare time, he was frequently invited to perform some of his impersonations with a local concert party. In 1929, he decided to go professional. For a while, he appeared at the Windmill. On the same bill, curiously enough, there was another bird imitator, a Scotsman, who impersonated a nightingale that he said he had heard at home. Percy put him right. Nightingales never nest north of Yorkshire. This was how a typical Percy Edwards routine began:

Hello, everyone. In the spring, a young man's fancy lightly turns to thoughts of love. That's what the poets would have us believe and I suppose there must be some truth in it. But what about the animal kingdom? Don't you think that they have their moments? Of course, they do. But whereas we are perhaps at bit quiet about our love-making, the animals must let the world and his wife know all about spring. This is the wolf, without his whistle, telling the age-old mountains and a full moon what a funny thing this thing called love is.[305]

But the work dried up for Percy and he returned to making ploughs. At the age of 37, he tried his luck again. This time, he succeeded. An appearance on BBC Radio's *In Town Tonight* led to other broadcasts, although even a bird imitator could fall foul of the censors. Percy had written one routine in which he described pond life: 'Now it's May, you'll see the water lilies appear. You'll see them poking through and breaking the surface of the water before unfolding and lying flat on top.' The producer looked worried. 'Poking through? It's not exactly BBC, is it. Couldn't Percy say "protruding"[306] instead?'

At first, Percy was worried about his stage career. He felt he was not getting the response that his fellow entertainers received. That was because his was a quiet act. A theatre manager in Halifax reassured him: 'You're making audiences realise how little they use their eyes and ears. An audience would sit quiet while I was on. It seemed unnatural, but they were listening and, thank God, loving it. But ... they never raised the roof for me. Then, I began to think. Well, why should they? I'm not a "sensation", just a gentle entertainer who loves to entertain.'[307]

In the end, Percy became such a revered figure that, whenever producers wanted the sound of a bird or an animal, they naturally thought of him first. In relatively old age, he provided 'voices' for the whales in the 1977 Richard Harris movie, *Orca*; the sheep and bird sounds for Kate Bush's song *The Dreaming* [1982]; and the reindeer in the 1985 picture, *Santa Claus: The Movie*.

Another entertainer who introduced birdsong into his act was Ronnie Ronalde. He took a song, sang one chorus, yodelled another, whistled another and impersonated some birds while the orchestra played the melody. Ronnie began impersonating birds when he was a child. At the age of 14, he joined a boys' choir, Arturo Steffani's Silver Songsters. When the choir disbanded in 1947, Steffani became his manager. His most popular songs were the traditional air, *If I Were a Blackbird*, and Arthur Ketelbey's *In a Monastery Garden*.

Ronnie Ronalde [Ronald Charles Waldron]

- Born Islington, North London, 29 June 1923
- Married Rosemarie Burschberger on Guernsey, Channel Islands, 15 April 1961
- Daughters, Carolyn and Christina
- Son, Ronnie

A tour of Britain in the late 1940s brought Ronnie his first taste of success and, in 1949, the BBC gave him his first radio series, *The Voice of Variety*. Like many entertainers, Ronnie had exaggerated views about his status and importance. Most showbiz people regard an invitation to take part in a Royal Variety show as a high point in their career, an opportunity to appear before the Queen and a good way to raise money for the Entertainment Artistes' Benevolent Fund. When Ronnie was invited in 1953, he learned that he was to appear for only a minute or two in a scene depicting music hall. Tessie O'Shea would represent Florrie Forde; the Scottish comedian, Jack Radcliffe, was to be Harry Lauder; and Ronnie would whistle like Albert Whelan.

He refused, insisting that he would have to do three numbers, one singing, one yodelling and one whistling. Astonishingly, he got his way.

When Peter Cook impersonated Harold Macmillan in *Beyond the Fringe* in 1961, everyone was told that this was the first time a serving Prime Minister had been lampooned on stage: not so. When the Vera Lynn/Max Miller show, *Apple Sauce!*, opened at the Holborn Empire in 1940, Winston Churchill was impersonated by a talented performer who is now almost completely forgotten, Afrique.

Afrique [Alexander Witkin]

- Born Johannesburg, 2 February 1907
- Married
- Four children, Robert Winston, Thames Morrison, Jacqueline Mirabelle and Elsie Grace
- Afrique died Lambeth, south London, 16 December 1961

He had trained as an opera singer and had developed such an amazing vocal range that he was able to imitate both the tenor, Richard Tauber, and the bass, Paul Robeson. His first variety appearance was at Vivian Van Damm's Windmill Theatre:

I picked Afrique at an audition because of his stage presence. That was really all he had then ... He had no act, no set routine. He came on dressed in a leopard skin, carrying a spear and made terrifying Zulu noises deep in his throat. From those small beginnings, we built up an act for him and very soon he had a ten-minute spot in each show and was a very big attraction.[308]

Afrique went on to appear in cabaret, where he impersonated the Prince of Wales, later Edward VIII. It was a good-humoured characterisation. Afrique had mastered all the Prince's mannerisms. Night clubs did not fall under the jurisdiction of the Lord

Chamberlain, who was irritated that he did not have the power to ban the impression, which he found 'most undesirable and in very bad taste.'[309] Afrique had no wish to court controversy and he voluntarily dropped the impersonation from his act. A heavy gambler, he died virtually penniless.

No act reached the top quite as quickly as Fayne and Evans. They first appeared in *Variety Bandbox* in 1948. Come 1951, they were part of the Royal Variety Show, they made a film with the Goons,[310] Peter Sellers, Harry Secombe and Spike Milligan, and they were a supporting act in a Palladium show starring Judy Garland.

They deserved success. They were fast, they were sophisticated and they were unique. At the start of their act, they asked their audience to imagine two radio sets side by side. They then performed a sports commentary in complete unison, mimicking well-known sportsmen and commentators with deadly accuracy. Their early lives ran in parallel too.

Tony Fayne and David Evans knew each other as boys. They were in the same class at the Cathedral School in Bristol, where they took great delight in imitating their teachers. After leaving school, they remained friends and put together a routine of impersonations. In 1940, they won a talent contest at the Bristol Empire and were booked to appear on Jack Payne's radio show, *Your Company is Requested*. Other broadcasts followed and they were just becoming well-known when they were called up for wartime service. They both joined the Fleet Air Arm, but were stationed in different places. They did not meet again until 1948 when [another coincidence] they were both working as clerks in insurance officers. Bored with clerical jobs, they decided to renew their showbiz careers.

A typical routine was one they performed in *Blackpool Night* on BBC Radio in 1956. They were played in to the melody of their signature tune, *Exactly Like You*. Speaking in unison, they presented their view of how radio might have sounded in the Sixteenth Century. In a cod *Radio Newsreel*, they cast Ken Platt as Sir Walter Ralegh and Sir Terence de Thomas [Terry-Thomas] as a court jester. A

Tony Fayne [Anthony Terence Alfred Senington]

- Born Bristol 18 January 1924
- Married Audrey Norma Collyer [died 2009]
- Six children, David, Jacqueline, Pamela and triplets Melinda, Teresa and Hazel
- Tony Fayne died 30 November 2009

David Evans [David Frank Evans]

- Born Bristol 10 March 1922
- Died Bristol 14 February 1980

joint impersonation of the cricket commentator, John Arlott, followed and they finished by singing *Friends* as Jimmy Wheeler and Gilbert Harding. Needless to say the two men fall out with each other.

Fayne and Evans went their separate ways in 1959. It had something to do with Evans' growing addiction to alcohol. It is unclear as to whether his drinking forced Fayne to end their association or whether Evans turned to drink as a result of the split. It was probably the former, but, whichever it was, this once famous double act was no more.

Fayne restructured his career. He issued a number of satirical LPs written by another old school friend, Philip Evans [aka Philip Bruce]; on television, he succeeded Nicholas Parsons as straight man to Arthur Haynes, who played a truculent tramp in excellent television comedies scripted by Johnny Speight; and, for 20 years, he was stooge to Albania's favourite comedian, Norman Wisdom, who found him ideal: 'with his schoolmasterly manner and commanding presence, he was the ideal foil. Tony is also particularly good at looking annoyed!'[311] Their entry for the Knokke Television Festival in 1976 won first prize.

Evans carried on drinking. He had a number of dead-end jobs, but on Sunday nights he went to his local club, the Chequers, in the Hanham area of Bristol, where ad lib shows were staged. He gave a first-rate impersonation of Winston Churchill delivering his wartime speeches, but his other victims, the cast of ITMA, Robb Wilton and the radio comedian, Stainless Stephen, who 'spoke'[312] each punctuation mark in his act, were becoming dated. Younger drinkers had to ask who he was impersonating. All the same, he was occasionally asked to appear elsewhere, but was often too drunk to turn up.

At a local church group, he did appear, but, as soon as he arrived, he fell over. The people who managed to get him on his feet again were alarmed to see that his shirt was covered in blood. They thought he had suffered a haemorrhage until they found he was carrying a piece of liver he had just bought from a butcher. Worse than that, when Tony Fayne was finishing his act at the Bristol Hippodrome, Evans staggered on from the wings and, possibly imagining they were still together, acknowledged the applause. Fayne hardly recognised him.

In 1980, Evans was found dead in his garden shed. His death certificate attributed the cause of death to heart trouble, but many of his friends independently attested that he had hanged himself.

CHAPTER TWENTY TWO

Life of Riley

Lucan and McShane

Alove affair between a Lincolnshire boy and a young Irish girl produced one of Britain's favourite comedy double acts, Old Mother Riley and her daughter, Kitty. It was enormously popular and brought fame and fortune to a couple from modest backgrounds, Arthur Towle and Kitty McShane. But the success turned Kitty, a pretty sweet-tempered girl, into a foul-mouthed vixen. In the end, she destroyed the act, then Arthur, and finally herself.

Arthur became interested in the stage while still a boy. Before he was seven, he hung around Shodfriars Hall, which housed a small theatre in the Lincolnshire town of Boston. After seeing his first pantomime there, he built a toy theatre at home and staged his own productions to amuse himself. The manager of the Shodfriars theatre was intrigued by the boy's enthusiasm and offered him a job sweeping the stage in the morning and selling programmes in the evening. Arthur accepted immediately, knowing he would be able to watch the shows there free. When he was ten, so many of the cast of *Robinson Crusoe* contracted 'flu that he was sent on in the role of a native and, when a music hall opened in Boston, he began selling programmes there and regularly appeared in its shows.

But the progress of Arthur's young theatrical career was not moving fast enough for him and, with his family constantly disapproving of the way of life he had chosen, he ran away from home. At first, he earned his living busking on the beaches of Skegness and Blackpool and then got to know Danny and Vera Clifton, who ran a concert party called the Musical Cliftons. Arthur joined them and learned the

HIPPODROME

TELEPHONE - 2447   **IPSWICH**   TELEPHONE - 2447
Lessee - A. A. SHENBURN   Licensee and Manager - R. A. SIMS

6.0   ✶   MONDAY, OCT. 9th   ✶   **8.10**
TWICE NIGHTLY

KITTY McSHANE presents

OLD MOTHER RILEY
AND HER **DAUGHTER KITTY**

Personal Appearance of your Stage, Radio and Screen Favourites

ARTHUR LUCAN
& KITTY McSHANE

WHITE & SIMONE ✶ DICK ✶ THE DUVAL GIRLS
Mrs. GINNOCHIE **CALKIN** GALE DOUGLAS
ROY ROLLAND ✶ ✶ EDDIE HART

WILLER NEAL as 'DANNY BOY'

rudiments of singing, dancing and working as a comic. In 1909, the troupe toured Ireland and, at some stage [accounts differ], Arthur met and fell in love with the winsome daughter of a Dublin fireman, Kitty McShane, who had been singing in small concert halls. Her family disapproved of her seeing a man who was considerably older, but, after Arthur had spent some time in England with the White Coons' concert party, he returned to Ireland and the couple married. Arthur was 28 and Kitty was 16.

Old Mother Riley and her daughter, Kitty.

Arthur then began formulating a sketch, entitled *Come Over*, in which they could combine their talents. He saw himself as a widowed Irish washerwoman and Kitty as his teenage daughter whom he has to support and protect. The birth of Old Mother Riley, however, was still a long way off. While Arthur and Kitty were touring halls and theatres around Ireland, they were seen by the ace talent scout, Danny Clarke. He immediately offered them £12 10s [£250] a week to appear at his hall, the Argyle Theatre in Birkenhead, a hall that marked a major step in the career of many entertainers. It was more than they had ever earned and they gratefully accepted. Soon, they became known all over Britain and, while touring, reached second billing, earning £18 [£360] a week.

By the time Kitty was 26, she became responsible for all business dealings associated with the act. Arthur, now 38, had no aspirations to be a star and was content just to jog along. During 1923, they were offered a tour of South Africa, Australia and New Zealand, but, in Cape Town, Arthur witnessed an aspect of Kitty's character he had never seen before. She grew angry at a poor review

---

Arthur Lucan [Arthur Towle]

- Born Sibsey, Lincolnshire, 16 September 1885
- Married Catherine McShane [professionally known as Kitty McShane] in Dublin 25 November 1913
- Son, Donald Daniel [who was born in Dublin in 1915 and who died in Redruth, Cornwall, 1975]
- Arthur Lucan died in Hull 17 May 1954
- Kitty McShane, who was born in Dublin 19 May 1897, died in London 24 March 1964]
- Arthur left £1,459 [£27,000]
- Kitty left £34,000 [£40,000]

she had received, lost her temper and stormed out, saying she was going to get drunk. Later, she apologised, but as the fame of Lucan and McShane increased, Kitty grew tougher and tougher.

By August 1925, *Come Over* was part of a bill at the Alhambra, London. Arthur had still not decided to devote his career to female impersonation. In March 1927, he was principal comedian in a revue, *Irish Follies*, at the Wood Green Empire. On his first appearance at the London Palladium in August 1932, he presented a sketch in which he staggered on stage as a dishevelled old woman declaring: Every man before wedlock should be padlocked. It was this character that finally developed into Old Mother Riley.

In 1934, Lucan and McShane were invited to take part in the Royal Variety Show. Arthur decided they needed a new act for the occasion and wrote *Bridget's Night Out*, which became the definitive Old Mother Riley sketch. In it, Riley stays up late, waiting for her daughter, Bridget [Kitty], to return home. She works herself in a lather of anger and concern:

> I wonder where she is. I wonder where she's gone. I wonder who's she with. I wonder what she's doing. I wonder what time it is. I hope she's all right. If only I knew what time it was, I'd be more settled in my mind. I don't know how long I've slept. I don't know how long she's been out and I can't read the clock until it strikes. That's where she has me. That's where she has me and she knows it. And here's me sitting pretty. I don't know whether it's daytime, night time, half time, summer time, early closing or next Wednesday. [The clock strikes three]. One o'clock three times.[313]

When Bridget returns, a row breaks out, culminating in 250 pieces of crockery being smashed. But farce turns to pathos as Kitty sings *Goodnight, Mother* to the tune of *Goodnight, Sweetheart* and Old Mother Riley collects her clothes in a bundle and shuffles upstairs to bed. Throughout the sketch, Arthur indulged in a series of acrobatic manoeuvres as he crosses and uncrosses his legs, hilarious activity ill befitting an old woman.

Watching film of the sketch now, it is clear that the talented member of the duo was Arthur. He created an endearing comic icon unlike any other character in the variety theatre. Kitty played Bridget competently and sang her song nicely, but any one of thousands of girls could have done the same. Yet increasingly, Kitty assumed the dominant role in the relationship and, however foul she became, Arthur forgave her.

The act made the Lucans wealthy. They bought a large home in Wembley and employed a butler, a cook, a maid, a cleaner, a gardener and a chauffeur. Arthur, softly spoken and smartly dressed, was admired by all who knew him. He spent hours pottering about in his garden. His only extravagance was collecting Dresden figurines. By contrast, Kitty, who was ill-mannered and self-centred, loved going to expensive restaurants and night clubs and spent lavish amounts of money on clothes and jewellery. She liked to behave and be treated as a star. Kitty's sister, Annie, shared the home at Wembley for many years: '[When touring] other members of the company [were] not [allowed to] stay under the same roof as Kitty … To stop it from happening she would pay for all the rooms in the hotel if necessary.'[314]

The 15 movies the Lucans starred in made them even richer.[315] When they worked the halls as Lucan and McShane, they commanded £700 [£24,500] a week. As Old Mother Riley and her daughter, Kitty, the figure rose to £1,000 [£35,000]. There were also shows on BBC Radio[316] as well as gramophone records.[317]

In spite of the success, Kitty's outrageous behaviour drove the couple apart. They stopped having sex and Kitty began looking elsewhere. Touring on her own in 1944, she was backed by a male quartet, one of whom, Billy Bleach, took her eye. Before the tour was over, they were lovers. She told Arthur that Billy was too good just to be part of a quartet. She thought he should join their sketches as Bridget's boyfriend. Arthur agreed. Kitty searched for a new name for her boyfriend, who was, incidentally, a married man with a family. His real name, she felt, made him sound like a detergent, but she invented a name that was equally odd, Willer Neal.

In Neal's presence, Arthur eventually voiced his concerns about the affair. Kitty responded by accusing Arthur of being gay, a charge utterly without foundation. Arthur went to hit her, but was stopped by Neal who beat him up so vigorously that he was left sobbing on the floor. Against this background, the finances of Lucan and McShane began to look less secure. Kitty was spending every penny they earned, squandering hundreds of pounds on Neal; the BBC declined the offer of a fourth radio series; [the third had centred mostly on Kitty singing]; and the Inland Revenue was demanding large sums in back taxes.

Kitty then decided to leave Arthur and set up home with Neal in an apartment she had bought in central London. Arthur begged her to return. She said she would, but only if she and Neal had their own bedroom. Unbelievably, Arthur agreed.

When the couple made their last film, *Old Mother Riley's Jungle Treasure*, they argued so frequently that the producer banned them from appearing in the studio together. Any scenes involving dialogue were to be shot on different days and then edited together. Arthur made one more film, *Old Mother Riley Meets the Vampire*, in which a young Dora Bryan played a maid:

> Dear Arthur Lucan … was such a nice man, but, like so many wonderful comics, his life was full of sadness … Kitty McShane … was barred by then from the film studios because it was said she caused trouble. But this did not stop her from turning up briefly each day in her Rolls Royce to give Arthur his day's pocket money.[318]

Arthur's life had become intolerable. To try to numb the misery, he turned to drink and only managed to get through each day with a constant supply of miniature bottles of gin. On the last tour he undertook with Kitty, he was made to stay in a small room at the back of a hotel while Kitty and Neal occupied a luxurious suite. Kitty treated Arthur as merely an employee of her production company and paid him just £30 a week.

In August 1953, Arthur was made bankrupt and was forced to sell his home. Most of the debts had been incurred by Kitty, who told a number of people, including her son, that she could no longer live with Arthur after discovering he was gay. A court hearing was arranged for 30 May 1954. In the meantime, Arthur had to hand his earnings to the Official Receiver.

A new tour started in Rotherham on 18 April 1954. It was devised by Gaston and Andree [see Chapter 26], who had by then given up their adagio act. It was a spectacular show and did good business. On May 17, it moved to Hull, where it was assured of success as Arthur had a good following there.

On the first night, Ellis Ashton, the stage manager for Gaston and Andree, who was also appearing in the show, announced: Ladies and gentlemen, Old Mother Riley. But, while waiting in the wings, Arthur dropped dead. His body was carried to his dressing room while Ellis told the audience that there had been a technical hitch. Arthur's wig was quickly removed and passed to his understudy, Frank Seton. Within a few minutes, the show started, the audience unaware of the backstage tragedy.

Kitty continued to stage shows with Roy Rolland playing Old Mother Riley. She also continued her affair with Neal, who had long made it clear that he would not divorce his wife. To the public, Kitty made out that life was tough for her. She was getting by on a widow's pension:

> Where has all the money gone? Has it been fast cars, rich living, champagne for breakfast and lavish parties? When Arthur Lucan died … it not only widowed me, but took away my income. The act died with my husband. And after his death, his bills came to me. I have settled them all now.[319]

Kitty maintained the last bill she had to pay was for £340 [£5,500]. That was an account with British Railways for transporting their scenery and props around Britain. Kitty said she had managed to reduce the debt to £39 13s 3d [£635], money she just could not raise. In the nick of time, the debt was settled and she avoided being sent to prison: all balderdash.

In December 1963, Neal was admitted to hospital and, within a few days, died of cancer of the bladder. Three months later, Kitty died too, a victim of chronic alcoholism.

CHAPTER TWENTY THREE

Their Lips Were Sealed

Top Vents Arthur Worsley, Saveen, Bobbie Kimber

As children, we enjoyed ventriloquists in much the same way as we enjoyed comic double acts. The only difference was that in ventriloquism one man played both parts: one was animate, the other was not. It was only when we started watching old movies that we began to believe that ventriloquism might embody something sinister. First, there was *The Great Gabbo* [1929], in which the vent, played by Eric von Stroheim, is able to express himself only through his dummy, Otto. As he becomes more dependent on Otto, he starts going mad. Then, there was *Dead of Night* [1945], in which a ventriloquist played by Michael Redgrave is possessed by his doll's malevolent spirit. Lastly, Richard Attenborough's film, *Magic* [1978], starred Anthony Hopkins as a vent whose dummy takes on a mind of his own.

The theme was sometimes mirrored in real life. The actress, Candice Bergen, whose father, Edgar, was one of America's most revered ventriloquists, was brought up as the younger sister of Edgar's dummy, Charlie McCarthy. Most spookily of all, the young Candice was made to sit on her father's knee and was encouraged to chat with Charlie on the other knee.

Saveen, one of the most accomplished ventriloquists in the British variety theatre, also elevated his best-known doll, Daisy May, onto a semi-human plane. She had her own bank account and her own telephone number, which received so many calls that Saveen had to close it. [At the same time, a real Daisy May was obliged to go ex-directory]. Showbiz people became accustomed to phoning Saveen only to have the call answered by Daisy May. Roy Hudd was one:

> I couldn't get him to speak as himself. Finally, I had to be satisfied with Daisy May saying, 'I'll ask Mr Saveen to phone you back.' He did and, after telling me she had given him my message, he carried on as if nothing had happened.[320]

Saveen eventually conceded that Daisy May had become an albatross around his neck.

Saveen was only seven when his parents took him to a penny concert to see music hall's greatest ventriloquist, Arthur Prince. He was immediately mesmerised and began practising ventriloquism in his bedroom with his teddy bear. In his teens, he performed as an amateur and was apprenticed to his father's trade as a printer. At work, his colleagues elected him as their social

Saveen [Albert Edward Langford]

- Born Southwark, south London, 27 May 1914
- Married Cynthia Ursula Edwina Lee in Wandsworth 17 March 1957 [dissolved]
- Daughter, Belinda
- Died Kingston-upon-Thames 14 April 1994
- Left £214,175 {£280,000}

secretary and he staged cabarets for them, appearing himself without charging a fee.

After he had saved some money, he bought his first dummy and inserted his father's top set of false teeth and his mother's bottom set into the doll, something he regarded as a memorial to his parents.

In May 1940, he secured his first professional engagement at the Coliseum, Portsmouth, but within weeks he was in the Royal Artillery. Six weeks later, he became the first in his regiment to be wounded. His chest was blown open when a 500lb bomb exploded only 25 yards [metres] from him. He was in hospital for a year and had to learn how to breathe again, using first one lung and then the other. He was so shell-shocked that he was unable to return to printing work. He was invalided out of the army and decided to become a ventriloquist full-time. 'If I could thank the German who dropped that bomb, I'd do so because he did me the greatest turn ever.'[321]

Saveen's first big chance came when he was booked by Archie Parnell's agency to appear at the Streatham Hill Theatre in 1943. He earned £25 [£625] a week. Val Parnell then gave him a 40-week engagement with Moss Empires at £35 [£875] a week. Saveen's first dummy was Andy the Spiv, who spoke in gruff Cockney tones. While playing Wolverhampton, he was shocked to find that only a few people in the audience were laughing. Most of them did not understand the East End patois. Saveen was out of work for 14 weeks and used the time to create Daisy May, a wooden doll with white stockings, plaits and a boater. She was painfully shy and spoke in a high, breathless, feminine voice, so different from Andy, who became her fiancé. The hospital exercises undertaken by Saveen allowed him to switch between voices instantaneously.

Although best known for Daisy May, Saveen's cleverest act involved two dogs. One, a dummy, barked incessantly. When Saveen told it to be quiet, it replied in a posh voice: 'No. I won't.' It sniffed the other dog, which sat totally still. At the end of the act, the second dog opened a false lower jaw, operated by Saveen, and said, 'Why don't you shut that ruddy dog up?' It then jumped down and walked away, having been trained by Saveen to be absolutely motionless.

Arthur Worsley was the ventriloquist's ventriloquist. He knew he might trick audiences into believing his dummy, Charlie Brown, was real, but he occasionally fooled fellow professionals too. In a television studio, he might leave Charlie propped up in a corner. Then, out of the blue, Charlie would let out a stream of filthy language. A worried producer often turned to Arthur and asked, 'He's not going to say that on air, is he?' Again, at a television rehearsal, a sound recordist who was testing levels asked Arthur to move Charlie closer to the mike.

Arthur had a clever gimmick. He never [well, hardly ever] spoke. Charlie did all the talking. Arthur sat by his side, looking rather bored. It was as though Charlie had nothing to do with him. He did not even look at Charlie, leading one young fan to ask: Why does that tall man stand beside him? He does nothing at all.

Arthur Worsley [Arthur Wilkinson Worsley]

- Born Failsworth, Greater Manchester, 16 October 1920
- Married Audrey Mary Hewitt in Blackpool 10 January 1950
- Son, Michael
- Died Blackpool 14 July 2001

The son of a car dealer, Arthur began working as a vent as a child. At the age of 11, he made his stage debut with a second-hand dummy: the venue, the Casino in Manchester. Over the next three years, he earned an average of £12 [£400] a week by winning competitions. Aged 14, he was billed as the youngest professional ventriloquist in the world.

Throughout the act, Charlie hectored Arthur: 'Look at me when I'm talking to you,' a line Eric Morecambe was happy to admit he 'borrowed' when addressing Ernie Wise: 'Whatever you do, son, don't talk at the same time as me. You'll strangle yourself;' and, bearing in mind that vents find the consonant 'b' one of the hardest to say, he repeatedly challenged Arthur to say 'bottle of beer'. 'Go on. Say it. Say bottle of beer. Say it. Go on. Bottle of beer. Bottle of Beer.' As he continued, Charlie got louder and louder. Ventriloquism is most easily practised in a soft voice. To shout is one of the hardest skills to accomplish. The letter 'm' is another one that vents dislike, but Charlie relished reciting English place names from Manchester to Macclesfield, ending with a magnificently measured Melton Mowbray.

By the 1940s, Arthur was one of the highest paid acts in variety. He played ten seasons at the London Palladium; he was a favourite in cabaret at the Dorchester and the Savoy; he became well-known in Australia, New Zealand and South Africa; and he appeared again and again on the *Ed Sullivan Show* in America.

He loved appearing on television. For years, BBC TV mistrusted him. They were suspicious that Charlie's voice was recorded, but Arthur's advanced perfectionism allowed him no fear of close-ups. Offstage, Arthur was never controlled by Charlie. When he retired in 1981, he put Charlie in the attic and left him there.

There were no female ventriloquists in variety. At least, there were none of any note, but there were two male vents dressed as women. One was the exotically named Lydia Dreams, the stage persona of Walter Lambert, who worked mostly with at least two dummies, Old Hewitt and Sammy. Walter/Lydia is better known for having painted *Popularity*, a vast work depicting 231 people, many of them well-known music hall entertainers gathered at Poverty Corner, a spot near the southern end of Waterloo Bridge, where many agents had their offices. It can be seen at the Museum of London.

For about 15 years, from just before the Second World War until the early 1950s, most people thought Bobbie Kimber was a woman. It was front page news when the 'hoax' was revealed. As time went by, Bobbie began to wear female clothing both on and off stage. In fact, by the end of his life, he was calling himself Roberta.

Bobbie started out as an artist in an advertising agency and then worked as a publicity officer with a firm of duplicator manufacturers, but he was sacked from both jobs. He had been interested in ventriloquism since he was a boy and practised, at first, without a dummy, in front of a mirror. Although his father, a clerk, wanted him to have a steady job, he encouraged him by buying a ventriloquist's doll and even writing dialogue for him.

Bobbie began appearing at church socials and cricket club dinners and was often working four nights a week, earning much more than he would have got in a Monday-to-Friday job. He then heard about a theatrical agent who had an office in his home city of Birmingham. This was Bert Hurran, who also worked as a comedian. He agreed to represent Bobbie and advised him to acquire more patter from writers who advertised in *The Stage*.

Within a short time, Bobbie was working seven nights a week with the occasional date at a variety theatre. In 1938, Bobbie joined an alfresco concert party, the Troubador Follies, at Weston-super-Mare. Originally, the troupe was to have included a soubrette and a comedienne, but, as backstage facilities were rudimentary, the local authority insisted that the company should be all-male. The Follies' director, Will Godfrey, wanted some female involvement and, as Bobbie, then only 18, was the youngest member of the troupe, he was told he would have to appear in drag.

One night, during some confusion, Bobbie had to present his ventriloquist act as a woman. He felt ill-at-ease and dreaded Godfrey's reaction. To his surprise, Godfrey was elated. This was something new: a female ventriloquist, and that was how Bobbie was to appear from then on. A friend introduced him to the

Bobbie Kimber [Ronald Victor Kimberley]

- Born Edgbaston, Birmingham, 27 May 1920
- Married Janette Dorothy Atherton Blatchley [professionally known as Jan Wynne] at Folkestone, Kent, 20 October 1941 [She was born in Camberwell 19 February 1910 and died in Shoreditch on 2 September 1985]
- Daughter, Christine, born 23 January 1949
- Died Hackney, London, 8/9 April 1993

comic singer, Randolph Sutton, who foresaw a great future for him and fixed him a booking at the Woolwich Empire. Ran also came up with Bobbie's billing: It Speaks for Itself.

By June 1939, Bobbie's career had progressed by leaps and bounds. After a trial appearance at the Shepherd's Bush Empire, Oswald Stoll booked him for a tour and then Moss Empires took him on. In July, he made his first broadcast for Radio Luxembourg with Vic Oliver and Sybil Thorndike. The following month, he made his first television appearance from Alexandra Palace. In 1940, he appeared in his first West End season at the Prince of Wales Theatre, but, for the next five years, he was a soldier.

He was sent to a garrison just outside Folkestone, where his sergeant major, who was responsible for entertainment in the sergeants' mess, became his manager-cum-agent. He once appeared at the Hippodrome in Dover in a charity show organised by Evelyn Laye. On another occasion there, he found he had no soap and so asked at the dressing room next to his if he could borrow some. That is how he came to meet his future wife, Jan Wynne, who was appearing in a sketch with her father, Jack. [For several years, he had been heard on radio as the Cockney batman to Stanelli in *Stanelli's Bachelor Party*: 'More sandwiches, Mr Stanelli, sir?']

After the war, Jack Wynne's agent, Audrey Thacker, fixed Bobbie a week at the Nottingham Empire and his career was successfully resumed. In 1947, he was invited to appear on the Royal Variety show at the London Palladium, the first time a female impersonator had been selected. Billy Russell, a wonderful comic who always appeared, according to his bill matter, On Behalf of the Working Classes, was also on the bill. But the stars were Laurel and Hardy, who were given a mixed reception. They were supposed to follow Dolores Gray and Bill Johnson, who were appearing at the Coliseum, but heavy traffic delayed them. So, Stan and Ollie performed their sketch straight after Bobbie. Reviewers said they failed to make an impression because they followed a strong comedy act.

Bobbie also appeared at the Palladium as a supporting act for Danny Kaye. By now, though, he had gained some weight and was looking less glamorous and more matronly. While appearing at the Theatre Royal, Portsmouth, he was made cruelly aware of his girth when he heard two sailors discussing his act. The opinion of one was: I liked the fat tart with the dolls.

Bobbie realised he could no longer rely on merely being a novelty. He needed to concentrate on being a first-rate ventriloquist. Up to then, he had worked with two dummies, Jock and Eddie, but Billy Russell made him a new one, Augustus Peabody, but neither Bobbie nor his wife liked the look of him and he was left on top of a wardrobe for two years. Eventually, Bobbie found a character for him: a dim-witted Midlands lad with a deep, throaty chuckle, who gently mocked Bobbie and laughed at his own jokes:

Hello, Gussie.
Hello, Miss Kimber. I say! You're getting fat.
I beg your pardon.
I said you're getting fat.
Let me tell you, that in the best places, they say 'plump'.
Alright. You're getting plump in the best places.[322]

It was a clever characterisation. Gussie enjoyed his own jokes so much that he kept returning to them. Every time, he got a bigger laugh than when he cracked the gag first.

During 1952, Bobbie regularly appeared on television so that, for the first time in his life, when he appeared in a theatre, he walked on stage to a round of applause. His fans had always harboured suspicions about his true sex. After all, he regularly imitated the cartoon sailor, Popeye, and sang a song in Popeye's deep gruff tones. Towards the end of 1952, he decided he should disclose his real sex.

The *Daily Mirror* splashed a story headed 'Biggest BBC Hoax Is Out', revealing that Bobbie, 'a full-bosomed creature with a plunging neckline … and shoulder length hair', was a man. 'I've been working as a woman ventriloquist since before the war. Most of the people booking me knew my real sex, but they kept my secret.'[323]

Most people in variety had known for at least four years. In January 1949, *The Performer* reported that Jan Wynne had given birth to a daughter. The press stressed the 'normality' of Bobbie: 'a strapping six-footer weighing about 14 stone … He has to take Mrs Kimber's advice about make-up … She even goes along with him to have clothes fitted.'[324]

Bobbie retired in the 1960s. He had no savings and so decided to become the licensee in succession of two pubs. This was not an ideal choice of profession as, by then, Jan was virtually an alcoholic and Bobbie almost matched her glass for glass. He then worked as a lorry driver and a bus driver, but hated both jobs. He longed to get back into show business. He worked in the northern clubs and even suffered the ignominy of appearing on the television amateur talent show, *Opportunity Knocks*. He failed to win, claiming that the clapometer, a device that measured the volume of the audience's applause, was not working properly.

Bobbie craved publicity. In the mid-1960s, he announced that he had had a sex change. A Sunday tabloid newspaper ran the story three weeks running.

Certainly, he was by then living as a woman and dressed as a woman for the rest of his life:

> I was blatantly doing the very thing I had carefully avoided for many years – taking the masquerade to extremes outside the theatre for considerable periods of time. I was becoming a freak and I began to be aware of the distaste created among people who had been aware of my real sex for many years. An occasional sortie in skirts could be accepted, but to be constantly attired as a woman and to expect them to treat me as one was an affront to their personal dignity.[325]

When Jan died in 1985, she was described on her death certificate as the wife of Roberta Kimber and, when Bobbie himself died eight years later, his name was given as Roberta Kimberley, otherwise Roberta Kimber, formally known as Ronald Victor Kimberley. On his death-bed, it was discovered he had not had a sex change.

Billy Russell, incidentally, worked until the very end. He had been booked to appear in a play with Michael Gambon for Yorkshire Television. The cast were having a coffee before the first read-through when someone noticed that Billy had gone quiet. He had not touched his coffee. In fact, he had died. Gambon commented later: A great judge of a script, Billy.

CHAPTER TWENTY FOUR

Two of a Kind

Doubling Up: Flotsam and Jetsam, Jewel and Warriss, Layton and Johnstone, Bob and Alf Pearson, Mike and Bernie Winters, Morecambe and Wise, the Two Leslies, the Western Brothers

The phenomenally successful television career of Morecambe and Wise, arguably the best loved British comic double act of all time, has been written about endlessly. These were, after all, two men whose Christmas shows attracted as many as 28 million viewers, but they were no overnight sensation. They first appeared as a double act in 1941 when they were 15. It took another 20 years to reach the top.

It was not even their idea to work together. That was the suggestion of Eric Morecambe's formidable mother, Sadie. In later years, she was fond of saying that, as a boy, Eric was a born entertainer. Apparently, he used to sneak out of the house, find a building site and entertain the men there with such songs as *Blue Moon* and *I'm Dancing with Tears in my Eyes*. Sadie took on extra work to pay for Eric to have dancing lessons. Together, they invented a routine for him and he earned his first fee at a working men's club. Sadie also bought the sheet music of a song made famous by the male impersonator, Ella Shields, *I'm Not All There*, and put together the costume she thought Eric ought to wear while singing it: a black beret, tortoiseshell spectacles, a bootlace tie over a white shirt, a tight jacket, pinstripe trousers, suspenders, red socks and black shoes. Week after week, Eric went from club to club singing a song he hated.

Early in 1939, Sadie entered Eric for a talent contest at a cinema at Hoylake near Birkenhead. The winner had the chance to be auditioned by Jack Hylton. Eric won and travelled to Manchester, one of the venues of Hylton's latest touring show.

There, he met another Northern lad, Ernest Wiseman, whose father, a railway porter, enjoyed performing song and dance routines at local clubs. At the age of six, Ernie began to learn such songs as *The Sheikh of Araby* and rehearse them endlessly. Aged seven, he teamed up with his father in a novelty double act. Together, they sang *It Happened on the Beach at Bali Bali*. On his own, Ernie had a repertoire that included *Let's have a Tiddley at the Milk Bar*.

Four years later, Ernie began taking part in amateur revues and was spotted by the impresario, Brian Michie, who was touring the north in search of young talent. At an audition at the Leeds Empire, Ernie told some jokes, sang *I'm*

Eric Morecambe [John Eric Bartholomew]

- Born Morecambe, Lancashire, 14 May 1926
- Married Joan Bartlett in Margate, Kent, 11 December 1952
- Daughter, Gail, born 1953
- Son, Gary, born 1956
- Son, Steven, adopted 1973
- Eric Morecambe died Cheltenham, Gloucestershire, 28 May 1984

Ernie Wise [Ernest Wiseman]

- Born Leeds 27 November 1925
- Married Doreen Blythe 18 January 1953
- Ernie Wise died Wexham, Berkshire, 21 March 1999

Knee Deep in Daisies and finished with a spirited clog dance. Several months elapsed before Ernie heard not from Michie, but from Hylton, who invited him to London. The result of the meeting was that Ernie joined Hylton's revue, *Band Waggon*, adapted from Arthur Askey's BBC Radio show. Ernie made a tremendous hit. One reviewer praised his timing and confidence: 'at 13, he is an old time performer.'[326]

From that moment, Hylton became Ernie's mentor. He gave him a five-year contract, starting at £6 [£170] a week, moved him into a central London flat and found him a chaperone. When *Band Waggon* closed, Ernie joined Hylton's band on tour and sat in on the audition Eric had in Manchester.

Both boys joined Michie's touring revue, *Youth Takes a Bow*, and became good friends. In time, Sadie, who travelled with Eric, became a surrogate mother to Ernie. Travelling from theatre to theatre, the boys told jokes, sang songs and impersonated other acts in the show. At first, Sadie enjoyed their boisterous behaviour, but there were times when she gritted her teeth.

In November 1940, the show reached Coventry, which had just suffered extensive enemy bombing. Each day, all three had to travel from Birmingham as the digs they had booked in Coventry had been flattened. The journey was often disrupted by damage caused by the bombing and one night, despairing of the endless antics of Eric and Ernie, Sadie suggested a better way of spending their time:

Have you ever tried travelling with two 15-year-old discoveries in a compartment in the blackout with both of them super-charged with adrenalin after a show? … In sheer despair one night, I said, 'Now, look, instead of all this malarkey, why don't you put your brains to some use? Try and do a double act of your own. All you need are a few fresh jokes and a song.'[327]

They agreed and made their debut together when *Youth Takes a Bow* reached the Liverpool Empire. By 1941, they had enough material to fill a seven-minute act, but then poor box office takings forced Hylton to close the show. They were without work until an agent suggested they went to the London Hippodrome, where George Black was holding auditions for a new show, *Strike a New Note*. George, who lived close to Hylton at Angmering-on-Sea in Sussex, already knew Ernie and he agreed to take both boys on, not as a double act, but working separately. All went well until they received their call-up papers.

Ernie joined the Merchant Navy, becoming a cook on ships taking coal from Newcastle to the Battersea power station. Eric was sent to the mines, but lasted less than a year. Heart trouble was diagnosed and he was discharged. Once he was well again, he went to work at a factory that made razor blades. Ernie took a number of short-term variety engagements during the war, billed as the Boy from the Brave Merchant Navy, and was discharged in 1945.

Oddly, there is more than one version about how they met again. Suffice to say they found work as a double act in another touring show. When it ended prematurely near the end of 1947, they were out of work until Vivian Van Damm booked them for the Windmill. They lasted a week.

In the six shows on Monday, starting at noon, we died six times. We stepped onto the apron of the stage to face not just a reluctant audience, but an audience with the concentrated hate of a lynch mob. Not one polite snicker met our collection of banal jokes.[328]

The jokes were banal, too. Before Associated Television and BBC Television paid for them to have top writers, the gags of Morecambe and Wise competed with mottoes in Christmas crackers for their banality: 'What's that?' 'A hanger.' 'What's it for?' 'An aeroplane.'[329] Eric and Ernie were then booked for two appearances each night in another nude revue, *Fig Leaves and Apple Sauce*, at the Grand in Clapham. As they had only 12 minutes of material, they had just enough time to write themselves a second turn. In the event, they were saved by a routine they had used before, Eric teaching Ernie how to sing *The [Woody] Woodpecker Song*.

But, in about 1950, Ernie decided he wanted to dissolve the act. He wrote to Eric, mysteriously saying that he was suffering a terrific amount of animosity at home and adding: I can't go on the way things are. According to Eric's son, Gary, Eric replied immediately saying he had never heard such rubbish. He advised Ernie to have a few days' rest and then get back to work.

After appearing on BBC Radio's *Workers' Playtime*, Eric and Ernie were invited to be guests on *Variety Fanfare*, transmitted by the BBC's North of England Home Service. It was produced by Ronnie Taylor, who gave them their first radio series, *You're Only Young Once*, in 1953. It was successful enough for them to be offered their first television series, *Running Wild*, which was also produced in Manchester. It was a huge flop.

Fortunately, television was then a comparatively rare medium in northern England and Eric and Ernie were able to return to their stage work largely unscathed. In 1961, they were offered a second television series, this time by Lew Grade's Associated Television. *Two of a Kind* was scripted by two brilliant writers, Dick Hills and Sid Green,[330] the first to understand how to make the best of Morecambe and Wise. Within two years, the show was second only to *Coronation Street* in the ratings. Grade offered them a second series, but Ernie felt the money was not good enough and they returned to the BBC, where they were teamed with Ken Dodd's former writer, Eddie Braben.

Then, the golden age began. The Morecambe and Wise Christmas shows became the highlight of the television year. Big names clamoured to be guests. Vanessa Redgrave played Josephine to Ernie's Napoleon; Shirley Bassey sang in size ten boots; and, best of all, Andre Previn rounded on Eric for playing all the wrong notes in Grieg's piano concerto. The riposte: I'm playing all the right notes, but not necessarily in the right order.

At one time, Jewel and Warriss were as corny as Morecambe and Wise, but, although they became big stars, they never properly succeeded in television. The BBC was pleased enough with their radio series, *Up the Pole,*[331] which ran from 1947 to 1952, but, apart from two television series [*Turn It Up* in 1951 and *Re-Turn It Up* in 1953], the Beeb did not consider them good enough to grant them all the facilities lavished on Morecambe and Wise. One factor that hampered their career was that Val Parnell did not rate them. He thought that Jimmy was a funny and versatile performer, but he felt that Ben was a poor straight man. All the same, Jimmy and Ben topped variety bills all over Britain, starred in pantomime and even had the lead cartoon strip in the children's comic, *Radio Fun.*

Jimmy was the traditional funny man. He wore baggy trousers and behaved gormlessly. Ben wore sharp suits, thought quickly and spoke fast. They were, in fact, cousins, born in the same bed in Sheffield within six months of each other. Their mothers were sisters. Jimmy's father wrote and produced touring revues. At first, Jimmy worked backstage, helping to make the sets and scenery and loading them on to horse drays and then into railway trucks en route for provincial theatres up and down the country. It was in a revue called *Explosions*, which opened at the Hippodrome in the Yorkshire town of Mexborough in 1925, that he decided he wanted to be a performer. Ben was also in the show, playing a miner's son, but, to save money, he was sacked and the part was given to Jimmy. Ben's dismissal caused a family rift that lasted for years.

With Jimmy now a professional, his father decided he needed proper tuition. A circus act coached him in somersaults and other acrobatics and an old friend of his father, Henry Vale, taught him tap, soft shoe and clog dancing. [Henry was something of a character. He carried everything he owned in a brown paper parcel and could fart to the tune of *Bye Bye Blackbird*].

Ben's parents were also in show business. Each week, he travelled with them from theatre to theatre and, in five years, attended 167 different schools. At the age of 11, he appeared in *Babes in the Wood* on the Palace Pier in Brighton and then developed an act in which he blacked up and did impressions. In 1934,

Jimmy and Ben found themselves appearing at the same theatre, the Palace in Newcastle. One night, a double act failed to turn up. So, Ben told the theatre's manager that he and Jimmy could do an extra spot together. They were booked for a revue, *Revels of 1934*, at a wage of £14 [£500] a week and went on a tour of Australia. They returned to Britain to tour for Moss Empires. They did so well they sought a rise to £35 [£1,200] a week. When this was refused, they terminated their contract. Not long after, Moss Empires thought again and were soon employing them at £100 [£3,500] a week.

Jimmy Jewel [James Arthur Thomas Jewel Marsh]

- Born Sheffield 4 December 1909
- Married Belle Bluett at Southend-on-Sea, Essex, 31 August 1939 [died 1985]
- Son, Kerry, born 1947
- Adopted daughter in 1955. Christened Piper in 1956.
- Jimmy Jewel died London 3 December 1995

Ben Warriss [Ben Holden Driver Warriss]

- Born Sheffield 29 May 1909
- Married [1] Grace Mary Skinner in Kent 22 September 1934 [dissolved]
- Married [2] Meggie Eaton in Marylebone, London, 22 May 1949 [dissolved]
- Married [3] Virginia Vernon, also known as Virginia Dixon, in west London 4 November 1964
- Son and two daughters
- Ben Warriss died Twickenham 14 January 1993

Theirs was a very physical, offbeat type of comedy. In one sketch, Jimmy needed a pen that could write under water. Ben, the forceful salesman, submerges him in a tank. Each time Jimmy came up for air, he was pushed back down again. After proving that the pen could work, Jimmy was bundled into an incinerator to see if it could write at 750 degrees Fahrenheit.

During the 1940s, Jimmy and Ben twice topped the bill at the London Palladium, starred in five pantomimes in Blackpool, and appeared in a Royal Variety Show. In 1950/51, they were the stars of the Palladium pantomime, *Babes in the Wood*. After the dress rehearsal, Val Parnell told them that he thought everything was right about the show, except Ben, who pulled funny faces all the time. On the last night of the panto, Ben could not appear as he had damaged his foot. Jimmy went on with an understudy and got more laughs than he had had for years. In his dressing room afterwards, Val Parnell's wife, Aileen,[332] urged Jimmy to split from Ben. In a restaurant a few nights later, Val said the same. Jimmy refused. He would not do anything that would upset Ben.

Four years later, the issue arose again. Jimmy and Ben were due to play the London Hippodrome, but the show was cancelled because the backer withdrew his money. Val told Jimmy he was glad because he did not think they were right for the West End. He had seen them recently at the Finsbury Park Empire:

[Ben] is paying no attention to you on stage. He's gagging. He's mugging. He's talking to the orchestra. He's talking to the people at the side of the stage. It wouldn't be right for you to come into the West End under those conditions. You come in on your own by all means because there's nothing you can't do. You sing. You dance. You do pathos. You should leave him.[333]

Again, Jimmy ignored the advice. By the time their television series finished, it was clear that their style and some of their material had not perceptibly changed for 25 years.

In 1967, Jimmy learned that Ben wanted to finish the act:

He wrote that he was buying a restaurant and that he wouldn't accept any more work as Jewel and Warriss ... I couldn't believe it. He lived just round the corner. Yet he hadn't come to see me. He hadn't even phoned. He had terminated the Jewel and Warriss partnership by letter. I was ill for a week.[334]

At first, Ben was happy with his restaurant, but the greasepaint still lured. He compéred a variety show in Blackpool and put together an hour-long solo routine. He also turned 'legitimate', taking the lead in John Osborne's play, *The Entertainer*. Jimmy did rather better. Apart from his television shows with the impossible Hylda Baker, he appeared in Arthur Miller's *Death of a Salesman* and Trevor Griffiths' *Comedians*, a brilliant analysis of class, politics and popular entertainment. At the Piccadilly Theatre in 1975, he teamed up with Alfred Marks for Neil Simon's comedy *The Sunshine Boys*, all about a comic double act who, over the course of 40-odd years, grew to hate each other:

In the play, I am asked why we stayed together for so long and I say 'Why? Because he was terrific. There will never be another one like him. Nobody could tell a joke the way he told it. Nobody could say a line the way he said it. He knew what I was thinking and I knew what he was thinking. One person we were.' Neil Simon could have written that play for Ben and me.[335]

Two brothers, Mike and Bernie Winters, born Weinstein, started out in very different ways. Mike went to the Royal Academy of Music to study the clarinet. Bernie worked as a salesman, while appearing by night as a stand-up comic in dance halls. In time, he became a 'pro', but enjoyed little success until he teamed up with Mike in 1949. Their father wanted them to be a comedy double act and he was a man who made sure he had his way. This was Samuel Weinstein, known to everyone as Pougie, a Russian word for 'naughty boy'. He once punched a huge navvy in the jaw for making anti-Semitic remarks and, when

Mike Winters [Michael Weinstein]

- Born Islington, North London, 15 November 1926
- Married Cathelene Mary Chaney in Kensington, West London, 21 October 1955
- Daughter, Chani

Bernie Winters [Bernard Weinstein]

- Born Islington, North London, 6 September 1930
- Married Sigrid Heine in London 28 February 1958
- Son, Raymond, born November 1961
- Bernie Winters died 4 May 1991
- Left £149,051 [£210,000]

a contract Mike and Bernie had signed proved useless, he went to their agent's office and 'persuaded' him to remove the contract from his safe and tear it into small pieces.

In their act, Mike was the straight man, always sharply dressed, and Bernie played the idiot, wearing clothes several sizes too large for him and pulling stupid faces. They teamed up just as the variety theatre was beginning to die. In the early 1950s, they split up several times to try to find other ways of earning a living, but they always ended up giving show business another try.

They made their first television appearance in 1955 and thought they had hit the big time two years later when they became resident comics on *Six Five Special*, BBC Television's first attempt at a rock show. The show was a hit, but they were not.

In 1959, the act broke up again. The movie mogul, Cubby Broccoli, had offered Bernie a five-year film contract worth £100,000 [£1.5 million]. Bernie promised Mike half his earnings, but Mike felt betrayed and deeply hurt. Bernie made four films, *Jazz Boat*, *In the Nick* and *Let's Get Married*, all with Anthony Newley,[336] and *Johnnie Nobody*, which Bernie called 'a complete embarrassment'.[337] But the contract was not all that it seemed and, in 1960, the double act was resumed. Over the next few years, Mike and Bernie became very popular on television with many series on ITV. But as *The Times* put it:

> They purveyed a boisterous, unsubtle form of humour with the emphasis on knockabout, rather than verbal wit … Their material was often not regarded as particularly original and their strength lay more in their presentation and comic timing.[338]

In spite of their success, Mike and Bernie began to grow apart. They disagreed about everything and both knew the final split was in sight. They delayed separating until after Pougie had died as they felt the split would break his heart. In fact, they kept going for another three years. Pougie died in 1975. Mike and Bernie made their last appearances together in a summer season at Sandown on the Isle of Wight in 1978. On the last night, Mike walked off to the left and Bernie to the right.

Mike moved to Florida to become a businessman and for years he and Bernie refused to speak to each other. Bernie proved successful on his own. He made his debut as an actor, playing Bud Flanagan in *Bud 'n' Ches*, a television play about Flanagan and Allen. Throughout the 1980s, he was frequently seen on television panel games, usually with an 11-stone St Bernard dog called Schnorbitz. In 1990, he contracted cancer, but, after an operation in which much of his stomach was removed, he returned to the stage to play Widow Twankey in a six-week run of *Aladdin* at a theatre in Basildon, appearing in up to three shows a day. Before he died, he and Mike were reconciled.

When Mike and Bernie were still toddlers, one of the most popular double acts in Britain was the Two Leslies, who sang comic songs, nonsense songs and happy feel-good songs, ideal material for the 1930s. Leslie Sarony and Leslie Holmes teamed up in 1935, Holmes playing the piano and singing with a broad smile, while the diminutive, energetic Sarony also sang and danced around the piano. Legendarily misanthropic, Sarony told anyone prepared to listen that, when he saw Holmes beaming at him across the piano, he wanted to hit him in the mouth.

Leslie Sarony [Leslie Legge Frye]

- [His mother's maiden name was Sarony]
- Born Surbiton, Surrey, 22 January 1897
- Married Anita Eaton in London 3 April 1939 [dissolved] [At his wedding, he called himself Leslie Sarony Frye]
- Leslie Sarony died London 12 February 1985

Leslie Holmes

- Born Newcastle 14 December 1901
- Married Joan Barrop in Liverpool 23 March 1940
- Leslie Holmes died in Hove, Sussex, 27 December 1960

Both men had established themselves individually before they formed their double act. Sarony had written many songs, including *Jollity Farm* and *I Lift up my Finger [and I say 'Tweet, Tweet'*] [both 1929]; *When the Guards are on Parade* [with Horatio Nicholls] and *Rhymes* [both 1931]; the grimly black *Ain't it Grand to be Blooming Well Dead?* [1932]; and *Wheezy Anna* [1933].

Sarony made his mark before the First World War, appearing in the revue, *Hullo, Tango*, at the London Hippodrome in 1913. After the Great War, in which he saw service in the Somme, he opted for a career in show business. He made his first dance band recordings with Teddy Brown in 1926 and went on to record for almost every label in Britain under his own name and many pseudonyms. He was intensely proud of having appeared in the original London production of *Show Boat*. He sang two great songs that have since become standards, *Make Believe* and *Why Do I Love You?*

Two years later, Sarony began a long tour throughout Britain and continental Europe with Jack Hylton's band and produced one of his greatest successes, *Rhymes*, a vocal setting of limericks. Sarony's gimmick was to omit the last line, allowing his audience to supply their most inventive and possibly most louche suggestions. His recording of *Rhymes* sold nearly 250,000 copies and remained Decca's biggest seller until Vera Lynn's *Auf Wiederseh'n, Sweetheart* 20 years later.

The question put most frequently to music hall researchers is 'How can I get hold of a song called *She Sits among the Cabbage and Peas*?' It was even the subject of a question on *University Challenge*. The teams were asked who had sung it, the answer being Marie Lloyd. One standard work on music hall song lists it as part of the repertoire of Bessie Bellwood, although without attribution. In fact, there was no such song. It was a line in a Sarony song, *Mucking about the Garden*. Aware of the controversy, Sarony registered the composer as Q. Cumber

---

As a child, Leslie Holmes taught himself to play piano and drums, but he began his professional life as a drapery assistant. From there, he moved into wholesale grocery; then he worked in an estate agent's; and after that he became a traveller in the millinery business. But he continued playing the piano and in 1920 obtained his first professional work with a band in a restaurant in Newcastle.

When his family moved to Manchester, he formed his own band at Cholrton's Palais de Danse, where he was seen by the Musical Director of London Midland Scottish Hotels, Henry Hall, who was impressed by Leslie's drumming and cheerful personality. Leslie made his first recordings with Henry Hall in 1925, but the following year, after suffering from depression that left him doubting whether he would succeed in the entertainment business, he moved to London to become a full-time representative for Peak Frean Biscuits.

Here he would have stayed had not the song publishers, Jimmy Campbell and Reg Connelly, asked him to run their newly-established office in Manchester. He was back in show business and, once they teamed up, it was clear that Holmes' repertoire included the sort of song favoured by Sarony: *Who's been Polishing the Sun? What can you Give a Nudist for her Birthday?* and *When it's Thursday in Egypt [it's Half Past Three in Spain]*.

The Two Leslies went their separate ways in 1946. Holmes became the publicity manager of the *News of the World*. Over Christmas 1960, there was a family row about his son's girlfriend. The following day, Holmes' wife found him dead in bed with a box of sleeping tablets by his side. The coroner recorded a verdict of death by misadventure, adding that Holmes may have mistaken the number of tablets he swallowed as he had been drinking.

After the separation, Sarony teamed up with a new partner, Michael Cole, for three years, but then reverted to being a solo performer. He turned 'legit', appearing in *As You Like It* and Samuel Beckett's *Endgame*. In 1979, at the suggestion of Roy Hudd, he returned to the studios to re-record 14 of his best-known songs. Aged 82 and sounding exactly as he had in the 1930s, he taped all 14 numbers in just one take each.

Flotsam and Jetsam were rather more urbane. They sang witty, sometimes topical songs that Flotsam, B.C. Hilliam, wrote. Their voices were in strict contrast, Jetsam, Malcolm McEachern, a basso profundo with a background in opera, Flotsam, a higher, more penetrating voice. All was explained in their short introductory song, which, by the time their 19-year-old career finished, they had sung more than 15,000 times:

> We'll tell you our names
> In case someone forgets 'em.
> I'm Jetsam. [I'm Flotsam].
> He's Flotsam. [I'm Jetsam].
>
> I sing all the low notes.
> [You'd wonder how he gets 'em].
> At the keyboard is Flotsam.
> So, I must be Jetsam.[339]

In his youth, Hilliam had a range of jobs: as a cub reporter in Bradford, he was the last journalist to interview the Victorian actor, Sir Henry Irving; he sang songs he had written and played the piano at hotels in Devon; and he had six weeks' work on a paper in Norwich, for which he drew cartoons of election candidates.

His parents separated when he was 15 and, when a neighbour, who had moved to Canada, sent back glowing accounts of life there, he and his mother crossed the Atlantic. Again, he found

Flotsam and Jetsam

work on a newspaper; he accompanied silent films at a cinema; he formed a double act with Hugh Aitchison Green, the father of the television presenter, Hughie Green; and he moved to New York, where he wrote two musicals. One evening, he went to Lambs theatre club, where McEachern asked for someone to accompany him in two songs, *The Floral Dance* and *In Cellar Cool*. Hilliam volunteered and the couple were greatly acclaimed.

McEachern, who was born in Australia, became the choirmaster at his local church and won two important singing competitions. At one point, he worked as a biscuit salesman, but, when he was 30, he met a young pianist, who helped him to begin a career in music. In time, he toured with the operatic soprano, Dame Nellie Melba. He arrived in London in 1921 and sang at the Albert Hall and at most music festivals throughout Britain. Five years later, Hilliam returned to Britain and, spotting an advertisement for McEachern at Queen's Hall, he went along. The two men had not seen each other for six years and, when they performed at a party, they were so well received that they were invited by Moss Empires to sing together in public.

B.C. Hilliam [Bentley Collingwood Hilliam]

- Born Scarborough 6 November 1890
- Married [1] Eleanor Young [dissolved]
- Married [2] Mona Constance Barrett Lennard in Lambeth, South London, 11 December 1926
- Daughter, Nancy Joan, born 16 April 1927
- B.C. Hilliam died Friern Barnet 19 December 1968

Malcolm McEachern [Walter Malcolm Neil McEachern]

- Born Albany, New South Wales, 1883
- Married Hazel Doyle 1916
- Son, Robert, killed in action 15 April 1945
- Malcolm McEachern died London 17 January 1945
- Left £2,978 [£75,000]

At the Victoria Palace, they soon realised that their real names were too unwieldy to appear on posters. They mulled over a number of choices: Mr Ebb and Mr Flow, Mr Null and Mr Void, even Mr Higgledy and Mr Piggledy. They eventually plumped for Flotsam and Jetsam. Hilliam wrote their signature tune and they sang it for the first time that night. They also broadcast for the first time in 1926 and became noted for their news bulletins, sung in verse. At five in the afternoon, Hilliam settled himself in the Langham Hotel opposite Broadcasting House and ran his eye over the evening papers. He then wrote a song, McEachern joined him and two-and-half hours later they sang it on the radio.

Between 1926 and 1945, Flotsam and Jetsam appeared at the London Coliseum, the Alhambra and at most London and suburban music halls. There was no contract between them, merely a gentleman's agreement, and they divided their responsibilities neatly. McEachern dealt with all business matters, deciding how much they should be paid and where they would appear without Hilliam having any say. For his part, Hilliam was to provide all their material and control their publicity without the intervention of McEachern. Of all their songs, *Little Betty Bouncer* proved to be their most durable:

> Little Betty Bouncer loves an announcer down at the BBC.
> She doesn't know his name, but how she rejoices,
> When she hears that voice of voices.
> Absolutely tireless, sitting at the wireless. Poor little Miss B.
> It's the man who announces with a lot of passion in it
> 'The Daventry shipping forecast will follow in a minute.'
> Little Betty Bouncer loves an announcer down at the BBC.

The partnership of Flotsam and Jetsam continued successfully until their last broadcast on 5 January 1945. Twelve days later, McEachern died after an operation.

Two upper-class coves wearing monocles and permanently disdainful expressions were the stage personae of the Western Brothers. They were 'the young [men] about town, raffish, unscrupulous, cynical, but, in reality, harmlessly good-natured [and] descended from a long line of knuts and mashers'[340] as *The Times* put it.

George Western [Ernest George Western]

- Born London 23 July 1895
- Married Irene Lilian Palmer in Edmonton, north London, 21 October 1922 [She died 25 December 1956]
- Three children, Pamela born 1926, Robert 1932 and Patricia 1933
- George Western died Weybridge, Surrey, 16 August 1969

Kenneth Western [Kenneth Alfred Western]

- Born London 10 September 1899
- Married Beatrice Florence Crowley in Islington, North London, 14 June 1924
- Four daughters, Joyce, Jill, Judith and Jane
- Kenneth Western died Bedford 24 January 1963
- Left £6,232 [£81,250]

The real Kenneth and George Western, not brothers, in fact, but cousins, could not have been more different. They came from ordinary families and were educated at secondary schools. They formed their act in 1925 and poked gentle fun at the trappings of the public school [their motto: Adsum Ard Labor], the BBC [two of their songs were *We're Frightfully BBC* and *No-one to Read out the News*] and, during the Second World War, the Germans [*Lord Haw-Haw, the Humbug of Hamburg*].[341] Kenneth wrote the music and George the lyrics of more than 400 songs. At the peak of their fame, they were earning £400 a week from the variety theatre and the BBC.

Forty years after they separated, all their recordings were transferred to a CD issued by the leading music hall expert, Tony Barker, on his Cylidisc label. It also has the Western Brothers in unconventional style in a song they wrote and recorded with the Billy Cotton band, *She Was Only Somebody's Daughter*: 'She was only a Corporal's daughter, but now she's an Officers' Mess' and 'She was only a bookie's daughter, but she came home at five to four.'

On film, the Western Brothers could be seen in the cinema adaptation of *Mr Cinders* [1934]; the *Radio Parade of 1935*, in which they briefly appeared as two weather forecasters; *Soft Lights and Sweet Music* [1936], described as a musical revue starring Ambrose and his Orchestra; and *Old Bones of the River* [1938].

During the 1940s, the Western Brothers' popularity declined. Kenneth once said: Old school ties have lost their point since they gave away the Empire. After Kenneth died, George ran a kiosk on Weybridge railway station.

Bob and Alf Pearson, who were real brothers, worked together for an amazing 57 years. They sang all sorts of songs, always introduced by their short signature tune: We bring you melodies from out of the sky, my brother and I. They recorded *Tears* 20 years before Ken Dodd made it his own and performed *Walkin' My Baby Back Home* 30 years before the gay American heart-throb, Johnnie Ray, sobbed his way through it.

They inherited their musicianship from their mother, a contralto, who sang under her delightful maiden name, Emily Smiles. Their father was a builder and they began their working lives as plasterers. In their spare time, they appeared with amateur concert parties in and around their home town, Sunderland, but, when their father won a big contract to work on houses being built on the Kingston bypass, the family moved to Surrey. They continued to fulfil engagements and made their first broadcast for the BBC from Savoy Hill in 1929.

Then, Emily entered them for a talent contest. The first prize was a recording contract with Columbia Records. They sang *Ol' Man River* and *Singing in the Rain* and won. At the time, a rather more famous double act, Layton and Johnstone, were two of Columbia's star recording artists and so they were handed over to a subsidiary label, Regal Zonophone:

We went to see the recording manager and he put on a record of two Americans … They were singing in thirds all the way through, even when it clashed with the harmonies in the music. He said, 'That's the way I want you to sing. The people who buy our records are people who eat fish and chips and that's

Bob Pearson [Robert Alexander Pearson]

- Born Sunderland 15 August 1907
- Married Vera Pauline Johnson [1905 – 1993] in Sunderland 8 June 1932
- Son
- Bob Pearson died 30 November 1985

Alf Pearson [Alfred Vernon Pearson]

- Born Sunderland 5 June 1910 [Bob married, but Alf remained single. 'My brother's wife, Vera, wasn't very open to the idea of there being another lady. I liked the company of girls and girls liked me as well. But Vera didn't want another lady in with Bob and Alf Pearson.'
- Shortly before she died, Alf's two sisters took him to visit her in a home. 'When I walked into the room, Vera took one look at me and said, "What do you want? Get out!" My sisters said, "Well, if that's what she wants, perhaps you'd better go." That was the last time I saw her. It was funny, wasn't it?']342
- Alf Pearson celebrated his centenary on 5 June 2010

what they sing and that's what they want to hear.' I said, 'Well, you can get someone else,' and that was the end of our connection with Columbia.343

Not long after, the music publisher, Bert Feldman, heard them and was sufficiently impressed to concoct an effective publicity stunt. They were asked to see Bert's manager, Frank Ruebens, and were told he would have 'something for them'. When they arrived, they found a room packed with journalists alongside Jack Hylton. The press were told that Ruebens had heard two plasterers singing while they were working and was so struck by their talent that he introduced them to Hylton, who was going to sign them up with his band. Nearly every paper carried the story and Bob and Alf were on their way to fame. They took a show round all the major theatres, they played summer seasons in Blackpool, they had their own television series and they were featured in Ted Ray's hugely successful radio series, *Ray's a Laugh*. In it, Bob was also heard playing a young girl named Jennifer.

In 1985, Bob and Alf were guests on Harry Secombe's television show, *Highway*, singing their last medley together, *Kiss Me Goodnight, Sergeant Major, I've Got Sixpence* and *It's a Lovely Day Tomorrow*. Bob died ten weeks later.

Before they hit the big time, Bob and Alf realised that their style was close to that of the honey-voiced black American act, Layton and Johnstone. In fact, they even considered trying to become Britain's Layton and Johnstone. One week, all four were appearing in Cardiff. Johnstone invited them to see him. He told them that, in his view, there would never be another Layton and Johnstone and added: We have our personality and you have yours.

Layton and Johnstone oozed sophistication. They were immaculately dressed and their voices blended superbly, one soft, the other somewhat harder. With Layton's thoughtful piano accompaniment, they turned apparently ordinary little ditties into songs of great appeal. There were no announcements and no gimmicks and, long before the introduction of microphones, they could be heard perfectly in all parts of even the largest theatres.

Turner Layton's place in the history of popular music was ensured even before he met Clarence Johnstone. The son of a Washington music teacher, he and Henry Creamer formed a vaudeville act in which they sang their own songs, including *After You've Gone* [1918], made popular by Sophie Tucker and *Way Down Yonder in New Orleans* [1922], which became a dance number in a Fred Astaire and Ginger Rogers movie.

Turner Layton [John Turner Layton]

- Born Washington 2 July 1894
- Married Emma Lee November 1915
- One daughter, Alelia
- Turner Layton died London 4 February 1978
- Left £32,940 [£124,000]

Clarence Johnstone [Clarence Nathaniel Johnstone]

- Born [?]
- Married [1] Raymonde Gilberte Defly Sandler
- Married [2]
- Clarence Johnstone died New York 21 September 1953

Clarence Johnstone, known as Tandy, was a qualified orthopaedic surgeon. Both he and Layton worked for the blues composer, W.C. Handy, and, when they were booked separately to appear at the same function, they decided to form a double act. During a season in Florida in 1923, an agent booked them for a show in which the American 'forces' sweetheart' Elsie Janis was to star at the Queen's Theatre in London in June 1924. Later, the Prince of Wales, the future Edward VIII, heard their act and was full of praise. When they appeared at the Café de Paris, a representative of Columbia Records signed them up on the back of a menu. They began recording for Columbia in December 1924 and, between 1925 and 1935, they sold over ten million records. Among the most popular were *It Ain't Gonna Rain no Mo'* [1923], *Bye Bye Blackbird* [1926], performed rather more classily than Jimmy Jewel's dance teacher, and *River Stay 'Way from my Door* [1931].

Temperamentally, Layton and Johnstone were very different men. Layton enjoyed the quiet life with an occasional round of golf. The profligate Johnstone lived the high life. Towards the end, they refused to speak to each other.

The act came to grief when Johnstone had an affair with the exotically named Raymonde Gilberte Defly Sandler, the wife of the Palm Court violinist, Albert Sandler, whose orchestra broadcast every Sunday evening from the Grand Hotel, Eastbourne. The pair eloped to America and, when Sandler[344] sued for divorce, he won substantial damages.

Layton then pursued a successful solo career with a regular spot at the Café de Paris. He retired in 1946. Johnstone, who married Mrs Sandler, but later divorced her, became a janitor at a block of flats in poor area of New York and died in poverty.

CHAPTER TWENTY FIVE

Par Excellence

Incomparable: Max Wall and Sid Field

T wo of the funniest comedians in the variety theatre were Sid Field and Max Wall. Their names are still intoned with great reverence. Sid Field's fame lasted for only eight years. He appeared in only four shows and three films, but the originality of his masterful routines will be treasured for many generations to come.

Max Wall came from a theatrical family. His father, Jack Lorimer, a fine Scottish character comedian, was a violent alcoholic. He had a brutal way of making people keep their word. The agent George Barclay used Jack to ensure his debtors paid up. Jack died of tuberculosis before reaching middle age. Max's mother, born Maudie Mitcheson, was an accomplished singer and pianist, who took the name, Stella Stahl. Max thought the world of her, but she advised him to stay single. 'Your father was mad and you are mad and you could never make a good husband.'[345] This was advice Max was to ignore three times.

Stella was a domineering stage mother, travelling with him everywhere and handling his business affairs. She once made a highly abusive phone call to Val Parnell, causing Max to offer a profuse apology in person. Parnell accepted it, but gave Max a stern warning about allowing his mother to interfere in his career. On the outbreak of the Second World War, Stella affected concern that the government would freeze personal assets. She advised Max to assign his endowment policies to her, saying she would continue to pay the premiums. As Max's career prospered, she also persuaded him to rent a four-storey house in Knightsbridge to show everyone he was doing well.

Stella deeply resented any other female involvement in Max's life. When he moved in with the woman who was to become his first wife, he decided to drive to Stella's bungalow in Staines to collect his belongings and the money she was supposed to be looking after on his behalf. Stella invited Jimmy Jewel to go too, so that he could persuade Max not to get married. 'He's at least 30 years old,' Jimmy said, 'I can't do that.'[346]

When Max arrived he found the door to his room locked and was told there was no money for him. A fight, instigated by Stella, then broke out between Max and his stepfather, Bill Tringham. It was a one-sided effort as Stella held on to Max while Bill landed his punches. Eventually, Max gathered his belongings, but failed to reclaim his insurance money. As he left, Stella followed him, screaming and throwing stones at his car. The attack left Max unable to work. His throat had been so damaged that he could neither sing nor speak properly.

Max Wall [Maxwell George Lorimer]

- Born Brixton, south London, 12 March 1908
- Married [1] Marian Ethel Pollachek [professionally known as Marion Pola] in Hampstead, north-west London 6 June 1942 [Dissolved 1956]
- Four sons, Michael, Melvin, Martin and Meredith
- One daughter, Maxine
- Married [2] Jennifer Schumacher, known as Jennifer Chimes, in Brighton 2 November 1956 [Dissolved 1969]
- Married [3] Christine Clements 1970 [Dissolved 1972]
- Max Wall died London 22 May 1990
- Left £193,004 [£290,000]

When Max next visited the house in Knightsbridge, he found the place had been trashed. Everything had been torn to pieces and the curtains had been ripped down. The whole house was a shambles, all the work of Stella.

Max, who was very good-looking when he was young, began as a song and dance man, billed as the Boy with the Obedient Feet. He made his London debut at the Lyceum in *The London Revue* [1925] and then appeared in *One Dam Thing after Another* [London Pavilion, 1927]; *Bow Bells* [London Hippodrome, 1932]; *Black and Blue* [London Hippodrome, 1939]; *Panama Hattie* [Piccadilly, 1943]; *Make it a Date* [Duchess, 1946] and *The Pajama Game* [London Coliseum, 1955] to name, as they say, just a few.

All the time, Max wanted to be a comic. His first opportunity came in a 40-week Moss Empires tour, starring Layton and Johnstone. Even Cissie Williams approved. From then on, his contracts referred to him as a comedian, rather than a 'dancing act, as known'.

Hello, everyone. Wall is the name. Max Wall. You've heard of my father, the Great Wall of China … He was the first man to tell me that, over in China, when a baby is born, they don't allow the mother in the room.[347]

It was during *Make it a Date* that Max introduced the only character he played, Professor Wallofski. Constantly embellished, it became the funniest routine in the variety theatre, as hilarious on the first viewing as it was on its one-hundredth. As a professor of music, Max wore a long wig, black tights and large boots. He was, in Max's own words, 'a weird spidery figure'.[348]

> Tonight, ladies and gentlemen, I've had one or two requests from thousands of people. It appears they require pianoforte music of the more classical nature and, believe me, I'm the lad to let 'em 'ave it.[349]

There was much comic business before the music even began. First, the Professor became concerned that one of his arms appeared to be longer than the other. Then, there were problems with the piano stool and half a conversation was held with a man offstage: Walter, the stooool. The stooooool, Walter!

Finally, the music started, usually played on two pianos, the Professor tackling the very simplest phrases and William Blezard, for instance, contributing the more complex passages. Once the music finished, Professor Wallofski signed off with what Max called the walking up and down bit, a sublime piece of eccentric dancing, accompanied only by a military drum roll. It was a superb act.

At the end of 1939, Max temporarily replaced Arthur Askey in a touring production of the BBC Radio show, *Band Waggon*, starring Askey and Richard Murdoch. [It was to allow Askey to fulfil a pantomime commitment.] Also on the bill were the Marian Pola Trio, a dance act. Marian, who had trained as a ballerina, had a superb figure and Max was greatly attracted to her. They married and had five children, but, by now, Max was working extremely hard. Like many rising stars in the variety theatre, he was allowed, for example, only very short Christmas breaks with his family. He might work, say, on Christmas Eve in Sheffield, drive home to Richmond Park, spend Christmas Day with Marian and their children and then head back to Sheffield on Boxing Day. He appeared regularly on *Variety Bandbox* and was fast becoming a name.

Marian, though, was unhappy. 'Why accept so much work? Work less and see more of your children.'[350] She should have known that Max had to accept whatever work was offered. Also, he was now able to provide his family with a good standard of living. 'You'd scream the place down if our standards dropped. The world doesn't owe me a living, you know.'[351]

In 1955, Max judged a beauty competition in Morecambe, one of the semi-finals for the Miss Great Britain contest. The winner he chose was Jennifer Chimes, whose 'poise and personality … left all the others standing like witches from Macbeth.'[352] In due course, Jennifer was named Miss Great Britain. That same year, *The Pajama Game*, with its hit songs, *I'm Not at All in Love*, *Hey There [You with the Stars in your Eyes]*, *Once a Year Day*, *Steam Heat*, and *Hernando's Hideaway*, was a big personal success for Max. But his marriage had by now almost collapsed.

After a particularly spectacular row with Marian, he moved out, first staying in a room at his agent's flat and then moving to a hotel. Marian was granted a divorce in the odd way the law worked then. Max had to stay for one night at the house of a woman he had never met, but it was enough to count as proof of adultery.

When Max took his doctor to the Café de Paris, he ran into Jennifer Chimes again. They began seeing each other. Max was 48. Jennifer, who was married, was 22. The tabloid press, which already knew Max had left Marian, now felt they had a major story and Max and Jennifer were roundly excoriated. In addition, they received piles of hate mail. Max's marriage was dissolved in May 1956; Jennifer was divorced by her husband in July; and the couple married in November 1956.

Max's showbiz chums rallied around him, among them, the harmonica player, Larry Adler: 'You'd've thought he'd been caught practising necrophilia on Queen Victoria.'[353] But, in the prudish 1950s, the shutters came down resoundingly on the career of Max Wall. Suddenly, he had no work at all.

Max, however, was undaunted. He found a new audience in the northern clubs, not ideal venues for as subtle a performer as Max, but he got by. His second marriage, however, failed too. This time, Jennifer moved out, leaving him a note that read: 'You will end up in one room, alone, with nothing.'[354] Max married a third time, but, in his autobiography, she was remembered only for twisting his trombone out of shape and throwing it in a dustbin. 'I can never forget my third marriage. Don't think I haven't tried.'[355]

Max had to wait until 1973 for the Establishment to forgive him. First, he was cast in *Cockie!* [Vaudeville], a revue about the career of C.B. Cochran. It did not last for long, but Max garnered some good reviews, including a spectacular one:[356] 'Mr Wall is, quite simply, the funniest comedian in the world.' The following year, Max played Archie Rice in *The Entertainer* at the Greenwich Theatre. John Osborne was to direct a season of his own plays and said he would do *The Entertainer* only if Max played Archie. During rehearsals, Max was appearing in Coventry at night and commuted every day to and from Greenwich. Osborne said Max learned the role as if he had been playing it all his life:

With his skill as a dancer came the gift of withholding, conjuring unimaginable surprise. He never made the smallest movement that was not felicitous and fastidious, whatever the comic outcome, whether it was opening a bottle of Dubonnet or leaning on his cane like a reflective, startled ape peering out through the bars of his remote cage.[357]

The problem was to stop Max being too funny. Archie was a failed comic, Max, a very successful one. The climax of his career was *Aspects of Max Wall*, his one-man show. The format was simple. During the first half, Max was a front-cloth comic, telling stories, exchanging banter with his pianist and drummer and perhaps singing to his own guitar accompaniment. In the second half, he was Professor Wallofski. Max was a dangerous performer who bent or ignored many of the rules of comedy. So, on some nights, he was hilariously funny and, on others, less so, but, however the show went, it was always a master-class. John Osborne rated Max among Britain's top two comedians:

> For my money, Max's only peer was the incomparable Sid Field. They shared the essential virtues unknown to modern comics, agility, grace and gravity.[358]

Before introducing Sid properly, here are three vignettes:

[1] As a boy, Sid was fascinated by Charlie Chaplin. When he went to the cinema to see a Chaplin movie, he never saw it once. He had to watch it two or three times before he left. Chaplin became his hero and he impersonated him as often as he could, first for the benefit of friends and neighbours and then in front of a crowd queueing outside a cinema. On that occasion, so many people gathered that traffic was blocked and the police were called.

[2] On the opening night of Sid's first West End appearance, George Black stood at the back of the stalls with Collie Knox, one of the most popular journalists of the day. The showman, C.B. Cochran, who was in the audience, spoke afterwards of 'the greatest laughter I have heard in a theatre for many years'.[359] [The critics provided supporting evidence. James Agate described Sid as 'immensely and unendingly funny'[360] and Kenneth Tynan said that 'no more naturalistic clown walked the land'.][361] As laughter filled the auditorium that evening, Knox turned to Black and shouted, 'That chap Field is a comic genius.' Black replied: 'Tomorrow morning, they will all hail Sid as a discovery, [but] success won't spoil him. He's been through too much.'[362]

[3] During a trip to America some years later, Sid was invited to dine with Charlie Chaplin, always a very private man. Chaplin gave him one of his photographs on which he had written 'as one of the members of the fraternity who've contributed to the much needed happiness of us poor humans, I salute you.'[363]

Sid used to say that his father, who had a great talent for mimicry, was the funniest man he knew. Later, Sid developed a mastery of accents. After hearing

---

Sid Field [Sidney Arthur Field]

- Born Birmingham 1 April 1904
- Married Constance Laura Dawkins 17 February 1933
- Three children, Diane, Elaine [known as Tootie] and John Nicholas
- Died Wimbledon south-west London 3 February 1950
- Left £31,736 {£650,000}

strangers speak only a few words, he knew where they were born to within a few miles. Sid's mother was a domineering woman. So domineering, in fact, that, after Sid married, he could visit her only on his own. Sid and his wife were even reluctant to tell her that their first child was due.

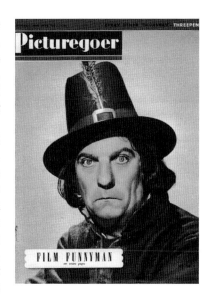

When he was a boy, his mother encouraged him to go on the stage and, at the age of 12, he joined the first of a number of juvenile troupes he worked with. He sang *Burlington Bertie from Bow*, the tale of a broken-down toff, made famous by Ella Shields and he understudied another music hall headliner, Wee Georgie Wood. Even as a youngster, Sid suffered from stage nerves and found it easier to have a sip of port before he made his entrance, a habit from which he should have been dissuaded. In 1929, he was seen in a revue at the Hammersmith Palace, *Hot Ice*, in which he played the feed to another obscure performer, George Norton, in a sketch about golfing. One night, Norton was so drunk he was sacked and Sid took his place.

In 1933, Sid edged tantalisingly closer to the West End when he appeared in *The Revue of the Moment* at the Finsbury Park Empire, billed as the Destroyer of Gloom. The stumbling block to national success was an exclusive contract with a provincial impresario, William Henshall. In 1942, he was free of it. In that year, he met Jerry Desmonde, a superb straight man. By then, he had developed the golfing sketch, the most famous of his routines, in which an irascible friend tries to teach him the rudiments of the game. When Jerry first read it, he could not see much humour in it. On paper, the sketch does indeed look thin. Much of it centres on confusion over the arcane rules and language of golf. But, as Jerry started losing his temper, Sid embellished the sketch so that it became much more than an ill-judged lesson:

> I do wish I hadn't come … I could have gone and had my music lesson with Miss Fanthorpe … Miss Fanthorpe's kind.
> She may be kind. But she can't play golf.
> No, but she can play the piano and the flute.
> But who wants to play the piano and the flute?
> Miss Fanthorpe … I can't understand what's come over you, Humphrey. You're not like this when we're painting together.[364]

Offstage, Jerry could not get on with Sid. He found him morose and difficult. Even when they were rehearsing for Sid's first West End appearance, *Strike a New Note*, in 1943, he found Sid's attitude hard to understand. 'The easier things went, the more he seemed to withdraw into his shell.'[365] Sid now needed more than a sip of port to get him on stage. An hour before curtain up, he was drinking large quantities of gin to try to steady his nerves. Thankfully, it did not make him slur his speech, but, as a nerve-steadier, it did not really work. On the first night of *Strike a New Note*, Sid was in such a state that he had to be practically thrown onto the stage.

He nonetheless gave a superb performance, as Jerry later recalled:

Jerry Desmonde dropped by Val Parnell.

> I've never heard such applause in the theatre … The laughs came like the waves of a rough sea, breaking on a shingled beach, and, when they came, they lasted … Even when the show was over, I couldn't tell exactly how Sid felt, but we found ourselves alone for a moment in the dressing room and I couldn't hold back. I took hold of him as if he were a brother and I must have had tears in my eyes. All I could say was: 'It's wonderful, so wonderful.'[366]

The reviews were more than encouraging. The *New Statesman* singled Sid out: 'Double-jointed wrists, a taking eye and patter fresh as a daisy complete the appeal of this new comedian,'[367] while *The Times* believed him to be 'definitely a "find". He is a versatile comedian, a Cockney [sic] with a touch of Mr Max Miller and capable of terrifying gentility.'[368]

Strike a New Note ran from March 1943 until April 1944, a total of 661 performances. It was followed by *Strike It Again* [434 performances], but now Sid could not go on stage without having had a drink.

> I'm dead nervous before every performance. I don't just get sick with stage fright. I get petrified, wondering if they'll still think I'm funny.[369]

Sid returned to the Prince of Wales in 1946 with *Piccadilly Hayride* [778 performances]. His co-star was Terry-Thomas, the gap-toothed comedian who specialised in roguish or inept aristocrats:

> Sid Field … had an underlying sadness, almost a desperation, beneath the comic façade. He was a morose character, not improved by the fact that he was a heavy drinker. I never saw him drunk, but, like Hancock, he would demolish whisky, crème de menthe, gin, barley wine, in fact anything with alcohol that came along.[370]

Finally, Sid appeared in *Harvey* [1949] [610 performances], again at the Prince of Wales, in which he played an alcoholic whose best friend is an invisible outsize rabbit. It is best remembered now as a movie starring James Stewart.

Many people believe that Sid made only two movies, *London Town* [1946] and *Cardboard Cavalier* [1948], but, before them, there was *That's the Ticket* [1939], which was made in three weeks and sank without trace. The Rank Organisation poured large amounts of money into *London Town*, the first big budget Technicolour musical to be made in Britain. More people than ever were going to the cinema and so Rank, with plenty of cash to spare, hired the Hollywood film director, Wesley Ruggles, who had made *Silk Stockings* and *I'm No Angel*, to write, produce and direct an original screenplay. First, he assembled an all-star cast, led by Sid. There were also Tessie O'Shea, a 12-year-old Petula Clark[371] and a beautiful newcomer, Kay Kendall. The songs were written by Johnny Burke and Jimmy Van Heusen, who had *Moonlight Becomes You*, *Aren't You Glad You're You?* and *Swinging on a Star* to their credit; the choreography was partly in the hands of Agnes de Mille; and for good measure, Britain's best big band, Ted Heath and His Music, were there as well.

But the film was a critical and financial flop, the whole being less than the sum of its parts. To try to recoup some of its losses, Rank cut 31 minutes of its original running time of 126 minutes, but, in doing so, lost one of Sid's best sketches, in which, as a professor of music, he played the tubular bells, renamed the tubercular bells. That left the golfing sketch and, as far as the author is concerned, a much funnier routine, in which Sid played an effeminate photographer: 'I've never been the same since my operation. Fourteen weeks on my back with my leg up.'

Sid's abuse of drink had now caught up with him and, after seven months, he left *Harvey* as a result of a nervous breakdown. He returned on Boxing Day, but died of a heart attack the following February, aged only 45.

Jerry then became Norman Wisdom's straight man, but he never worked for Val Parnell again. Terry-Thomas worked for Parnell many times:

Val … had a reputation for being the toughest man in the business. He was! He once disagreed with Jerry Desmonde … over some trifling matter. After Sid's death, Val never used Jerry again. As Jerry was as big a name as Sid Field had been, this took a bit of believing, but that's how Val was.[372]

Jerry, born James Sadler, had other work. He was one of the panel in the first edition of the television show, *What's My Line?* [1951]: his association with the show continued until 1954. Then, in 1956, he hosted ATV's *The 64,000 Question* [not The $64,000 Question, which is how it is popularly remembered], in which competitors could win up to £3,200 plus a number of premium bonds. Jerry often swept off his glasses with a flourish as he interviewed contestants, a mannerism that irritated some viewers. After 54 appearances, ATV's Lew Grade replaced him.

Jerry's involvement with Norman Wisdom's films began with Norman's first movie, *Trouble in Store* [1953] and continued with *Man of the Moment* [1955], *Up in the World* [1957], *Follow a Star* [1959], *A Stitch in Time* [1963] and *The Early Bird* [1965]. During those 12 years, Norman relished working with Jerry, not just in the movies, but in countless television appearances too:

Jerry Desmonde [was] one of the world's great straight men, someone who could keep his dignity intact even when being soaked with a soda siphon … He was as fastidious about his appearance in real life as his acting persona would suggest. Always immaculately attired, with his shoes polished like mirrors, he could have stepped out of any of his screen roles.[373]

All this sounds like a success story, but there was not enough work to sustain Jerry. He became a mini-cab driver and, in 1967, he took an overdose of barbiturates, washed down with alcohol, and killed himself.

CHAPTER TWENTY SIX

A Dancing Mood

Molto Adagio: Ganjou Brothers, plus international stars Wilson, Keppel and Betty

One of the most popular dance acts in variety was the Ganjou Brothers and Juanita. Their routine was based on adagio dancing, a cross between dance and acrobatics, in which, most commonly, a woman is thrown into the air by her male partner, caught and then swung around. The lovely Juanita, as she was called, was thrown about by three real-life Polish brothers, Serge, George and Bogdan [Bob] Ganjou, born Ganjoulevitch. They appeared at the London Palladium, travelled all over the world and, during the 1940s, they were one of the highest paid acts.

Their best known routine was entitled *A Romance in [Dresden] Porcelain*, in which Juanita, wearing very little, was lifted high over the heads of the lithe and handsome brothers. Some reviewers referred to it as poetry in motion, although, late in his life, Serge was realistic enough to admit: 'We were a sort of refined circus act, [which was] supposed to be very tasteful ... It would be rather difficult for anyone today to [take it] seriously.'[374]

As a young man in Warsaw, Serge Ganjou appeared in concert parties and toured village halls, singing and playing gypsy songs to his own guitar accompaniment. George and Bob emigrated to America, where George found work in a symphony orchestra and Bob started an adagio act. Sometime later, Bob initiated a similar act with George, a Danish acrobat and 'Juanita' Richards, who had worked as a ballerina and an artist's model. When the act arrived in London in 1933, Serge replaced the Dane. Not long after, there was yet another change of personnel. The original Juanita left and was replaced by Joy Marlowe, whom Serge married.

Another of their acts, set in an Eighteenth Century ballroom, can be seen in the movie, *Variety Jubilee*, made in 1943. It depicts a huge mantelpiece with a clock at its centre. To the strains of the *Blue Danube* waltz, played by

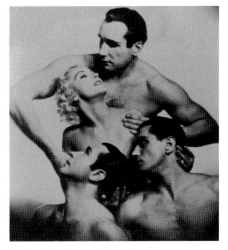

Ganjou Brothers and Juanita.

an 18-piece orchestra, Juanita is first seen as the clock's pendulum before the brothers, wearing powdered wigs, billowing shirts, decorated waistcoats and tights, fling her from one to another, tossing her over their heads from shoulder to shoulder. Finally, they throw her high into the air, spin her round, catch her and then freeze in a pose that brings the house down.

In their heyday, the Ganjou Brothers and Juanita were in great demand. Their act was both lavish and expertly choreographed, but, when the variety theatre began to lose its appeal, they disbanded in 1957. George became an agent and played a part in the early career of Cliff Richard. On his advice, Cliff made a demo disc which impressed him. He sent it to the record producer, Norrie Paramor, who immediately signed Cliff up for Columbia Records. Cliff's first hits soon followed. Serge found a new career too. He opened a successful Polish restaurant, the Daquise, in south Kensington. Bob died in 1972, leaving £38,131 [£325,000], George in 1988 and Serge in 1998. He left £1,246,007 [£1,270,000].

No other adagio act ever equalled the Ganjou Brothers and Juanita, but a one-man one-woman turn, Gaston and Andree, also topped bills. Jimmy Gaston was born James Thomas, the son of a Welsh dairy farmer. He started out as a wrestler, but then formed an acrobatic act with a male partner. When he teamed up with a female partner, the adagio act was formed. Like the Ganjou Brothers, they also appeared at the London Palladium. In all, there were five Andrees, but Jimmy believed the best was Rosemary Andree, who set up a theatrical agency with him when they retired from the stage. Gaston died in 1966 at the age of 79 and Rosemary in 1974.

Wilson, Keppel and Betty, the supreme eccentric dance act of the 1930s, 1940s and 1950s, still hold sway 50 years after their disbandment. Theirs is a remarkable achievement. Many speech-based comedy routines of that period now appear to be resoundingly awful, their jokes no better than those found in children's comics.

But Wilson, Keppel and Betty created something new, the appeal of which seems ageless. They were sand dancers, who established a routine they called Cleopatra's Nightmare, performed to the music of *Ballet Egyptien* by the French composer, Alexandre Luigini. It was carefully constructed over several years. The common view now is that it was immutable just like other music hall and variety acts, able to travel throughout Britain never needing to change their routines: all that is wrong. Wilson, Keppel and Betty did alter their act, although the changes were mostly cosmetic. Their followers were happy to watch their turn time and time again and demand nothing very much different.

Basically, the act ran along these lines. Betty began with a voluptuous dance, playing finger cymbals, while Jack Wilson and Joe Keppel, played whistles and tambourines. Then, the two men, looking soppy and somewhat camp, danced themselves, wearing long nightshirts and fezzes. The sand dance followed with Wilson and Keppel in shorter tunics and head cloths. While they changed costume, Betty danced a solo. All three finished with a far more energetic dance.

Modern accounts of Wilson, Keppel and Betty often refer to them as being risqué or suggestive without explaining what they mean. According to *The Daily Telegraph*,[375] 'the Cleopatra routine [had] the sense of a vaguely obscene joke which never quite reaches its conclusion.' These references may suggest that, when Wilson and Keppel danced close together [knees bent, one behind the other], there was a hint of sexual intimacy between the two men.

None of the above gives any idea of the act's unique wit. For that, you had to see them. Fortunately, the Internet's incomparable YouTube carries more than one clip.

The publicity material of Jack Wilson says he was born in Liverpool on 29 January 1894, but his death certificate of 1970 gives his date of birth as 30 June 1894. It is impossible to say whether either of these dates is correct. There is no corresponding birth entry in the registers of 1894. [Jack's true forenames were John William]. Joe was said to have been born in Cork on 10 May 1895. We do know that this date is wrong. He was, in fact, born John Keppel on 5 May 1894, the son of Michael, a labourer, and his wife, Ellen, whose maiden name was Sullivan.

There are several accounts of their early years. One says they first worked together as a clog-dancing act, touring minor halls in Lancashire. They are then said to have joined a troupe going to Berlin and, after a year in mainland Europe, travelled to America. Another account says Jack made his stage debut as a high-kicking dancer in Bristol, Connecticut, in 1909 before making his way to Australia where he joined Colleano's Circus. Joe is also said to have emigrated to America at an early age, making his first stage appearance as a tap dancer with a minstrel troupe in Albany in 1910. This account maintains he met Jack when he also joined Colleano's Circus.

What is certain is that the British agent, Harry Foster, saw them at the Palace, New York, in May 1932 and immediately booked them for four weeks' work in Britain. They opened at the London Palladium in August 1932 in a bill topped by Layton and Johnstone and the Roy Fox band. They were so successful that they decided to make Britain their base. One sign of their enduring popularity is that they appeared in three Royal Variety shows [1933, 1945 and 1947].

It is impossible to say how many Bettys there were. People lost count. We do, however, know the details of the first two, who were mother and daughter. Betty Knox teamed up with Wilson and Keppel in 1928. She was born Betty Peden and outraged her family by becoming a theatre dancer. She fled to Omaha, where she married a young mechanic, Donald Knox. They were later divorced. Wilson, Keppel and Betty Knox apparently first worked in Des Moines, Iowa, and between them they developed the Cleopatra's Nightmare routine. Betty was part of the act until 1941 when she left to begin a successful career in journalism. She became a regular contributor to the London *Evening Standard*, filed despatches from Normandy in the latter stages of the Second World War and covered the Nuremburg Trials. She was among the first to report the suicide of Hermann Goring. [She eventually settled in Germany and died in Dusseldorf in 1963 at the age of 56.]

The original Betty was replaced by her 17-year-old daughter, Patricia [Patsy], who, as well as working as a dancer, was an accomplished dress designer. One account says she stayed with the act until 1950, although another Betty, Edna May, claimed to have been the third member of the trio between 1945 and 1947.

Then, there were Irene Edwin-Scott, a classically trained dancer from Glasgow; Jean Bamberger, an acrobatic dancer; Valerie Cottrell, a youngster from Bristol; and Maureen Drew. The last Betty, possibly the eighth, was Jean McKinnon, a Windmill girl, who joined the act about ten years before it broke up and who played two years with them at the Crazy Horse strip club in Paris. In an Anglian TV feature, *Bygones*, she recalled that audiences at the Glasgow Empire always loved Betty. That was fortunate for her given the treatment that hall meted out to most English performers. When Jean left showbiz, she became a barmaid in Birmingham. George Melly believed Wilson and Keppel deliberately changed their Bettys every ten years or so.

Because [like many magicians] the act was wordless, it could travel the world. There were few countries that failed to welcome them. One exception was Germany in the 1930s. When they appeared at the Wintergarten, Berlin, in 1936, Josef Goebbels found the bare legs of Jack and Joe a threat to the morals of the Nazi Youth Movement.

On stage, Jack Wilson and Joe Keppel looked like undernourished twins, something Joe had to work at. He did not smoke or drink and ate mostly nuts, cereals, radishes and honey. On the other hand, Jack smoked all his life, ate anything he was offered and enjoyed rum and Guinness. They were dissimilar in other ways too. Joe was always immaculately dressed and very retiring by nature. Jack, who could have been mistaken for a stagehand in appearance, was more gregarious: the life and soul of the party. As for hobbies, the two men enjoyed sport, especially boxing and wrestling.

They were both apparently yoga fanatics and it was not unusual to find them standing on their hands in their dressing room, which they always turned into a workshop.

They possessed every conceivable carpenter's tool and wiled away the hours between shows making their own props, such as staffs, spears and shields. [In time, they cut the number of props they used to make the act fit on smaller stages as well as to make it easier to move between venues.] They also spent much of their spare time working on their 'sand carpet', a large wooden tray with raised edges to keep the sand from littering the stage. After each performance, they meticulously sifted the sand to remove any particles of dust deposited during their dance.[376]

The trio had a strict division of duty. Wilson was in charge of their bookings; Betty took care of their costumes; and Keppel controlled the sand. In fact, he became quite an expert, in particular in relation to the texture of sand needed by the act. He eventually found that Deep Sea Sand

Wilson, Keppel and Betty.

and that used by the Metropolitan Water Board were ideal. [The glue that stuck the sand to the tray had to be exactly right too]. Even when the act went to Las Vegas, a city surrounded by sand, Keppel took his own.

> The bag produced some suspicion when seen by an American customs officer. The sand was sifted for narcotics very carefully before being released.[377]

The trio appeared twice nightly at the Desert Inn. After their first show, the club's manager told them to drop the sand dance from their act. Incredulous, they sought a reason. 'The customers near the stage complained. The sand was getting in their soup.'[378]

In 1948, Wilson, Keppel and Betty played the London Casino, now the Prince Edward Theatre. Each half of the show was opened by the Freddie Carpenter Dancers, one of whose number, Mary Logan, took every opportunity to watch the act from the wings:

> When it was time for their slot, they placed their props carefully in a chosen position, which did not seem to differ by so much as a centimetre on any night … Costume changes were kept on hangers and wrapped in dust sheets. They were hung on the back struts of the scenery from where the trio made their exits and entrances. Stagehands were forbidden to come anywhere near or touch anything. In fact, the only thing Wilson, Keppel and Betty needed to rely on was the band in the pit. When they needed any of their props during the act, they incorporated bringing them on into the routine being performed … In the famous sand dance … the mat was carried on to music and sand scattered from a container, all carried out in perfect unison. Afterwards, they folded the mat and danced off without missing a beat.[379]

The act was much imitated, but never equalled. Wilson, Keppel and Betty appeared to regard impersonators as a compliment rather than a threat. In the summer of 1933, when they were playing the Alhambra, Leicester Square, Jack Wilson came out of the stage door with Bert Ross, who worked for *The Performer* and later became the first Historian of the British Music Hall Society:

> A considerable crowd was enjoying the antics of three buskers who were presenting a commendable take-off of the Wilson, Keppel and Betty act … Their bottler came round the crowd and was doing quite well when he reached

the spot where Jack and I stood. Recognising Jack Wilson, he shamefacedly and hurriedly attempted to depart ... but Jack gripped his arm and held tight. Then, with his free arm, he extracted his wallet from an inside pocket and without a word handed a note to the bottler. The relief on the man's face was a sight to see. He just managed to say 'Thanks, Jack' and hurried away.[380]

Wilson, Keppel and [more often than not] Betty made several movies, three of which, *In Town Tonight*, *On the Air* [both 1934] and *Merrygoround* [1948] are now amazingly considered to be "lost." Those that survive are *Pathetone Weekly No. 164* [1933], a short showing the act performing their Ballet Egyptien; *Soft Lights and Sweet Music* [1936]; *Starlight Serenade* [1943] in which Bonar Colleano, of the circus family, appeared; and *Variety Jubilee* [1943]; [*Highlights of Variety {Nos. 24 and 25}* [1944] and *For Old Times' Sake* [1948], both reissues of footage from *Variety Jubilee*, are also considered "lost"]; *The Peaceful Years* and *Variety Makers* [both 1948]; *Scrapbook for 1933* [1949]; and *A Ray of Sunshine* [1950], linked by Ted Ray.

Luke McKernan, who worked at the National Film and Theatre Archive for a number of years and who gave illustrated talks about the act, believes that film clips of the trio were probably the most requested items from the Archive. Indeed, when the NFT staged an evening in which every known piece of footage of the act was shown, it was so popular that it had to be repeated.

Besides movies, Wilson, Keppel and Betty appeared in a series of pantomimes, most notably *Aladdin* at the Blackpool Opera House [1936/37] and the Princes Theatre, Manchester [1937/38]; *The Sleeping Beauty* at the Royal, Glasgow [1947/48] and at the Royal, Newcastle [1948/49]; *Aladdin* again at the Kings Theatre, Hammersmith [1950/51]; *Cinderella* at the Bristol Hippodrome [1954/55]; *Aladdin* once again at the New, Cardiff [1956/57]; and *Dick Whittington* at the Derby Hippodrome [1957/58].

They made their television debut in *The Max Wall Show* on 1 April 1956 and appeared in Norman Evans' series, *Saturday Comedy Hour*, which began on 13 October 1956.

Great personal strain could be imposed on music hall, variety and vaudeville acts when they worked together week in, week out, all over the world. Sometimes, inevitably, the relationship broke down completely [vide Mike and Bernie Winters and the fictional Lewis and Clark in Neil Simon's superb play, *The Sunshine Boys*]. Barry Grantham, a variety entertainer, met Wilson and Keppel when they shared a bill together:

One of them ... invited Barry to his dressing room for a drink between shows. At this time, Wilson and Keppel weren't speaking [to each other]. So, Barry found them at each end of the room. 'What do you want?' asked Wilson. 'Mr Keppel invited me for a drink.' Keppel stared at Barry ... 'Oh, yes,' he said and took the top off a bottle of Guinness. Barry drank it in silence and neither of them ever said another word to him.[381]

As the variety theatre declined in the 1950s, Wilson, Keppel and Betty became accustomed to playing theatres they would have previously considered beneath them. Eric Midwinter wrote:

> I was prepared to travel at some length to watch them and eventually found myself in dilapidated halls scheduled for closure ... I last saw their names posted low on a bill for a third-rate revue in a declining Lancashire mill town ... Suddenly, there was really no place for [their act] and a torn poster on the derelict wall of a now declining once humming textile centre told it all.[382]

In 1962, however, Wilson, Keppel and Betty joined the company of a summer show guaranteed to be popular, *Secombe Here*, starring Harry Secombe, at the Wellington Pier Pavilion, Great Yarmouth. During the run, Wilson began feeling tired and ill. He decided he wanted to retire. Keppel was still very fit and both he and Jeannie McKinnon would have liked to continue, but Wilson's decision was final. All three pulled out of the show, bringing a partnership of more than 50 years to an end. Their departure, incidentally, provided a young Ronnie Corbett with a lucky break. There was suddenly a five-minute gap in the show and Secombe suggested Corbett could work up a short spot to fill it. Together with Don Arroll, a one-time compère of *Sunday Night at the London Palladium*, Corbett put together five minutes of jokes and patter, his first solo spot ever. But it lasted only three or four nights. The management wanted a bigger name and the magician, Donald B. Stuart, was brought in to replace him.

Wilson and Keppel went their separate ways. In 1967, Wilson moved into Brinsworth House, the retirement home in Twickenham for actors and variety performers. There, on 31 August 1970, he died from cancer of the throat. Reg Swinson, the General Secretary of the Variety Artistes' Benevolent Fund, paid tribute:

> He was a prince among men: always kind, gentle and utterly selfless in his consideration for his loved ones and friends. Never physically robust, within his slender frame burned a spirit of courage that few can emulate.[383]

Joe Keppel returned to Cork, where he spent the rest of his days. He made a particular impression on one lad, Jim Hastings, whose father ran a grocery shop in the centre of the city.

> [He was] very well dressed, wore black gloves [and smoked his cigarettes through] a long cigarette holder. In those days, most grocery shops had sawdust on their floors and [Joe] would always make his entrance by shuffling in on the sawdust much to the amusement of my father and [any] customers present ... Immediately, he and my father adjourned to the pub.[384]

Joe's non-smoking, teetotal days were now evidently behind him. Another man from Cork, John Turner, remembered Joe as a man 'who liked his Dimple Haig and Bass's barley wine. [He] could tell a good yarn and make people laugh.'[385]

In 1977, Joe was admitted to St Finbarr's Hospital, Cork, with prostate cancer. He survived for six weeks and died on 14 June. Two days later, he was interred at St Joseph's cemetery in a plot where the bodies of one of his sisters, Nora, and his brother-in-law, Jack Buckley, had been buried. Incredibly, no inscription was added. A third of one of the most famous and most loved variety acts in the world lies in an unmarked grave.

By the time of his death, Joe must have severed most of his links with the world of variety as *The Times* did not publish its short obituary of him until two months later. It honoured Wilson, Keppel and Betty as 'a top-of-the-bill act in almost every variety theatre and music hall in Britain.'[386] In this, *The Times* was wrong. Wilson, Keppel and Betty were very rarely the stars of a show, but a world-class supporting act. As long as their films continue to be shown, they will be remembered, for the humour of Wilson, Keppel and Betty is timeless.

CHAPTER TWENTY SEVEN

Downhill All the Way

Time to Say Goodbye

T he face of popular entertainment began to change with the arrival of pop music. Britain's first pop idol was Donald Peers, an unlikely figure to acquire the title largely because he had to wait until he was 39. He did not share the sex appeal of Frank Sinatra or Johnnie Ray. Nor did he sing the sort of song guaranteed to excite female fans. He favoured such evergreens as *[In a Shady Nook] By a Babbling Brook*, which became his signature tune. All the same, legions of girls and women swooned and screamed for him long before rock stars appeared.

Donald's father, a clerk at a sawmill and a lay preacher for the Plymouth Brethren, who disapprove of all forms of entertainment, would have been appalled. As a boy, Donald sang a sacred song at a Sunday School function and, encouraged by the applause, followed it with an impromptu comedy number. For this transgression, his father beat him soundly. Later in life, he spoke warmly of both of his parents, although strangely he failed to attend his mother's funeral.

On the eve of his 16th birthday, Donald fled the harsh regime at home and moved from one cheap boarding house to another, finding work as a painter and decorator on the way. He began singing at local dances and thought he had had a lucky break when he broadcast for the first time in 1927, but, even after he had signed a contract with His Master's Voice, he merely continued touring small-time theatres outside London.

Donald Peers [Donald Rhys Hubert Peers]

- Born Ammanford, Dyfed, 10 July 1908
- Married Marie --- 7 June 1930 [Separated 1953]
- Daughter, Sheila, born 1931
- Donald Peers died Brighton 9 August 1973
- Left £12,401 [£100,000]

During the Second World War, he travelled to Bangor in north Wales to sing on a variety show. On the outbreak of hostilities, the BBC's Variety Department decamped first to Bristol and then to Bangor. Donald was paid ten guineas [£260] for the engagement, augmented, as he openly admitted, by plug money at the rate of £5 song. This was cash the publishers gave him if he sang one of their songs on a BBC show.[387]

But Donald's career, it seemed, was stillborn. It was not until he recorded *By a Babbling Brook* in 1945 that he made any impact. He began touring better halls and did so well that, in 1948, he was given his first radio series, *Cavalier of Song*. Britain's bobby-soxers claimed him as their own. At one recording at the Kings Theatre, Hammersmith, 1,500 girls and women screamed his name. 'His secret? He sings in a robust light baritone, does not croon and has a strange personal magnetism that makes each girl think he is singing for her.'[388]

Donald's career was now moving quickly. In 1949, he signed the biggest individual BBC contract ever awarded. It was calculated to add £1,500 to his annual earnings already estimated to be about £15,000 [£350,000] a year. His producer, Roy Speer, said: 'When we've finished the recording, the fans make Donald sing more. Then, the band packs up and goes home, but Donald goes on singing. In the end, he has to sing the National Anthem to get them out of the theatre.'[389]

In terms of songs, it is difficult to gauge the popularity of any singer in the late 1940s and early 1950s. At first, the charts reflected only sales of sheet music. After tentative attempts, the leading music paper, *Melody Maker*, began printing alphabetical lists of the week's best-selling 15 published songs in July 1946. It was not until November 1952 that its rival, the *New Musical Express*, published its first list of best-selling records. As for records sold, Donald featured only three times: *Games that Lovers Play* [1966]; *Please Don't Go* [1968] and *Give Me One More Chance* [1972].

A much clearer picture of his popularity is gained from the sheet music listings, which between 1945 and 1953 show his success with many popular songs of the day, including *Far Away Places [With Strange Sounding Names]* ; *Dear Hearts and Gentle People*; *[Put Another Nickel in] Music! Music! Music!* ; *[If I Knew You Were Comin'] I'd've Baked a Cake*; *Enjoy Yourself [It's Later than You Think]* ; *Rudolph the Red-Nosed Reindeer* [recorded with Hattie Jacques]; and *Mockin' Bird Hill.*

The twin peaks of Donald's career came in 1950: a one-man show at the Albert Hall and a spot in the Royal Variety show. The press gave him rave notices: 'After 20 years spent touring the provincial halls, he is now a polished entertainer and is winning audiences with his sunny personality, his sincerity and, of course, his mellow pleasing voice.'[390] 'Donald Peers ... proved that a Welshman with an English accent can triumphantly interrupt the American film star ascendancy at the Palladium.'[391]

During the 1950s, the closure of variety theatres continued relentlessly: the Accrington Hippodrome; the Bow Palace; the Bradford Empire; the Alhambra, Brighton; the Bristol Empire; Bedford, Camden Town; the Empress, Brixton; Camberwell Palace; the Cardiff Empire; the Chelsea Palace; Chiswick Empire; the Croydon Hippodrome; the Grand, Derby; the Dewsbury Hippodrome; the

Royal Hippodrome, Dover; the Winter Garden, Drury Lane; the Durham Empire; the East Ham Palace; the Ealing Hippodrome; the Granville, Fulham Broadway; the Gateshead Empire and the Alexandra, Gateshead; the Hartlepool Empire; the Grand, Halifax; the Ilford Hippodrome; the Ipswich Hippodrome; the Palace, Hull; Collins, Islington; the Kingston Empire; the Leicester Palace; the Gaiety and Alhambra, Leith; Lewisham Hippodrome; the New Cross Empire; the Queens, Poplar; the Sheffield Empire; the South London Palace of Varieties; the Royal Standard, Whitehaven; and the Wood Green and Woolwich Empires.

Although many blamed the arrival of pop music for the death of variety, it helped, paradoxically, to provide a stay of execution. Once new recording stars reached the charts, their fans [as had happened with popular radio entertainers] wanted to see what they looked like. Nationwide tours were arranged with the latest pop sensation at the top of the bill and old variety lags filling the rest of the time. Some veterans complained that the arrivistes lacked stagecraft and musicianship, but they would have been drawing the dole were it not for a new generation's interest in the latest idols. All the same, it was galling for a seasoned variety entertainer to play to a bored audience merely waiting for an inexperienced star.

As it turned out, some of the first generation of pop singers were every bit as colourful as the variety entertainers they were replacing. One was Ruby Murray, who set a new record by having five hits in the Top Twenty at the same time, a feat equalled only by Elvis Presley and Madonna. She topped variety bills for 20 years in spite of a growing addiction to alcohol and tranquillisers. She was twice admitted to psychiatric hospitals and, when she was arrested for being drunk and disorderly, she entertained the police by singing a medley of her hit songs from her cell.[392]

The beautiful Joan Regan, who was regularly in the charts in the 1950s, was rudely shocked on her first appearance on the variety stage. Unaware of such things as safety curtains, she was knocked unconscious by one being lowered without her knowledge. In 1963, she suffered a nervous breakdown after her second husband, Harry Claff[393], the box office manager at the London Palladium, was sent to prison for five years for embezzling £62,000 [£870,000] from Moss Empires. He had a gambling addiction. Over the previous four years, he had lost £13,500 [£190,000] on the horses. Joan divorced him, married a doctor and moved to Florida, where she suffered a brain haemorrhage that left her paralysed and without the power of speech. Part of her programme of recovery involved her miming to her old records.

The handsome Dickie Valentine had 14 hits between 1953 and 1960, including two chart-

Ruby Murray.

toppers, *Finger of Suspicion* and *Christmas Alphabet*. He was killed in a car crash at the age of 41.

Michael Holliday, who modelled himself on Bing Crosby, had an enormous hit in 1958 with *The Story of My Life* and presented a controlled and relaxed image on stage. Offstage, he was sexually compulsive and had to pick up women constantly. He allowed tax problems to grow and, in 1963, he drove to a club run by his friend, Freddie Mills, once the light-heavyweight boxing champion of the world, to tell him that he was contemplating suicide. That night, he died from an overdose of drugs. Two years later, Mills, who was alleged to have had an affair with Holliday, shot himself dead.

David Whitfield, who topped the charts with *Cara Mia* and *Answer Me*, was another singer who could not resist the groupies. Eric Morecambe witnessed him in action at the Winter Gardens, Blackpool:

> Girls were hanging round the stage door, but I didn't realise why … I was pushing my way up the stairway [and] wondered what these giggling girls were queuing up for … When I got to the doorway and looked inside, David and three of his mates were hard at it with about six half-naked teenagers … David … shouted for me to come inside and help myself. I said, 'Thanks very much, but I've already had some … at the vicar's coffee morning.'[394]

Later in life, Whitfield drank heavily, a habit that deterred potential employers from giving him work. They distanced themselves even further when he was fined for indecently exposing himself to an 11-year-old girl in 1966. During a tour of Australia, David Whitfield died of a brain haemorrhage in 1980 at the age of 54.

There were survivors, most notably, Tommy Steele, who was engaged by Moss Empires for a nationwide tour while he was enjoying his first hit, *Rock with the Caveman*. Before his first date at the Sunderland Empire, he had to appear before members of the local Watch Committee. Its spokesman told him he would not be allowed to have his amplifier on stage.

> 'Why not?' 'Because there are electricals coming from it into your banjo.' 'It's a guitar.' 'I don't care if it's a pookin' piccolo. It's a firetrap.' 'But it's rock-and-roll. I sing rock-and-roll.' 'You can sing "Rock of Ages" for all I care, but not with electricals.'[395]

A compromise was reached. Tommy made his theatrical debut with his amplifier on stage together with a fireman in full uniform, standing alongside, holding a smoke blanket and a fire bucket.

David Whitfield.

The stars saw different reasons for variety's decline. The bandleader, Jack Payne, thought the rot had set in when movies became predominant: 'How can you expect people to pay, say, 7s 6d to go to a music hall when they can get a better seat for, say, 2s4d at a picture house?'[396] Jack was also critical about the physical condition of some variety theatres, citing poor lighting, dirty paintwork, tatty scenery and incompetent pit orchestras. Morecambe and Wise blamed the Second World War: 'A lot of brilliant acts disappeared and the Palladium embarked on a policy of using only American tops of the bill.'[397] Val Parnell imported the likes of Judy Garland and Bob Hope.[398] Filmgoers had seen them on the screen and, once again, they wanted to see them in the flesh. Some succeeded. Danny Kaye was a huge hit. Others failed, none so ignominiously as Mickey Rooney. Asked why he brought big American names to London, Parnell said he was primarily a businessman. His job was to fill theatres.

Others found further reasons for variety's demise. According to Barry Cryer, the strip shows were the main factor: 'People stopped taking their children. The man didn't take his wife and so on. It all changed.'[399] Alf Pearson believes that skiffle and rock and roll sounded the death knell. What he really meant was that his style of music had suddenly gone out of fashion. Certainly, Lonnie Donegan, Britain's leading exponent of skiffle, was heading variety bills as soon as he released his first hit record, *Rock Island Line*, at the start of 1956.

Issy Bonn knew when he had to retire:

I went on the stage of the Chiswick Empire and started to do my act. All through the show, up in the gallery, the kids were jiving and singing … So, I stopped the show and said to them 'I want you to enjoy yourselves and have a good time … Years ago, when I was young … I used to go to the gallery in the Holborn Empire and my pals and I would do our best to upset the artists of the day … I told myself that one day I would get the same treatment. I see that day has arrived.'[400]

Movies, music and girlie shows all played their part in making variety less popular, but a major reason was an increasing interest in television. At the start of the 1950s, about 350,000 households had TV sets. By the end of 1952, that figure had grown to nearly 1.5 million. It leaped again just before the Coronation of the Queen. About 10,000 viewers had watched the Coronation of her father, George VI, in 1937. In 1953, no fewer than 27 million people watched Elizabeth's.

Ironically, television allowed variety its last hurrah. When the BBC's television service faced competition for the first time in 1955, ITV screened Val Parnell's *Sunday Night at the London Palladium*, in its first week, giving the best variety entertainers a much-needed new outlet. Viewers had never seen a TV show as spectacular as this and it immediately climbed to the top of the ratings. Val Parnell continued to import big American stars.

The compère was the veteran variety comedian, Tommy Trinder, whose name had been linked with the Palladium throughout his long career. Tommy was a master of the ad lib and was as effective without a script as he was with one. With a long thin face and a jutting chin, his trademark was a trilby hat, which he wore even with evening dress. Tommy's comedy was abrasive: 'If it's laughter you're after, Trinder's the name. You lucky people!'[401] One night, a power failure blacked out the entire ITV network. Tommy ad-libbed for two hours. When the picture was eventually restored, his first words were 'Welcome to Monday morning at the London Palladium.'[402]

A young Bruce Forsyth.

In 1958, when Tommy was 51, Parnell began looking for a younger compère. Enter, Bruce Forsyth. In his twenties, he worked in variety, usually as the second spot comic. At the age of 27, he played his first summer season at the Babbacombe Theatre in Devon. On Sunday nights, a different show was staged. Besides the usual acts, Bruce had the opportunity of organising games with members of the audience, similar to the Beat the Clock segment of *Sunday Night at the London Palladium*. Bruce was brilliant at playing one member of the audience against another. He found an Ethel in the stalls and an Ada in the gallery and maintained a running gag involving both of them. Three years later [1958], Bruce moved along the coast to play a summer season at the Hippodrome, Eastbourne, but he was becoming dispirited with show business and, in fact, gave himself five years to succeed. Otherwise, he would find another job.

He got to know an act called Francois and Andre, who were friends of the top-line agent, Billy Marsh, and they convinced him that he ought to see Bruce at work. Marsh was evidently impressed as Bruce was invited by Brian Tesler, the director of *Sunday Night at the London Palladium* to appear in another TV show, called *New Look*, featuring performers at the start of their careers. They were well selected. Besides Bruce, Des O'Connor, Roy Castle and Lionel Blair took part. In time, Bruce was asked to appear on *Sunday Night at the London Palladium* and, after that, to take over from Tommy:

> That is how in September 1958 at the age of 30 I left that dowdy old theatre … the Hippodrome, Eastbourne, where I worked sometimes to 40 or 50 people, to go to the London Palladium, which seated 2,500 people and had a 30-piece orchestra … The contrast was unbelievable.[403]

If only today's showbiz moguls were as adventurous in their talent-spotting. As its popularity increased, *Sunday Night at the London Palladium* became one of the few presenters of variety. As former theatre-goers sat at home and watched variety on television, the theatres continued to close: the Ardwick Empire; the Alhambra and the Grand, Blackpool; the Grand, Bolton; the Hippodrome, Brighton; the Bristol, Chatham, Dewsbury, Finsbury Park and Leeds Empires; the Lewisham Hippodrome; the Newcastle and Woolwich Empires; and, most tragically of all, the Metropolitan, Edgware Road, which was demolished for a road widening plan that never materialised.

When Val Parnell said he was importing American stars because he had to fill theatres, he was by implication suggesting that there were not enough British stars. There was – and is – a love of and a need for variety, as witnessed by the current glut of such incredibly popular television shows as *The X Factor* and *Britain's Got Talent.*

The talent is there. It just needs an outlet. Although cinema and television did Old-Time Variety no favours, they did not kill it. Variety committed suicide.

Notes

Chapter 1: New Readers Start Here
1. Thomas Burke, Son of London, London, Herbert Jenkins, 1947, pp. 250–251.
2. One restriction that has never been lifted is the twice-yearly charade of changing the clocks.
3. W.J. MacQueen Pope, The Melodies Linger On, London, W.H. Allen, 1950, pp. 434–435.

Chapter 2: Amazing Gracie
4. James Agate, Immoment Toys, London, Jonathan Cape, 1945, p. 227.
5. James Agate, Ego 2, London, Gollancz, 1936, p. 223.
6. J.B. Priestley, English Journey, London, Heinemann, 1934, p. 253.
7. Jessie Merrilees married Jack Pleasants [1874–1924], who sang I'm Twenty-One Today and I'm Shy, Mary Ellen, I'm Shy.
8. Gracie Fields, Sing As We Go, London, Frederick Muller, 1960, p. 37.
9. Ibid., p. 45.
10. The Era 25 February 1924.
11. The Sunday Chronicle 29 September 1935.
12. Matthew Sweet, Shepperton Babylon, London, Faber and Faber, 2005, p. 123.
13. Gracie Fields, Sing As We Go, London, Frederick Muller, 1960, p. 89.
14. Ibid., p. 89.
15. Florence Desmond by Herself, London, Harrap, 1953, p. 52.
16. Henry Kendall, I Remember Romano's, London, MacDonald, 1960, p. 133.
17. Stanley Holloway, Wiv a Little Bit o' Luck, London, Leslie Frewin, p. 166.
18. Basil Dean, Mind's Eye, London, Hutchinson, 1973, p. 207.
19. Ibid., p. 90.
20. Ibid., p. 90.
21. Film Weekly 8 May 1937.
22. "Big-hearted" Arthur Askey did not according to one account always live up to his sobriquet. Michael Hurll said he was the worst pantomime dame he had ever worked with: "A grumpy, unfunny, lazy performer, [he] had no regard for the theatre audience. To see him 'walk through' a matinee panto performance was a disgrace to the theatrical profession. One very foggy night before one show, he counted the house and realised that there were more people on stage than in the audience … Askey invoked the ancient rule that, if the cast outnumbered the audience, we could cancel the performance. The dancers and 'true' pros in the cast argued with him that 'the show should go on,' but the wretched little cynical 'so-called' star said the curtain stays down." Hurll's criticism was countered by many rebuttals. The Call Boy Spring 2007 Volume 44 No. 1.
23. Joan Moules, Our Gracie London, Robert Hale, 1983, p. 90.
24. Daily Mail 1 June 2007.
25. Radio Times 18 July 1947.

Chapter 3: Funny Girl

26. Denis Gifford [1927–2000] wrote 50 books, including The British Film Catalogue 1895–1985, which lists every British film made during that period for public entertainment; The Golden Age of Radio [both 1985]; and Entertainers in British Films [1998].
27. Issued on a Cylidisc CD, Live Music Hall, in 2004. [Cylidisc albums are available from Tony Barker, 68 Hawkes Road, Mitcham, Surrey].
28. For the BBC, they were Radio's Two Cockney Kids.
29. Music Hall BBC Radio 28 June 1942.
30. 'Just Two Big Kids' by Ethel Revnell Radio Pictorial 16 July 1937.
31. Radio Times 8 December 1939.
32. My Alf, recorded as a 78 rpm disc 1 July 1938.
33. A mixture of feature films and variety turns.
34. TV Mirror 20 October 1956.
35. Graham Payn and Sheridan Morley, The Noel Coward Diaries, London, Weidenfeld and Nicholson, 1982, p. 552.
36. Renee Houston, Don't Fence Me In, London, Pan Books, 1974, pp. 33–34.
37. Radio Pictorial 15 January 1937.
38. London Laughs, BBC Radio 28 May 1961.
39. Alan Melville, Merely Melville, London, Hodder and Stoughton, 1970, p. 166.
40. Years later, Joan Turner and Jimmy Edwards, in his time, a huge radio star, announced that they were to marry. Joan did not know then [nor did the general public] that Jimmy was gay. A newspaper revealed his sexuality. When the critic, Sheridan Morley, referred to him coming out of the closet, Jimmy bellowed back: "Out of the closet? Of course, I didn't come out of the bloody closet. They broke the bloody door down and dragged me out." [The Spectator, 5 May 2001]. Towards the end of his life, Jimmy Edwards drank two bottles of whisky a day.
41. Holiday Music Hall, BBC Radio, 8 August 1959.

Chapter 4: Black and Blue

42. Momus was the Greek God of mockery, faultfinding and unfair criticism. He is also the patron of writers and poets.
43. The Performer Christmas edition, 1928.
44. Patrick Pilton, Every Night at the London Palladium, London, Robson Books, 1976 p25.
45. The Palace represented the pinnacle of vaudeville, America's equivalent of music hall, from 1914 to 1934.
46. Sophie Tucker, Some of These Days, London, Hammond, 1948 p. 174.
47. Theatre World May 1933.
48. John Bull 9 July 1938.
49. The Performer 11 April 1923.
50. The [London] Evening News 4 May 1923.
51. Tommy Handley, one of the greatest of all radio comedians, is mostly remembered for his morale-boosting series, ITMA [It's That Man Again], in the Second World War. But he began his broadcasting career with an appearance in a radio revue in 1926. The following year, he acted as a commentator on the Royal Variety Show, the first time a complete show was broadcast. "Tommy Handley handled his part well, cracking several jokes off his own bat, but never interpolating unnecessary comment." [The Encore 9 February 1928]. For 20 years, he toured with a musical scena, The Disorderly Room, compiled by Eric Blore, later to be seen in American movies playing a haughty waiter or a petulant butler.

52. Reith created the BBC as a public service broadcaster. It set high standards and was copied by many other broadcasting stations around the world. However, the moral strictness Reith imposed on his staff made him look ludicrous. Employees who divorced, for instance, were expected to resign. But Reith, the archetypal dour Scot, was not above reproach himself. He treated his wife shamefully and was estranged from his daughter for many years. Later in life, he had several flirtatious relationships with women, but his first love was a 17-year-old schoolboy, Charlie Bowser. For nearly 10 years until each of them married, Bowser was the most important person in his life.

53. Eric Maschwitz wrote three London musicals that ran for more than 500 performances, Balalaika [1936], Zip Goes a Million [1951] and Love from Judy [1952]. He is best known for the songs, These Foolish Things [1936] and A Nightingale Sang in Berkeley Square [1940].

54. BBC Sound Archive LP 24976.

55. Radio Times 15 January 1926.

56. Four complete editions of Music Hall survive: [1] the broadcast of 14 November 1936 with Arthur Askey and Will Hay; [2] that of 29 March 1941 with Issy Bonn, Arthur Prince, Norman Long, Elsie and Doris Waters and Anne Ziegler and Webster Booth; [3] 10 January 1942 with Gwen Farrar, Horace Kenney and the Two Leslies; and [4] 8 June 1946 with Cicely Courtneidge, Ronald Frankau, Jewel and Warriss, Tommy Handley and Anne Ziegler and Webster Booth. Other complete editions are held by private collectors and should be in the BBC Archive as well. The BBC also has excerpts from fourteen editions of Music Hall: [1] the broadcast of 28 October 1933 with Jack Payne and his Band; [2] that of 19 November 1938 with Ben Lyon and Bebe Daniels; [3] 19 April 1939 with Tommy Handley and Ronald Frankau; [4] 24 January 1941 with Suzette Tarri; [5] 22 March 1941 with Stainless Stephen; [6] 9 September 1941 with Jeanne de Casalis; [7] 15 November 1941 with Donald Peers, Suzette Tarri, Tommy Handley and Ronald Frankau; [8] 4 January 1942 with Suzette Tarri; [9] 26 April 1942 with Ronald Frankau; [10] 28 June 1942 with Nosmo King and Revnell and West; [11] 2 October 1948 with Vic Oliver; [12] 17 December 1949 with Ted Ray and Jimmy Wheeler; [13] 8 November 1950 with Peter Cavanagh; [14]; and 14 September 1952 with George Robey and Percy Edwards.

57. Workers' Playtime was a lunchtime entertainment for factory workers. As it was presented from a different factory every week, those involved sometimes worked with great ingenuity. An edition from Batchelors Food in the Kentish town of Ashford in 1960 was a case in point. Paul Gouldstone was one of the engineers: "Batchelors had to build a temporary stage in the works canteen of cardboard boxes of tinned peas to raise the artists above floor level so that the audience could see everything. At the rehearsal, the stage creaked from the [sound of] boxes of peas rubbing against each other and the works manager dashed home, removed his entire stair carpet and came back and laid the carpet across the front of the stage for [the singers] Pearl Carr and Teddy Johnson to broadcast without any unwanted sound effects." [Prospero, the magazine for retired BBC staff, October 2004]. Four complete editions of Workers' Playtime survive: [1] the broadcast of 29 October 1942 with Leonard Henry and Elsie and Doris Waters; [2] that of 6 February 1943 with Claude Dampier and Billie Carlyle and Elsie and Doris Waters; [3] 6 June 1946 with Jack Warner and Renee Houston and Donald Stewart; [4] 23 October 1962 with Eve Boswell, Peter Goodwright and Elsie and Doris Waters. The BBC also has excerpts from three other editions of Workers' Playtime: [1] the broadcast of 17 April 1945 with Maudie Edwards; [2] that of 15 May 1945 with Cyril Fletcher; and [3] 16 August 1945 with Norman Long.

58. Nine complete editions of Variety Bandbox survive: [1] the broadcast of 3 October 1948 with Frankie Howerd and Billy 'Uke' Scott; [2] that of 16 October 1949 with Frankie Howerd, Richard Attenborough and Peter Brough and Archie Andrews; [3] 6 November 1949 with Suzette Tarri, Reg Dixon and Betty Driver; [4] 13 November 1949 with Frankie Howerd, Charlie Chester, Florence Desmond, Eve Boswell and Bill Kerr; [5] 27 November 1949 with Frankie Howerd, John Hanson, Charlie Kunz and Janet Brown; [6] 15 January 1950 with Cardew Robinson, Reg Dixon, Kay Cavendish and Albert and Les Ward; [7] 22 January 1950 with Frankie Howerd, Peter Sellers and Bill Kerr; [8] 29 January 1950 with Harry Secombe, Peter Cavanagh and Reg Dixon; and [9] 19 February 1950 with Frankie Howerd, Dirk Bogarde, Dick Emery, John Hanson and Ivy Benson. Other complete editions are held by private collectors and should be in the BBC Archive as well. The BBC also has excerpts from two editions of Variety Bandbox: [1] the broadcast of 15 August 1948 with Charles Clark and [2] that of 17 December 1951 with Al Read.
59. Patrick Pilton, Every Night at the London Palladium, London, Robson Books, 1976, p. 26.
60. Hughie Green's son, Christopher, remembers watching the Coronation on television with Miss Leddington. She fell asleep and snored loudly. When she woke up, she waved a small Union Jack in the air, repeatedly said "God bless her" and farted loudly. Christopher Green with Carol Clerk, Hughie and Paula, London, Robson, 2003, pp. 102–103.
61. The Stage 29 September 1966.
62. John Fisher, Always Leave Them Laughing, London, Harper Collins, 2006, p. 86.
63. Variety Programme Policy Guide for Writers and Producers [London, BBC, 1949].

Chapter 5: Gang of Six

64. George Black writing in The Sunday Chronicle 6 October 1935.
65. They included Umbrella Man written by Vincent Rose, Larry Stock and James Cavanagh and recorded in 1937. [Umbrella Man was a nickname for Neville Chamberlain, Britain's Prime Minister from 1937 to 1940. He often carried an umbrella in public and was always shown with one in cartoons]; Nice People written by Nat Mills and Fred Malcolm; F.D.R. Jones, written by Harold Rome; If a Grey-Haired Lady [Says "How's Your Father?] written by Ted Waite; and Home Town, written by Jimmy Kennedy and Michael Carr.
66. The Sunday Chronicle 6 October 1935.
67. Bud Flanagan, My Crazy Life, London, Frederick Muller, 1961, p. 143.
68. The Golden Years of British Comedy, a three DVD set, issued by Universal Pictures.
69. John Fisher, Funny Way to be a Hero, London, Frederick Muller, 1973, p. 65.
70. Bud Flanagan, My Crazy Life, London, Frederick Muller, 1961, p. 140.
71. Terry-Thomas with Terry Daum, Terry-Thomas Tells Tales, London, Robson, 1990, p. 78.
72. The Call Boy Vol 30 No 3 Autumn 1993.
73. Caryll and Mundy were in only the first of the Crazy shows. Many veterans of variety regard Billy Caryll as the best stage drunk. From 1921, he appeared in a double act with his wife, Hilda Mundy. Caryll died in 1953 after his right leg was amputated above the knee. Mundy died in 1969.
74. Bud Flanagan, My Crazy Life, London, Frederick Muller, 1961, p. 159.
75. Ibid., p. 184.
76. Val Guest, So You Want to Be in Pictures, London, Reynolds and Hearn, 2001, p. 56.

Chapter 6: There'll Never Be Another

77. Max at the Met, an LP made at the Metropolitan Theatre, Edgware Road, in 1958.
78. John Osborne, A Better Class of Person, Harmondsworth, Penguin, 1982 p. 204.
79. John Fisher, Funny Way to be a Hero, London, Frederick Muller, 1973, p. 90.
80. Music Hall BBC Radio 26 December 1942.
81. Max left £7,000 to his mistress, Ann Graham, who was described in his will as his secretary.
82. Frederick Jester Barnes was a big star. He was gay and was known throughout the profession as Freda. Alcoholism led to his downfall. He lost everything and died in lodgings in the Essex seaside town of Southend.
83. The Performer 5 November 1930.
84. BBC Radio Two Arts Programme 20 November 1994.
85. Max Bygraves, I Wanna Tell You a Story, London, W.H. Allen, p. 176.
86. Those pensioners did not include his first showbiz employer, Jack Sheppard, who, towards the end of his life, lived in two rooms in Brighton, entirely dependent on his old age pension and National Assistance, totalling £3 10s [£45] a week. Jack, whose real name was Thomas Gomm, died in Brighton in 1968 at the age of 94.
87. Daily Mail 9 May 1963.
88. BBC Radio Two Arts Programme 20 November 1994.
89. Bob Monkhouse, Crying with Laughter, London, Century, 1988, p. 58.
90. East was an intelligent and highly complex man. At one stage in his life, he was involved in soft-core porn movies. He wrote one, directed another and even appeared with the likes of Mary Millington, who committed suicide at the age of 33. A senior BBC Radio producer, who employed him as a researcher, referred to his "irresistible sleaziness." His literary career rests on the highly readable 'Neath the Mask, an account of the East family, who played an important role in the early days of the British film industry. Yet, John was not an East. His real surname was Baker. The cinema historian, Matthew Sweet, while researching his book, Shepperton Babylon, spent many hours with East, but, as time went by, he grew increasingly sceptical about the relentless flood of anecdotes. East died on April Fool's Day 2003 and left £715,000. He left some material to the British Film Institute and the London Theatre Museum and made 25 individual bequests. The residual beneficiary was a young German man East got to know at the BBC although there had been little contact since the reunification of Germany in 1991.
91. There was a short verse attributed to Max: "When roses are red, They're ready for plucking. When a girl is sixteen, she's ready for …. 'ere!" Again, it is too coarse for Max.
92. Leslie Irons, who helped to compile the Max Miller Appreciation Society's Blue Book, says he remembers the furore at the time of the broadcast. "[Max said] 'They should not have faded me out because I was not going to use that ending.' So, obviously the joke was in his repertoire." [Not necessarily. He may have heard the joke, but never used it. Ed.] Another of the Society's members, Ronald Jones, is equally convinced: "I remember it vividly because, when I went out to play, the other kids were asking each other [whether] they had heard it on the radio." There'll Never Be Another, the magazine of the Max Miller Appreciation Society, Vol. 5, Issue 1, Spring 2003.
93. Of course, Max **knew** dirty jokes. Most men do. Barry Cryer recalled sharing a bill with Max on BBC Radio's Midday Music Hall. "During rehearsals, Max told a joke about a bus breaking down … The driver lifted the bonnet to discover the cause of the breakdown. After 10 minutes, the conductress, looking at the

impatient passengers, joined him and asked 'Do you want a screwdriver?' 'No, we're 10 minutes late already,' replied the driver.' ... The producer held his head in his hands and nervously asked Max to delete the joke." Barry Cryer, You Won't Believe This But ..., London, Virgin, 1998, p. 80.
94. Daily Mail 8 December 1949.
95. The programme, transmitted on 6 May 1951, also featured Gracie Fields, Danny Kaye, Frankie Howerd, George Robey, Ted Ray, Robb Wilton, Elsie and Doris Waters, G.H. Elliott, Donald Peers, Albert Whelan and Anne Ziegler and Webster Booth.
96. Gracie Fields, Billy Cotton, Terry-Thomas and Josef Locke also appeared.
97. John Fisher, Funny Way to be a Hero, London, Frederick Muller, 1973, p. 92.
98. Lord Delfont, Curtain Up! London, Robson, 1989 p. 90.
99. Evening Standard 7 November 1958.
100. Time and Tide 7 September 1940.
101. News Chronicle 21 December 1959.
102. Ibid.

Chapter 7: A Class of their Own
103. A 78 rpm gramophone record, The Police Station, made 24 September 1931.
104. A 78 rpm gramophone record, The Fire Station, made 24 September 1931.
105. A 78 rpm gramophone record, The Home Guard, made 6 September 1943.
106. The Call Boy Vol. 26 No. 3 Autumn 1989.
107. A collection of Robb Wilton's scripts [1951–54], biographical documents [1956/57] and photographs is held by Warwick University.
108. Top of the Bill BBC Radio Two 10 February 1980.
109. John Fisher, Funny Way to be a Hero, London, Frederick Muller, 1973, p. 189.
110. Ibid.
111. Casey wrote and produced The Clitheroe Kid, a BBC Radio comedy show that ran from 1957 to 1972. It starred the diminutive Jimmy Clitheroe as a cheeky schoolboy, a latter-day Wee Georgie Wood. He died on 6 June 1973, the day of his mother's funeral. An inquest found that he had accidentally taken an overdose of drugs.
112. John Fisher, Funny Way to be a Hero, London, Frederick Muller, 1973, p. 194.
113. Ibid., p. 195.
114. Mike Craig, Look Back With Laughter, Manchester, Mike Craig, 1996, pp. 48–49.
115. Workers' Playtime BBC Radio 16 February 1943.
116. Billie Carlyle, Claude Dampier, Mrs Gibson and Me, Staines, Billie Carlyle, 1978, p. 43.
117. Music Hall, BBC Radio, 4 January 1941.
118. Cape Argus 2 February 1949.
119. James Agate, Immoment Toys, London, Jonathan Cape, 1945, pp. 225–226.
120. The Era 19 March 1924.
121. T.W. Connor's real name was Thomas Widdicombe. He died on 24 January 1936 and left £16 [£550].
122. His most famous song was She Was One of the Early Birds [1895], which he wrote for George Beauchamp.
123. The word was not considered offensive then.
124. Radio Pictorial 10 July 1936.
125. The distinguished character actress.
126. Hawley Harvey Crippen was hanged for murdering his wife, a minor music hall singer, Belle Elmore, in 1910.

127. My Mother Doesn't Know I'm on the Stage, a 78 rpm recording made on 24 August 1929.
128. James Agate, Immoment Toys, London, Jonathan Cape, 1945, p. 226.
129. Radio Times 5 June 1931.
130. A BBC interview, recorded in August 1971, but never transmitted.
131. A 78 rpm gramophone record made 1 October 1928.
132. BBC Radio's Music Hall 17 December 1949.
133. Will Wyatt went on to be the deputy of the controversial Director General of the BBC, [Lord] John Birt.
134. Will Wyatt, The Fun Factory, London, Aurum Press, 2003 p. 44.
135. Bill Pertwee, By Royal Command, Newton Abbot, David and Charles, 1981, p. 121.
136. The Sunday Times 14 May 1972.

Chapter 8: Infinite Variety

137. Eric Morecambe and Ernie Wise, Eric and Ernie, London, W.H. Allen, 1973, p. 92.
138. Detroy, who was born in the Lancashire town of Stockport, died in Las Vegas in 1986.
139. The Stage 11 March 1954.
140. Charlie Chester, The World is Full of Charlies, London, New English Library, 1974, pp. 107–108.
141. TV Mirror 31 December 1955.
142. Leslie Welch died in 1980.
143. Sheila Van Damm, We Never Closed, London, Robert Hale, 1967 p. 117.
144. TV Mirror 30 July 1955.
145. Cue 9 January 1954.

Chapter 9: When Harry wrote *Sally*

146. A flivver was a car. The song is about the joys of cheap pre-war motoring.
147. Richard Armitage inherited his father's music publishing company and turned it into the biggest theatrical agency in Europe. His clients included David Frost, Jonathan Miller, John Cleese and Rowan Atkinson.
148. Radio Pictorial 29 January 1937.
149. Eddie Rogers, Tin Pan Alley, London, Robert Hale, 1964, p. 90.
150. The Sunday Times 11 October 1955. [A review of a London Palladium show, Fun and the Fair, in which Formby sang the song.]
151. Harry Gifford died on 8 January 1960.
152. Fred Cliffe died on 22 September 1957.
153. A revised version of Me and My Girl [1985] ran for more than 4,000 performances at the Adelphi Theatre. Some of Noel's other songs, including Leaning on a Lamppost and The Sun Has Got His Hat On, were interpolated. [The original line in the latter song "He's been tanning niggers out in Timbuktu" was replaced by "He's been roasting peanuts out in Timbuktu."] A young Stephen Fry, who rewrote the book, became a millionaire in the process.
154. The Siegfried Line was a line of fortifications built by the Germans before and during the Second World War. It was named after a character in German mythology.
155. Radio Pictorial 15 January 1937.
156. David [1872–1940] wrote for a number of music-hall stars. With George Arthurs, he produced I Want to Sing in Opera [1910] for Wilkie Bard; with Bert Lee and

Harry Fragson, he was responsible for Hello! Hello! Who's Your Lady Friend? [1913] for Fragson; and with C.W. Murphy he wrote Hold Your Hand Out, Naughty Boy [also 1913] for Florrie Forde.

Chapter 10: George and the Dragon

157. The Life and Wartimes of George Formby, a DVD issued by Mastersound in 2004.
158. George also played the banjulele. It is similar to the ukulele, but is fitted with a drum of calfskin vellum and a resonator so that it sounds louder.
159. He recorded six songs in 1926: Rolling Around Piccadilly; John Willie's Jazz Band; I Was Always a Willing Young Lad, all written by Robert Hargreaves, who died in Hendon in 1934, aged 40, and Stanley Damerell [otherwise known as John Edward Stanley Stevens], who died in Twickenham in 1951, aged 73; I Parted My Hair in the Middle by C.W. Murphy, who died in Blackpool in 1913, aged 38, and Worton David, who died in Worthing in 1940, aged 68; John Willie, Come On by George Formby senior; and The Man Was a Stranger to Me.
160. George had, in fact, appeared in two films in 1915 made by his father's friend, Will Barker. They were five-reelers entitled By the Shortest of Heads and No Fool Like an Old Fool. Only one print of the former is believed to have survived, but it is apparently in a private archive and unavailable for public viewing. Nothing is known about the latter. Barker, who was a pioneer of the British film industry, bought land in Ealing in 1902 and built his first studio there five years later.
161. Beryl also appeared in these two films.
162. Basil Dean, Mind's Eye, London, Hutchinson, 1973, p. 212.
163. Michael Balcon, Michael Balcon Presents …, London, Hutchinson, 1969, p. 118.
164. Basil Dean, Mind's Eye, London, Hutchinson, 1973, p. 213.
165. The BBC banned this record until it learned that the Queen Mother liked it. The record was then reinstated.
166. Florence Desmond by Herself, London, Harrap, 1953, pp. 135–136.
167. Patricia Kirkwood, The Time of My Life, London, Robert Hale, 1999, p. 63.
168. Ibid., pp. 62–63.
169. Alan Randall and Ray Seaton, George Formby, London, W.H. Allen, 1974, p. 85.
170. London Evening Standard 26 October 1951.
171. The Sunday Times 11 October 1953.
172. Harry Scott was George's valet for 29 years: "My first week's wage with the Formbys was £5. It was still £5 a week nearly 30 years later when George died. The number of hours of work and companionship I gave George and Beryl must have been colossal. I went with them everywhere and enjoyed every moment. We had our disagreements and I walked out on them more than once. But I would do it again, even for a fiver a week." [The Vellum, the magazine of the George Formby Society, Winter 2005].
173. Will's father warned his children never to patronise music halls because he believed they were all disreputable and vulgar.
174. At the age of 22, Eppie died of consumption, which had claimed the life of her sister, Nellie, on her nineteenth birthday.
175. John Mills, Up in the Clouds, Please, Gentleman, London, Weidenfeld and Nicolson, 1980, p. 122.
176. Billie Carlyle, Claude Dampier, Mrs Gibson and Me, Staines, Billie Carlyle, 1978, p. 42.
177. Marcel Varnel was killed in a car accident in 1947 while on his way to the studios at Walton-on-Thames.
178. The Times 19 April 1949.

Chapter 11: By 'Eck

179. www.btinternet.com/~nigel.ellacott/gardenwall.html.
180. The Era 14 November 1934.
181. The Tatler 15 November 1939.
182. Sandy Powell and Harry Stanley, Can You Hear Me, Mother? London, Jupiter Books, 1975, p. 117.
183. Most of Sandy's films were made by British Lion, one of Britain's major movie makers. Founded in 1927, it made more than 150 pictures, including In Which We Serve [1942].
184. In the Brains Trust, the panel discussed questions from listeners, such as "What is the difference between fresh air and a draught?" and "How does a fly land upside down on a ceiling?" Commander Campbell's catch phrase became "When I was in Patagonia…".
185. The Decorator, an EMI Gold CD, Right Monkey: The Best of Al Read.
186. The Times 11 September 1987.
187. Daily Mirror 18 September 1933.
188. 78 rpm gramophone record, Albert Before the Means Test, recorded on 10 October 1933.
189. One was the comedienne, Sally Barnes, who was best known for her portrayal of a charwoman. She made two films with Frank – Holidays with Pay and Somewhere in Politics. In the 1950s, she became one of television's first comedy stars. She died in 1985.
190. Recorded at Feldman's Theatre, Blackpool, in August 1938 and released by Regal Zonophone as a 78 rpm gramophone record.
191. During the Second World War, British newspaper readers grew accustomed to the phrase "Somewhere in …" Local paper reports of enemy action were censored to prevent the Germans knowing details of the damage they caused. So, when, for example, the Argyle music-hall in Birkenhead was all but destroyed in 1940, a local paper, The Birkenhead Advertiser and Wallasey Guardian [28 September 1940] had to report: "Commercial buildings, a well-known variety theatre and other public buildings were damaged by incendiary bombs which were scattered over a wide area in a north-west coastal district."
192. All Frank's films are extant with the exception of Somewhere in Politics. A private collector may have a copy, but, if he does, he is keeping it secret.
193. Blakeley converted a disused Wesleyan church in the Rusholme district of Manchester. The church itself became the main set, while the church hall was converted into a subsidiary set. Most of the cost was met by a government grant aimed at propping up the ailing British film industry. In 1954, the BBC bought the studio and produced a range of television programmes there, including Top of the Pops.
194. Diana Dors, Swingin' Dors, London, World Distributors [Manchester], 1960, pp. 86–87.
195. Randolph Sutton [1888–1969] was the original singer of On Mother Kelly's Doorstep. Twice married, he spent his latter years with a male partner, Terry Doogan, best known for playing a cat in pantomime. Doogan died in 2005.
196. The Times 5 February 1952.
197. The Observer 10 February 1952.
198. Roy Castle, Now and Then, London, Robson, 1994, pp. 61–62.

Chapter 12: With a Little Bit of Locke
199. I'll Take You Home Again, Kathleen, composed by an American songwriter, Thomas P. Westerndorf, was first published in 1876. It adopted an Irish dimension when it was made by popular by another Irish tenor, John McCormack.
200. Goodbye is from Im Weissen Rossl, produced at the Grosses Schauspielhaus, Berlin, in 1930. The show came to the London Coliseum as White Horse Inn in 1931.
201. Hear My Song, Violetta was written by Rudolf Luckesch and Othmar Klose in 1936. Its English lyric was the work of Harry S. Pepper.
202. Jimmy Jewel, Three Times Lucky, London, Enigma Books, 1982, p. 119.
203. It was part of the 1921 operetta, Der Vetter aus Dingsda, composed by Eduard Künneke. As The Cousin from Nowhere, it was staged at the Princes Theatre in London in 1923.

Chapter 13: Musical Mayhem
204. Roy Hudd and Philip Hindin, Roy Hudd's Cavalcade of Variety Acts, London, Robson, 1997, p. 122.
205. Daily Telegraph 20 August 2004.
206. Ibid.
207. TV Mirror 26 May 1956.
208. Sid had a son, born in 1955 and christened Rance Lancelot.
209. Cyril Lagey died in March 1999, aged 81.
210. Toni Traversi died in March 2004, a few days short of his 90th birthday.
211. Morton Fraser died 10 June 1972.
212. Two members of the Gang went on to achieve far greater fame. Dave King became a top-rate comedian in the 1950s and early 1960s before establishing himself as a respected serious actor in such television dramas as Dennis Potter's Pennies from Heaven. Gordon Mills became Tom Jones' manager and co-wrote his first hit, It's Not Unusual.
213. Jimmy Prescott was replaced by David Conway in 1961.
214. Les Henry [Cedric Monarch] died 12 January 2007.
215. Eric Yorke died 5 March 1998.
216. Daily Telegraph 19 February 1994.
217. Skiffle was a form of folk music heavily influenced by blues and jazz. Home-made or improvised instruments were used such as the washboard, a bass made from a tea chest, a musical saw, comb and paper as well as more conventional instruments such as the banjo and the acoustic guitar.
218. The Stage 11 October 2001.
219. Bob Monkhouse, Over the Limit, London, Century, 1998 p. 259.

Chapter 14: Hutch – Too Much
220. Hutch also favoured the work of some British songwriters, most notably, Ray Noble [I Hadn't Anyone Till You] and Eric Maschwitz [These Foolish Things].
221. Only one artiste refused to yield to Hutch's top-of-the-bill status, Jose Collins, the star of Maid of the Mountains. She stayed away from the Coliseum in spite of two court actions and was never forgiven by the variety world.
222. Leslie Sarony saw a song in this gimmick, The Night That Hutch Forgot His Handkerchief. He also impersonated Hutch singing White Christmas.
223. Charlotte Breese Hutch, London, Bloomsbury, 1999, p. 154. This chapter is based almost entirely on this superb biography.

Chapter 15: The Day War Broke Out
224. The Times 5 September 1939.
225. The compulsory closure of theatres lasted only until 16 September 1939.
226. An abbreviation of the German word, blitzkrieg, meaning 'lightning war'.
227. Jimmy Jewel, Three Times Lucky, London, Enigma Books, 1982, p. 94.
228. Hermione Gingold, How to Grow Old Disgracefully, London, Gollancz, 1989, pp. 89–90.
229. They are now called customers since gypsies, once proud of their history and tradition, have become travellers.
230. Stations were not entirely safe. Sixty-eight people were killed when a bomb fell near Balham Station in October 1940; 111 died when the booking hall at Bank station was bombed in January 1941; and in March 1943, 173 people were crushed to death at Bethnal Green station.
231. Richard Fawkes, Fighting for a Laugh, London, Macdonald and Jane's, 1978, p. 187.
232. Sunday Despatch 10 October 1943.
233. Sunday Despatch 17 October 1943.
234. Richard Fawkes, Fighting for a Laugh, London, Macdonald and Jane's, 1978, p. 188.
235. Ibid., p. 187.

Chapter 16: Bare-Faced Chic
236. Even in its latter years, the Lord Chamberlain's office committed many nonsenses, such as its refusal to license Jean Genet's The Maids [sadism and Lesbianism] and John Osborne's A Patriot For Me [homosexuality].
237. Between 1932 and 1935, John Tilley made a number of 78rpm gramophone records and a short film.
238. Pearson's Weekly 10 September 1932.
239. The Stage 24 November 2005.
240. Sheila Van Damm, We Never Closed, London, Robert Hale, 1967, pp. 62–63.
241. Michael Bentine, The Reluctant Jester, London, Bantam Press, 1992, p. 180.
242. Arthur English, Through the Mill and Beyond, Basingstoke, The Basingstoke, Press, 1986, p. 69.
243. Eric Morecambe and Ernie Wise, Eric and Ernie, London, W.H. Allen, 1973, p. 71.
244. Sheila Van Damm, We Never Closed, London, Robert Hale, 1967, p. 175.
245. Ibid., p. 176.
246. Ibid., p. 182.
247. Wallace Parnell was a son of Fred Russell, the father of modern ventriloquism, and a brother of Val Parnell. He specialised in staging spectacular revues and at one time had no fewer than 16 of them on the road simultaneously. For six years, he was the production manager for the Tivoli circuit in Australia and then he moved to Hollywood, where he built up a number of joint business ventures with his secretary, Beryl Erickson. He eventually sold his interest in them to Mrs Erickson. On 20 May 1954, he shot her dead and then committed suicide.
248. For the record, Jack was five foot [150 cms] tall. Phyllis was five foot three-and-a-half inches [159 cms]. Her vital statistics: 34 23 36.
249. Sunday Dispatch 16 September 1956.
250. Lord Chamberlain's papers deposited with the British Library.
251. Frances Day [1908–84] was an American actress and singer who was highly popular in Britain in the 1930s.

252. Howard Thomas, With an Independent Air, London, Weidenfeld and Nicolson, 1977, pp. 106–107.
253. Sunday Dispatch 16 September 1956.
254. Philip Purser and Jenny Wilkes, The One and Only Phyllis Dixey, London, Futura Publications, 1978, p. 144.
255. Sunday Chronicle 16 September 1951.
256. H.G. Pelissier founded The Follies concert party. A gay alcoholic, he was the first husband of the distinguished actress, Fay Compton, before dying in 1913 at the age of 39.
257. Reg Stone died of pneumonia in 1934. He was 40.
258. Brighton Standard and Fashionable Visitors' List 15 May 1919.
259. Daily Express 5 August 1919.
260. There were three Splinters movies: Splinters [1929]; Splinters in the Navy [1931]; and Splinters in the Air [1937].
261. James Edwin Slater: born 4 November 1896; died Yeadon, West Yorkshire, 17 December 1996.
262. Chris Sheen, whose real name was Christopher Shinfield, died in 1983.

Chapter 17: From the Heart of my Bottom
263. W.J. MacQueen Pope, The Melodies Linger On, London, W.H. Allen, 1950, pp. 116–17.
264. A 78 rpm gramophone record made on 11 January 1923. All of Hayes' Monty records were re-released on a CD on the Windyridge label, The Meanderings of Monty. Windyridge CDs can be ordered on line at www.musichallcds.com or you can contact Mr W.J. Clark, Windyridge, Kettleburgh, Woodbridge, Suffolk IP13 7JR.
265. W. Buchanan-Taylor, Shake it Again, London, Heath Cranton, 1943, p. 29.
266. The Era 21 February 1925.
267. "Cheap, tawdry and over-elaborate."
268. W. Buchanan-Taylor, Shake it Again, London, Heath Cranton, 1943, p. 29.
269. Williams recorded it twice: in June 1913 and April 1926.
270. Bransby Williams by Himself, London, Hutchinson, 1954, p. 47.
271. Radio Pictorial 27 November 1936.
272. Henry Hall's Hour BBC Radio 19 December 1936.

Chapter 18: Nothing Up My Sleeve
273. John Wade, The Trade of the Tricks, London, Elm Tree, 1974, p. 93.

Chapter 19: Use of Cruet, Threepence
274. 11,081,977 radio licences were issued in 1948. It was reckoned that about 21,000,000 people tuned in to Variety Bandbox each week. The number of radio licences reached a record 11,819,190 in 1950. After that, the growing popularity of television began to force the figure down. "[The producer of Variety Bandbox,] Joy Russell-Smith, won't forget the day one newcomer turned up for an audition. 'He was a shambling, distraught young man who didn't know one side of the mike from the other. But he made me laugh. Goodness, how I laughed!' It was Frankie Howerd, of course. Joy booked him for three fortnightly broadcasts, but listeners agreed with her and Howerd has appeared on every other Sunday since." Radio Times 2 April 1948.
275. Graham McCann, Frankie Howerd, London, Fourth Estate, 2004 p. 73.

276. Stagedoor, the newsletter of the Scottish Music Hall and Variety Theatre Society. Issue 66. Autumn 2004.
277. Roy Hudd's Book of Music Hall, Variety and Showbiz anecdotes, London, Robson, 1993, p. 93.

Chapter 20: High Camp, Low Farce
278. This theatre stood at the corner of Oxford Street and Tottenham Court Road in central London. It closed in 1926 and was demolished a year or two later.
279. The Times 17 March 1983.
280. Douglas Byng, As You Were, London, Duckworth, 1970, p. 111.
281. 78 rpm disc recorded on 17 December 1928.
282. In his highly entertaining book, The Krays and Bette Davis, Dougie's last agent, Patrick Newley, gives an hilarious account of how Dougie tried to look after Alice Delysia when they both lived in Brighton in their old age. She was always cross when he called on her while she was watching Crossroads.
283. 78rpm disc recorded on 8 February 1935.
284. 78 rpm disc recorded on 27 November 1932.
285. The Guardian 23 December 1983.
286. Ibid.
287. The Place To Be Seen, an article written by Patrick Newley in Capital Gay 27 July 1990. The Duke of Kent [1902–42], the fourth son of George V, was a promiscuous, bi-sexual alcoholic, who at one time was addicted to cocaine. Coward had an affair with him and Dougie admitted to a "dalliance". At the age of 39, he was killed when his plane crashed in Caithness in northern Scotland.
288. The Times 26 August 1987.
289. Michael Kilgariff, Grace, Beauty and Banjos, London, Oberon, 1988, p. 278.
290. The Independent 8 May 1995.
291. Hereford Times 2 January 1953.
292. An e-mail to the author dated 21 November 2004.
293. Look in at the Local, a Decca long-playing record released in 1967.
294. Ibid.
295. The Epilogue was a short religious broadcast at the end of each evening's television transmissions.
296. A Drop of the Hard Shuff, a Decca long-playing record issued in 1973.
297. The Amazing Mrs Shufflewick p. 77.

Chapter 21: Indelible Impressions
298. To help her, Marie's sister, Alice, who was as popular in America as Marie was in Britain, gave Dessie the shawl in which Marie had sung the sung.
299. Florence Desmond by Herself, London, Harrap, 1953, p. 47.
300. Ibid., p. 49.
301. TV Mirror 5 September 1953.
302. Florence Desmond by Herself, London, Harrap, 1953, p. 285.
303. Ally Sloper's Half Holiday, which was first published in 1884, was the first comic to be named after and feature a regular character. Ally Sloper was a ne'er-do-well, always trying to avoid his creditors. The comic ceased publication in September 1916, although it was later briefly revived.
304. The word was not considered offensive then.
305. Workers' Playtime 3 May 1956.
306. Percy Edwards, The Road I Travelled, London, Arthur Barker, 1979, p. 72.
307. Ibid., p. 81.

308. Vivian Van Damm, Tonight and Every Night, London, Stanley Paul, 1952, p. 169.
309. An undated and untitled newspaper clipping held in the Mander and Mitchenson. Theatre Collection.
310. This was London Entertains, a tour of the Battersea Festival, a BBC studio, a nightclub and the Windmill Theatre.
311. Norman Wisdom, My Turn, London, Century, 1992, p. 246.
312. "Somebody once said inverted commas Comedians are born not made. Well, slight pause to heighten egotistical effect comma let me tell my dense public [innuendo] that I was born of honest but disappointed parents in anno domini eighteen ninety something." John Watt quoting Stainless Stephen in Radio Variety, London, J.M. Dent, 1939, p. 19.

Chapter 22: Life of Riley
313. Bridget's Night Out [1936], produced by Butcher's Film Service.
314. Steve King with Terry Cavender, As Long As I Know It'll Quite Alright, Blackpool, Lancastrian Transport Publications, p. 66.
315. Old Mother Riley and Kitty were first seen in the cinema in Stars on Parade [1936], together with Jimmy James, Robb Wilton and Albert Whelan. Their own movies started the following year: Old Mother Riley [1937]; Old Mother Riley in Paris [1938]; **Old Mother Riley MP** and Old Mother Riley Joins Up [both 1939]; **Old Mother Riley in Society** and Old Mother Riley in Business [both 1940]; **Old Mother Riley's Circus** and **Old Mother Riley's Ghosts** [both 1941]; Old Mother Riley Overseas and **Old Mother Riley Detective** [both 1943]; **Old Mother Riley at Home** [1945]; **Old Mother Riley's New Venture** [1949]; **Old Mother Riley Headmistress** [1950]; Old Mother Riley's Jungle Treasure [1951]; and **Old Mother Riley Meets the Vampire** [1952]. This last film featured Arthur without Kitty. The vampire was played by Bela Lugosi. One horrific figure was replaced by another. Movies shown in bold print have been reissued on DVD. Contracts were being negotiated for Old Mother Riley's Trip to Mars when Arthur died.
316. The first series, Old Mother Riley Takes the Air, which was written by Arthur and produced by Tom Ronald, began on 21 June 1941. The second, Old Mother Riley and her Daughter, Kitty, began on 6 June 1942. The third, using the same title, also featured Willer Neal. But the scriptwriter was now Kitty. It began on 20 September 1948.
317. Old Mother Riley's Past and Old Mother Riley in the Police Force [both recorded 4 July 1941]; Old Mother Riley on the Farm, Old Mother Riley's Budget and Old Mother Riley Takes her Medicine [all three recorded 6 August 1941]. All these recordings have been reissued on CD by the Windyridge label.
318. Dora Bryan, According to Dora, London, Bodley Head, 1987, pp. 74–75.
319. Sunday Dispatch 28 October 1956.

Chapter 23: Their Lips Were Sealed
320. Roy Hudd and Philip Hindin, Roy Hudd's Cavalcade of Variety Acts, London, Robson, 1997, p. 162.
321. It's a Funny Business BBC Radio Two 7 December 1988.
322. Up and Coming BBC Radio 23 January 1952.
323. Daily Mirror 15 December 1952.
324. TV Mirror 29 August 1953.
325. Unpublished autobiography with the working title, The Lady Was a Gentleman, written between 1956 and 1965.

Chapter 24: Two of a Kind
326. Daily Express 7 January 1939.
327. Eric Morecambe and Ernie Wise, Eric and Ernie, London, W.H. Allen, 1973, p. 38.
328. Ibid., p. 71.
329. Ibid., p. 39.
330. As well as Two of a Kind, Dick Hills [1926–1996] and Sid Green [1928–1999] wrote the first colour BBC series for Morecambe and Wise. They also appeared in some of the sketches. In addition, they wrote the three disappointing movies Morecambe and Wise made, The Intelligence Men [1965], That Riviera Touch [1966] and The Magnificent Two [1967].
331. At various times, Up the Pole featured Claude Dampier, Jon Pertwee [later to play Dr Who and Worzel Gummidge on television] and the ITMA stalwart, Fred Yule.
332. For 20 years, Val Parnell had a relationship with Noele Gordon, who appeared in the cheaply made television soap opera, Crossroads. After Parnell died, Aileen married the millionaire carpet manufacturer, Cyril Lord [1911–84].
333. Jimmy Jewel, Three Times Lucky, London, Enigma Books, 1982, p. 147.
334. Ibid., p. 146.
335. Ibid., p. 149.
336. Bernie was also in Idol on Parade with Tony Newley.
337. Bernie Winters, One Day at a Time, London, BCA, 1991, p. 44.
338. The Times 6 May 1991.
339. A 78 rpm record, issued 14 June 1927, their first recording session.
340. The Times 25 January 1963.
341. Lord Haw-Haw was the nickname of several announcers on the English language propaganda programme, Germany Calling, broadcast by Nazi Germany to audiences in Britain. The name generally refers to William Joyce, who was hanged for treason in 1946.
342. The Oldie January 2006.
343. Roger Wilmut, Kindly Leave the Stage, London, Methuen, 1985, p. 71.
344. Albert Sandler died of heart failure on 30 August 1948. He was 42.

Chapter 25: Par Excellence
345. Max Wall with Peter Ford, The Fool on the Hill, London, Quartet Books, 1975, p. 98.
346. Jimmy Jewel, Three Times Lucky, London, Enigma Books, 1982 p. 89.
347. John Fisher, Funny Way to be a Hero, London, Frederick Muller, 1973, p. 212.
348. Max Wall with Peter Ford, The Fool on the Hill, London, Quartet Books, 1975, p. 184.
349. John Fisher, Funny Way to be a Hero, London, Frederick Muller, 1973, p. 216.
350. Max Wall with Peter Ford, The Fool on the Hill, London, Quartet Books, 1975, p. 143.
351. Ibid., p. 143.
352. Ibid., p. 163.
353. Larry Adler, It Ain't Necessarily So, London, Collins, 1984, p. 87.
354. The Fool on the Hill p. 219.
355. Ibid., p. 223.
356. International Herald Tribune 15 December 1973.
357. The Independent on Sunday 27 May 1990.
358. Ibid.

359. John Fisher. What a Performance! [London, Seeley, Service and Co., 1975] p. 101.
360. James Agate, Ego 9, London, Harrap, 1948, p. 186.
361. Kenneth Tynan, Profiles, London, Nick Hern Books, 1989, p. 12.
362. Collie Knox, People of Quality, London, MacDonald, 1947, p. 165.
363. [The grammar was wrong, but you know what he meant]. John Fisher. What a Performance! London, Seeley, Service and Co., 1975, p. 170.
364. A 78 rpm gramophone record of Sid Field Plays Golf was released on 3 January 1945. It formed part of a Sepia Records CD of London Town in 2006.
365. John Fisher. What a Performance! London, Seeley, Service and Co., 1975, p. 82.
366. Ibid., p. 88.
367. New Statesman 1 April 1943.
368. The Times 19 March 1943.
369. The Tatler and Bystander 4 February 1948.
370. Terry-Thomas with Terry Daum, Terry-Thomas Tells Tales, London, Robson, 1990 p. 74.
371. To Pet, he became Uncle Sid. "He was an absolute darling." This is My Song, a Biography of Petula Clark by Andrea Kon, London, W.H. Allen, 1983 p. 51.
372. Terry-Thomas with Terry Daum, Terry-Thomas Tells Tales, London, Robson, 1990 p. 34.
373. Norman Wisdom, My Turn, London, Century, 1992, p. 187.

Chapter 26: A Dancing Mood

374. The Stage 26 November 1998.
375. The Daily Telegraph 9 May 1998.
376. Patrick Pilton, Every Night at the London Palladium, Robson, 1976.
377. Norman Quilliam, Tops, Bottoms and Middles III: Wilson, Keppel and Betty, The Call Boy, Vol. 20, No.3, Autumn 1983.
378. Hubert Gregg, Maybe It's Because…? Pen Press Publishers, 2005.
379. The Stage 7 October 1999.
380. Bert Ross, letter to The Stage 14 September 1978.
381. There'll Never Be Another, the journal of the Max Miller Appreciation Society, Winter 2005, Issue 4, Volume 7.
382. Eric Midwinter, Make 'Em Laugh, George Allen and Unwin, 1979.
383. The Stage 17 September 1970.
384. E-mail to the author dated 14 August 2008.
385. E-mail to the author dated 26 August 2008.
386. The Times 16 August 1977.
387. Song plugging had been a problem for the BBC since 1935. Top variety singers earned anything between £30 and £50 from plugs. The racket eventually became the subject of an expose in a Sunday newspaper: "sheet music tsars – to boost their sales – direct their own 'black market' at a minimum estimate of £250,000 [£5 million] a year." [The People, 12 May 1946]. As a result, a government inquiry was set up largely to see whether BBC staff employees were involved. It concluded that there was no foundation for any charge of bribery, corruption or partiality against BBC staff, but ruled that its head of dance music, Mrs D.H. Neilson, had been unwise to allow a band leader to take her to a furrier "where she chose two blue fox skins which were made up into a fur and for which he paid £41 13s 4d. [£1,000]" [Daily Telegraph, 27 November 1947].
388. Daily Herald 7 March 1949.
389. Daily Mirror 5 March 1949.
390. Daily Mirror 5 March 1949.

391. Ivor Brown writing in The Observer 13 August 1950.
392. Ruby Murray died in Torquay on 17 December 1996.
393. His father, also Harry Claff, led the singing of the National Anthem at the first Royal Command Performance in 1912.
394. Bob Monkhouse, Over the Limit, London, Century 1998, pp. 34–36.
395. Tommy Steele, Bermondsey Boy, London, Michael Joseph, 2006, p. 252.
396. Jack Payne, This is Jack Payne, London, Sampson Low, Marston, undated, p. 118.
397. Eric Morecambe and Ernie Wise, Eric and Ernie, London, W.H. Allen, 1973, p. 84.
398. Bob Hope was British by birth, but, to all intents and purposes, he was an American entertainer.
399. The Stage 3 February 2005.
400. Eddie Rogers, Tin Pan Alley, London, Robert Hale, 1964, pp. 36–37.
401. The Times 11 July 1983.
402. John Fisher, Funny Way to be a Hero, London, Frederick Muller, 1973, p. 184.
403. Bruce Forsyth, Bruce, London, Sidgwick and Jackson, 2001, p. 110.

Bibliography

Adair, Ian. *The Encyclopedia of Dove Magic, Volume Three* [Bideford, Devon, Supreme Magic Company, 1975]

Adler, Larry. *It Ain't Necessarily So* [London, Collins, 1984]

Agate, James. *Immoment Toys* [London, Jonathan Cape, 1945]

    Ego 2 [London, Gollancz, 1936]

    Ego 9 [London, Harrap, 1948]

Andrews, Val. *Life … Dull It Ain't* [no place of publication, Magical Treasury, 1983]

Baker, Richard Anthony. *Marie Lloyd, Queen of the Music Halls* [London, Robert Hale, 1990]

    British Music Hall: an Illustrated History [Stroud, Gloucestershire, Sutton Publishing, 2005]

Baker, Roger. *Drag* [London, Triton Books, 1968]

Balcon, Michael. *Michael Balcon Presents …* [London, Hutchinson, 1969]

Band, Barry. *Blackpool's Comedy Greats [1 and 2]* [Blackpool, Barry Band, 1995 and 1999]

Barker, Tony. *Music Hall* [John Tilley] [Mitcham, Surrey, Tony Barker, 2001]

Beckett, Ian. *Home Front 1914–1918* [Kew, Richmond, Surrey, The National Archives, 2006]

Bennett, Alan. *Untold Stories* [London, Faber and Faber, 2005]

Bentine, Michael. *The Reluctant Jester* [London, Bantam Press, 1992]

Betts, Graham. *Complete UK Hit Singles 1952–2005* [London, Collins, 2005]

Bevan, Ian. *Top of the Bill* [London, Frederick Muller, 1952]

Blacklock, R.S. *Which Song and When* [Edinburgh, Bandparts Music Stores, 1975]

Braddon, Russell. *The Piddingtons* [London, Werner Laurie, 1950]

Breese, Charlotte. *Hutch* [London, Bloomsbury, 1999]

Bret, David. *Gracie Fields* [London, Robson Books, 1995]

    George Formby [London, Robson, 1999]

Briggs, Asa. *The History of Broadcasting in the United Kingdom: The Birth of Broadcasting* [London, Oxford University Press, 1961]

    The History of Broadcasting in the United Kingdom: The Golden Age of Wireless [London, Oxford University Press, 1965]

Britland, David. *The Mind and Magic of David Berglas* [Burbank, California, Hahne Publications, 2002]

Britton, Alan. *Cara Mia, the David Whitfield Story* [Beverley, Highgate Publications, 1993]

Bryan, Dora. *According to Dora* [London, Bodley Head, 1987]

Buchanan-Taylor, W. *Shake it Again* [London, Heath Cranton, 1943]

Burgess, Bernie and Bowles, Frank. *Ruby [Murray Ed.] – My Precious Gem* [Derbyshire, the Derwent Press, 2006]

Burgess, Muriel with Tommy Keen. *Gracie Fields* [London, W.H. Allen, 1980]

Burke, Thomas. *Son of London* [London, Herbert Jenkins, 1947]

Busby, Roy. *British Music Hall* [London, Paul Elek, 1976]

Bygraves, Max. *I Wanna Tell You a Story* [London, W.H. Allen, 1976]

Byng, Douglas. *As You Were* [London, Duckworth, 1970]

Carlyle, Billie. *Claude Dampier, Mrs Gibson and Me* [Staines, Middlesex, Billie Carlyle, 1978]

Carstairs, John Paddy. *Honest Injun!* [London, Hurst and Blackett, 1942]

Castle, Roy. *Now and Then* [London, Robson, 1994]

Chester, Charlie. *The World is Full of Charlies* [London, New English Library, 1974]

Christopher, Milbourne and Maureen. *The Illustrated History of Magic* [Portsmouth, New Hampshire, Heinemann, 1973]

Cochrane, Peggy. *We Said It With Music* [Bognor Regis, New Horizon, 1980]

Craig, Mike. *Look Back with Laughter* [Manchester, Mike Craig, 1996]

Crossland, Ken. *The Man Who Would Be Bing* [Lewes, Sussex, the Book Guild, 2004]

Crowther, Leslie. *The Bonus of Laughter* [London, Hodder and Stoughton, 1994]

Cryer, Barry. *You Won't Believe This But …* [London, Virgin, 1998]
    Pigs Can Fly [London, Orion, 2003]

Cullen, Frank. *Vaudeville Old and New* [New York, Routledge, 2007]

Dawes, Edwin A. *The Great Illusionists* [Newton Abbot, David and Charles, 1979]

Dean, Basil. *The Theatre At War* [London, Harrap, 1956]
    Mind's Eye [London, Hutchinson, 1973]

Delfont, Lord. *Curtain Up!* [London, Robson, 1989]

Desmond, Florence. *Florence Desmond by Herself* [London, Harrap, 1953]

Donovan, Paul *The Radio Companion* [London, Harper Collins, 1991]

Dors, Diana. *Swingin' Dors* [London, World Distributors {Manchester}, 1960]

Driver, Betty. *Betty* [London, Granada Media, 2000]

Dunn, Kate. *Exit Through the Fireplace* [London, John Murray, 1998]

Dunville, T.E. *The Autobiography of an Eccentric Comedian* [London, Everett, 1912]

Earl, John and Sell, Michael. *Guide to British Theatres 1750–1950* [London, A. and C. Black, 2000]

East, John M. *Max Miller* [London, W.H. Allen, 1993]

Edwards, Jimmy. *Take it From Me* [London, Werner Laurie, 1953]

Edwards, Percy. *The Road I Travelled* [London, Arthur Barker, 1979]

English, Arthur. *Through the Mill and Beyond* [Basingstoke, The Basingstoke Press, 1986]

Evans, Peter. *The Mask Behind the Mask* [London, Leslie Frewin, 1969]

Farrer-Brown, Malcolm. *Channing Pollock* [privately printed, 2000]

Farson, Daniel. *Marie Lloyd and Music Hall* [London, Tom Stacey, 1972]

Fawkes, Richard. *Fighting For a Laugh* [London, Macdonald and Jane's, 1978]

Felstead, S. Theodore. *Stars who Made the Halls* [London, T. Werner Laurie, 1946]

Fergusson, Jean. *She Knows You Know* [Derby, The Breedon Books, 1997]

Fields, Gracie. *Sing As We Go* [London, Frederick Muller, 1960]

Fields, W.C. *W.C. Fields by Himself* [London, New York, 1974]

Fisher, John. [Born 1909]. *What a Performance!* [London, Seeley, Service and Co., 1975]

Fisher, John. [Born 1945]. *Funny Way To Be a Hero* [London, Frederick Muller, 1973]
    George Formby [London, Woburn-Futura, 1975]
    Paul Daniels and the Story of Magic [London, Jonathan Cape, 1987]
    Always Leave Them Laughing [London, Harper Collins, 2006]
    Cardini, the Suave Deceiver [Los Angeles, The Miracle Factory, 2007]
    Tony Hancock, the Definitive Biography [London, Harper Collins, 2008]

Flanagan, Bud. *My Crazy Life* [London, Frederick Muller, 1961]

Fletcher, Cyril. *Nice One Cyril* [London, Barrie and Jenkins, 1978]

Forsyth, Bruce. *Bruce* [London, Sidgwick and Jackson, 2001]

Foster, Andy and Furst, Steve. *Radio Comedy 1938–1968* [London, Virgin, 1996]

Fuld, James J. *The Book of World-Famous Music* [New York, Crown Publishers, 1966]

Gammond, Peter, *The Oxford Companion to Popular Music* [Oxford, Oxford University Press, 1991]

Ganzl, Kurt. *Encyclopedia of the Musical Theatre* [Oxford, Blackwell, 1994]
   The British Musical Theatre [Basingstoke, Hampshire, MacMillan, 1986]

Gifford, Denis. *The Golden Age of Radio* [London, B.T. Batsford Ltd., 1985]
   The British Film Catalogue 1895–1985 [Newton Abbot, David and Charles, 1973]

Gingold, Hermione. *How to Grow Old Disgracefully* [London, Gollancz, 1989]

Goldin, Horace. *It's Fun to be Fooled* [London, Stanley Paul, 1937]

Goldstein, Murray. *Naked Jungle* [London, Silverback Press, 2005]

Gottfried, Martin. *Nobody's Fool* [New York, Simon and Schuster, 1994]

Green, Christopher with Clerk, Carol *Hughie and Paula* [Robson, London, 2003]

Green, Stanley. *Encyclopedia of the Musical Theatre* [New York, Mead Dodd, 1976]

Gregg, John. *The Shelter of the Tubes* [Harrow Weald, Capital Transport, 2001]

Guest, Val. *So You Want to Be in Pictures* [London, Reynolds and Hearn, 2001]

Hall, William. *Titter Ye Not!* [London, Harper Collins, 1992]

Harding, James. *Cochran* [London, Methuen, 1988]
   George Robey and the Music Hall [London, Hodder and Stoughton, 1990]

Harris, Eric. *History of Southampton's Theatres and Music Halls* [A typescript copy held by Southampton Reference Library]

Hasler, Adrienne. *Muffin the Mule* [No place of publication given, Jeremy Mills, 2005]

Henson, Brian and Morgan, Colin. *First Hits* [London, Boxtree, 1989]

Hickman, Charles. *Directed By –* [Bognor Regis, Sussex, New Horizon, 1981]

Hillerby, Bryen D. *The Lost Theatres of Sheffield* [Barnsley, South Yorkshire, Wharncliffe Publishing, 1999]

Hilliam, B.C. *Flotsam's Follies* [London, Arthur Barron, 1948]

Hoare, Philip. *Noel Coward* [London, Sinclair Stevenson, 1995]

Holloway, Stanley. *Wiv a Little Bit o' Luck* [London, Leslie Frewin, 1967]

Houston, Renee. *Don't Fence Me In* [London, Pan Books, 1974]

Howard, Diana. *London Theatres and Music Halls* [London, Library Association, 1970]

Hudd, Roy. *Roy Hudd's Book of Music-Hall*, Variety and Showbiz Anecdotes [London, Robson, 1993]

Hudd, Roy and Hindin, Philip. *Roy Hudd's Cavalcade of Variety Acts* [London, Robson, 1997]

Hughes, John Graven. *The Greasepaint War* [London, New English Library, 1976]

Hulbert, Jack. *The Little Woman's Always Right* [London, W.H. Allen, 1975]

Jacobs, Dick and Harriet. *Who Wrote That Song?* [Cincinnati, Writer's Digest Books, 1994]

Jewel, Jimmy. *Three Times Lucky* [London, Enigma Books, 1982]

Kavanagh, Ted. *Tommy Handley* [London, Hodder and Stoughton, 1949]

Kilgarriff, Michael. *Sing Us One of the Old Songs* [Oxford University Press, 1998]
   Grace, Beauty and Banjos [London, Oberon Books, 1998]

Kendall, Henry. *I Remember Romano's* [London, MacDonald, 1960]

King, Steve assisted and edited by Terry Cavender. *As Long As I Know, I'll be Quite Alright [The Life Stories of Lucan and McShane]* [Blackpool, Lancastrian Transport Publications, 1999]

Kirkwood, Patricia. *The Time of My Life* [London, Robert Hale, 1999]

Knox, Collie. *People of Quality* [London, MacDonald, 1947]

Kon, Andrea. *This is My Song* [London, W.H. Allen, 1983]

Larkin, Colin. *The Virgin Encyclopedia of 50s Music* [London, Virgin Books, 2002]

La Rue, Danny. *From Drags to Riches* [London, Viking, 1987]

Leeman, Dicky. *What's My Line?* [London, Allan Wingate, 1955]

Leishman, Marista. *My Father, Reith of the BBC* [Edinburgh, Saint Andrew Press, 2006]

Lewis, Eric. *The Genius of Robert Harbin* [Pasadena, California, Mike Caveney's Magic Words, 1997]

Lewis, Eric and Warlock, Peter *P.T. Selbit: Magical Innovator* [Pasadena, California, Magical Publications, 1989]

Linnane, Fergus. *The Encyclopedia of London Crime and Vice* [Stroud, Gloucestershire, Sutton Publishing, 2003]

   London's Underworld [London, Robson, 2003]

Lynn, Vera. [London, W.H. Allen 1975]

MacQueen Pope, W. J. *Theatre Royal, Drury Lane* [London, W.H. Allen. 1945]

   The Melodies Linger On [London, W.H. Allen, 1950]

Mander, Raymond and Mitchenson, Joe. *Theatrical Companion to Coward* [London, Rockliff, 1957]

   British Music Hall [London, Gentry Books, 1965]

   Musical Comedy [London, Peter Davies, 1969]

   Revue: A Story in Pictures [London, Peter Davies, 1971]

Mann, Leslie. *My Song Goes Round the World* [Belfast, Ellen Publications, 1997]

Maschwitz, Eric. *No Chip on my Shoulder* [London, Herbert Jenkins, 1957]

McBrien, William. *Cole Porter* [London, Harper Collins, 1998]

McCann, Graham. *Morecambe and Wise* [London, Fourth Estate, 1998]

   Frankie Howerd [London, Fourth Estate, 2004]

   Morecambe and Wise Untold [London, Harper and Collins, 2007]

McIntyre, Ian. *The Expense of Glory* [London, Harper Collins, 1993]

Mellor, Geoff J. *They Made Us Laugh* [Littleborough, Lancashire, George Kelsall, 1982]

   The Northern Music Hall [1970]

Melville, Alan. *Merely Melville* [London, Hodder and Stoughton, 1970]

Messiter, Ian *My Life and Other Games* [London, Fourth Estate, 1990]

Mills, John. *Up in the Clouds, Please, Gentlemen* [London, Weidenfeld and Nicolson, 1980]

Monkhouse, Bob. *Crying with Laughter* [London, Century, 1993]

   Over the Limit [London, Century, 1998]

Moore, James Ross. *Andre Charlot* [Jefferson, North Carolina, McFarland, 2005]

More, Kenneth. *Happy Go Lucky* [London, Robert Hale, 1959]

Morecambe, Eric and Wise, Ernie. *Eric and Ernie* [London, W.H. Allen, 1973]

Moules, Joan. *Our Gracie* [London, Robert Hale, 1983]

Murrells, Joseph. *Million Selling Records* [London, Batsford, 1984]

Nathan, David. *The Laughtermakers* [London, Peter Owen, 1971]

Newley, Patrick. *The Krays and Bette Davis* [Sandy, Bedfordshire, Authors On Line, 2006]

   The Amazing Mrs Shufflewick: the Life of Rex Jameson [London, Third Age Press, 2007]

   You Lucky People! The Tommy Trinder Story [London, Third Age Press, 2008]

Nobbs, George. *The Wireless Stars* [Norwich, Wensum Books, 1972]

Nown, Graham. *When the World Was Young* [London, Ward Lock, 1986]

Nuttall, Jeff. *King Twist: a Portrait of Frank Randle* [London, Routledge and Kegan Paul 1978]

Osborne, John. *A Better Class of Person* [Harmondsworth, Penguin, 1982]

Owen, Maureen. *The Crazy Gang* [London, Weidenfeld and Nicolson, 1986]

Parsons, Nicholas. *The Straight Man* [London, Weidenfeld and Nicolson, 1994]

Partridge, Eric. *A Dictionary of Catch Phrases* [London, Routledge and Kegan Paul, 1977]

Payn, Graham and Morley, Sheridan. *The Noel Coward Diaries* [London, Weidenfeld and Nicolson, 1982]

Payne, Jack. *This is Jack Payne* [London, Sampson Low, Marston, undated]

Peers, Donald. *Pathway* [London, Werner Laurie, 1951]

Perry, George. *Forever Ealing* [London, Pavilion, 1981]

Perry, Jimmy. *A Stupid Boy* [London, Century, 2002]

Pertwee, Bill. *By Royal Command* [Newton Abbot, David and Charles, 1981]

Pilton, Patrick *Every Night at the London Palladium* [London, Robson Books, 1976]

Powell, Sandy and Stanley, Harry. *Can You Hear Me, Mother?* [London, Jupiter Books, 1975]

Price, David. *Magic: a Pictorial History of Conjurers in the Theatre* [New Jersey, Cornwall Books, 1985]

Price, Victor J. *Birmingham Theatres, Concert and Music Halls* [Studley, Warwickshire, KAF Brewin Books, 1988]

Priestley, J.B. *English Journey* [London, Heinemann, 1934]

Pulling, Christopher. *They Were Singing* [London, George G. Harrap, 1952]

Purser, Philip and Wilkes, Jenny. *The One and Only Phyllis Dixey* [London, Futura Publications, 1978]

Randall, Alan and Seaton, Ray. *George Formby* [London, W.H. Allen, 1974]

Read, Al. *It's All in the Book* [London, W.H. Allen, 1985]

Reid, Beryl. *So Much Love* [London, Hutchinson, 1984]

Rhodes, Joan. *Coming on Strong* [Darlington, Serendipity, 2007]

Richards, Jeffrey. *The Age of the Dream Palace* [London, Routledge and Kegan Paul, 1984]

Rogers, Eddie. *Tin Pan Alley* [London, Robert Hale, 1964]

Ronalde, Ronnie *Around the World on a Whistle* [Auckland, New Zealand, Blackbird Publications, 1998]

Rose, Clarkson. *Red Plush and Greasepaint* [London, Museum Press, 1964]

Rust, Brian. *British Music Hall on Record* [Harrow, Middlesex, General Gramophone Publications, 1979]
 The Complete Entertainment Discography [New York, Arlington House, 1973]
 and Forbes, Sandy. *British Dance Bands on Record 1911 to 1945* [Harrow, Middlesex, General Gramophone Publications, 1989]

Ryan, Brendan. *George Formby: A Catalogue of His Work* [no details]

Saunders, Andy. *Jane, a Pin-up at War* [Barnsley, South Yorkshire, Leo Cooper, 2004]

Schwartz, Charles. *Cole Porter* [London, W.H. Allen, 1978]

Seaton, Ray and Martin, Roy. *Good Morning, Boys* [London, Barrie and Jenkins, 1978]

Secombe, Harry. *Arias and Raspberries* [London, Robson, 1989]

Seeley, Robert and Bunnett, Rex. *London Musical Shows on Record 1889 –1989* [Harrow, Middlesex, General Gramophone Publications, 1989]

Shellard, Dominic and Nicholson, Steve. *The Lord Chamberlain Regrets ...* [London, British Library, 2004]

Short, Ernest. *Fifty Years of Vaudeville* [London, Eyre and Spottiswoode, 1946]

Smith, John. *The Benny Hill Story* [New York, St Martin's Press, 1989]

Solomon, Clive. *Record Hits* [London, Omnibus Press, 1979]

Steele, Tommy. *Bermondsey Boy* [London, Michael Joseph, 2006]

Sutton, David. *A Chorus of Raspberries* [Exeter, University of Exeter Press, 2000]

Sweet, Matthew. *Shepperton Babylon* [London, Faber and Faber, 2005]

Sykes, Eric. *If I Don't Write It, No-one Else Will* [London, Fourth Estate, 2005]

Terry-Thomas with Terry Daum. *Terry-Thomas Tells Tales* [London, Robson, 1990]

Thomas, Howard. *With an Independent Air* [London, Weidenfeld and Nicolson, 1977]

Took, Barry. *Star Turns* [London, Weidenfeld and Nicolson, 1992]
   Laughter in the Air [London, Robson, 1976]
Tucker, Sophie. *Some of These Days* [London, Hammond, 1948]
Tynan, Kathleen. *The Life of Kenneth Tynan* [London, Weidenfeld and Nicolson, 1987]
Tynan, Kenneth. *Profiles* [London, Nick Hern Books, 1989]
Underwood, Peter. *Life's a Drag!* [London, Leslie Frewin, 1974]
Vahimagi, Tise. *British Television* [Oxford, OUP, 1994]
Van Damm, Sheila. *We Never Closed* [London, Robert Hale, 1967]
Van Damm, Vivian. *Tonight and Every Night* [London, Stanley Paul, 1952]
Wade, John. *The Trade of the Tricks* [London, Elm Tree, 1974]
Wagg, Stephen [editor]. *Because I Tell a Joke or Two* [London, Taylor and Francis {Routledge}, 1998]
Wall, Max with Peter Ford. *The Fool on the Hill* [London, Quartet Books, 1975]
Warner, Jack. *Jack of All Trades* [London, W.H. Allen, 1975]
Waters, T.A. *The Encyclopedia of Magic and Magicians* [Oxford, Fact on File, Publications, 1988]
Watt, John. *Radio Variety* [London, J.M. Dent] 1939
Wearing, J.P. *The London Stage 1910 – 1919* [Metuchen, New Jersey, The Scarecrow Press, 1982]
   The London Stage 1920 – 1929 [Metuchen, New Jersey, The Scarecrow Press, 1984]
   The London Stage 1930 – 1939 [Metuchen, New Jersey, The Scarecrow Press, 1990]
   The London Stage 1940 – 1949 [Metuchen, New Jersey, The Scarecrow Press, 1991]
   The London Stage 1950 – 1959 [Metuchen, New Jersey, The Scarecrow Press, 1993]
White, Mark. *You Must Remember This* [London, Frederick Warne, 1983]
Wilcox, Herbert. *Twenty-Five Thousand Sunsets* [London, Bodley Head, 1967]
Williams, Bransby. *Bransby Williams by Himself* [London, Hutchinson, 1954]
Williams, Philip Martin and David L. *Hooray for Jollywood* [Ashton-under-Lyne, History on Your Doorstep, 2001]
Wired to the Moon [Ashton-under-Lyne, History on Your Doorstep, 2006]
Wilmut, Roger. *Tony Hancock 'Artiste'* [London, Methuen, 1978]
   Kindly Leave the Stage [London, Methuen, 1985]
Winters, Bernie. *One Day at a Time* [London, BCA, 1991]
Winters, Mike and Bernie. *Shake a Pagoda Tree* [London, W.H. Allen, 1976]
Wisdom, Norman. *My Turn* [London, Century, 1992]
Woodward, Chris and Mark, Richard *Maurice Fogel in Search of the Sensational* [Seattle, Hermetic Press, 2007]
Wyatt, Will. *The Fun Factory* [London, Aurum Press, 2003]

Index